THE CHRISTMAS

By Nick van der Leek and Lisa Wilson

Copyright (c) 2016 by Nick van der Leek

All rights reserved. No part of this book may be used, reproduced or transmitted in any form or by any means, electronic or mechanical, including photocopying, recording, or by any information storage or retrieval system, without the written permission of the author, except where permitted by law, or in the case of brief quotations embodied in critical articles and reviews.

Every effort has been made to trace copyright holders. The author would be grateful to be notified directly of any corrections that should be incorporated in future editions of this book.

Cover design: Nick van der Leek
"The death of JonBenét Ramsey was a tragedy but everything that's happened since is horrendous." — Fleet White, former friend of John Ramsey <u>and exonerated three times on charges relating to JonBenét Ramsey's murder</u>

"At thirty-six years old, I thought my life's passion as a police officer was carved in stone. I realize that although I may have to trade my badge for a carpenter's hammer, I will do so with a clear conscience. It is with a heavy heart that I offer my resignation from the Boulder Police Department, in protest of this continuing travesty." — Detective Steve Thomas, August 7, 1998 [excerpt from Thomas' <u>letter of resignation</u> to Boulder Police Sheriff Beckner]

"Do roses know their thorns can hurt?" — JonBenét Ramsey to Ramsey family landscaper and gardener, Brian Scott in October 1996

Important Note to the Reader:

The #SHAKEDOWN books are unique. Although available in print, it's recommended these narratives are read on Kindle or other smart devices as the authors have provided hyperlinks to relevant resources including documents, photographs and videos to enhance your interactivity with the story. It is the authors' intention to take you on a thoughtful journey of discovery; one that not only encompasses the lives of the subject matter, and the insights drawn from them, but also your own.

TABLE OF CONTENTS

Introduction 4
Key Individuals 7
CHRISTMAS LIGHTS 14
Cogne #1 15
The Riddle of the "Baseball Bats" 17
Items 3 GLI and 74 BAB on the Search Warrant 26
A Hand in the Death of Another 28
Overcoming the Reluctance to Kill 32
CAROLS & KILLOGY 35
Cogne #2 36
The Day After Christmas 40
The Psychology of Killing 43
Computer Games - Classical or Operative Conditioning? 47
JonBenét Ramsey murder - thirteen familiar flourishes present in other famous cases 54
HOLLY & CANDYSTICKS 58
Cogne #3 59
Why was Patsy still wearing the same outfit on December 26th? 62
Why would you pretend to be asleep when your sister is missing/dead? 64
Under the Christmas Tree 80
Baseball Bats, Footprints and Tracks in the Snow 89
Into and Out of Intruder Territory 100
A War of Words Part 1 112
Did Burke Break the Basement Window? 121
BELLS & BAUBLES 148
Cogne #4 149
Pam Paugh and the Attack of the Cardboard Boxes 152

Gentlemen Prefer Blondes 162
Who is Kim Ballard? Part 1 167
Revisiting Plausible Deniability 183
"Zonked" 196
FEUDS & FUNERALS 200
Cogne#5 201
The Feud Against Fleet 203
Two Funerals for Lazarus 235
Cogne #6 245
Doug's Back to School Announcement [on behalf of Burke] 249
UNDERWORLD 251
Cogne #7 252
JonBenét's Medical History 254
Back to the Future of Injustice 266
"Attorney of the Damned" 271
Silent Aftermath #1 278
Cogne #8 287
Acknowledgements 289

Introduction

Before we begin our journey to that after-Christmas-place that was Boulder in 1996 we have a final psychological stop to make: *where does the urge to kill come from and how do we get it if we don't have it?*

This narrative focuses on the events immediately following the discovery of JonBenét Ramsey's small blonde corpse lying in the basement by her father and "a family friend".

Exactly how did John Ramsey conduct himself? Exactly what did Patsy say and do according to police officials *on the scene*? Exactly where was Burke, and when did he leave, and who spoke to him on the 26th?

The Day After Christmas trilogy examines the aftermath of the six year old's murder over a three year period – in other words the period from the discovery of the dead child to the publication of their first book and the filing of the first lawsuits in 1998 and 1999*.

In *The Craven Silence 3* we used a case file to demonstrate what a real murder-kidnapping looks like, how it is investigated and how it is prosecuted. In this narrative we will use a different case file – the Cogne case – as guidance. The Cogne case involves similar circumstances to the Ramseys and JonBenét: the death of a young child discovered by his mother in bed at a home in Italy.

After introducing the Cogne case we will attempt to tie up the events as they unfolded on December 26th, 1996 just after 13:00 at 755 15th street in Boulder. Our first order of business is that final psychological house call.

In *The Craven Silence 3* we interrogated the psychologies of sibling rivalry and the possibility of peer pressure in the six year old girl's death. We still need to examine *the psychology of killing* itself. We may think the urge to kill is innate in man and woman [and boy], but is it? When last did you kill an animal, and did you do so with impunity?

On our way to establishing exactly this territory we must also address glaring errors made in *The Craven Silence Trilogy*. These errors were not only ours, but part of the fabric of the police investigation. These errors are integral to why we feel the case has been stuck in an unsolved state for two decades and counting.

In this narrative we attempt to prove three prime errors above all:

1. The baseball bat is not a baseball bat and it did not belong to Burke Ramsey**.

2. The broken window was not broken months before the murder and it wasn't broken by John Ramsey.

3. The window grate was not a point of entry or exit and was not "the metal scraping sound" heard by Luther Stanton near midnight on the morning after Christmas.

By the end of this narrative we address exactly *where* JonBenét was murdered.

*Defamation Lawsuit filed February 1998. [Boulder photographer and neighbor Stephen Miles vs John Ramsey and the National Enquirer]. $25 Million Libel Suit filed in November 1999. [Burke Ramsey vs Star and American Media].

**On the Dr. Phil Show [September 13th, 2016] Burke asserted that the bat belonged to him.

Key Individuals

"I've never lost a homicide case." — Retired Detective Lou Smit

"I believe there's evidence of an intruder, and I believe people should still be looking for him. There's a dangerous guy out there." — Retired Detective Lou Smit

Most of the 90+ names mentioned below occur in the continuing narrative.

Many additional key individuals have been left out of the list for reasons of efficacy.

Family

1. JonBenét Ramsey [deceased 1996, age 6]
2. JonBenét's father John Ramsey, former CEO of ACCESS GRAPHICS*, engineer, pilot, naval officer, businessman, author
3. JonBenét's mother Patsy Ramsey, former Miss West Virginia [deceased 2006, age 49]
4. JonBenét's brother, Burke Ramsey

John Ramsey - Extended Family

5. JonBenét's half-sister - Elizabeth 'Beth' Pasch Ramsey [deceased 1992, age 22]
6. JonBenét's older half-sister - Melinda Ramsey, sometimes resided in Ramsey family home.
7. JonBenét's older half-brother – John Andrew, resided in Ramsey family home, when not at college.

8. JonBenét's uncle and <u>John Ramsey's</u> brother – Jeff Ramsey

9. John Ramsey's first wife - <u>Lucinda Pasch</u>

Patsy Ramsey - Extended Family

10. Patsy's mother – <u>Nedra Paugh</u> [<u>deceased</u>]

11. Patsy's father – Donald Paugh [deceased]

12. Patsy's younger sister – <u>Pamela Paugh</u>, former Miss West Virginia

Friends

13. <u>Fleet Russell White, Jr.</u>, identified by <u>John Ramsey as possible suspect</u>

14. <u>Priscilla Brown White</u>, wife of Fleet and identified by John Ramsey as possible suspect

15. <u>Fleet White III</u> , son of Fleet and Priscilla, friend of Burke and identified by John Ramsey as possible suspect

16. <u>Daphne White</u>, daughter of Fleet and Priscilla and friend of JonBenét Ramsey

17. Glen Stine

18. <u>Susan Stine</u>, wife of Glen and identified as possible suspect

19. Doug Stine, son of Glen and Susan, friend of Burke and identified as possible suspect

20. Evan Colby, friend of Burke Ramsey, next door neighbor and identified as possible suspect by John Ramsey

21. Kyle Colby, Evan's brother, friend of Burke Ramsey and next door neighbor.

22. Mike Archuleta, John Ramsey's pilot and friend

23. Pam Archuleta, [refers to herself as "Pam Barday" in Dateline documentary] Mike's ex-wife and friend of Patsy

24. Stewart Walker, friend of the Ramseys

25. Roxanne Walker, friend of the Ramseys

26. Bill McReynolds, Santa, identified as possible suspect [deceased]

27. Janet McReynolds, Santa's wife and identified as possible suspect

28. Rev. Rolland [Rol] Hoverstock, Episcopal minister in Boulder, Ramsey's pastor

29. Leslie Durgin, Mayor of Boulder

30. Jay "Pasta" Elowsky, John Ramsey's business associate, owner of Pasta Jay's

31. Judith Phillips, family photographer and long-time friend of Patsy [sold portraits of JonBenét after her death to the media without Patsy's consent]

Neighbors

32. Joe Barnhill, took care of JonBenét's dogs

33. Betty Barnhill, wife of Joe [deceased]

34. Glenn Meyer, boarded with the Barnhills

35. Luther and Melody Stanton, neighbors and ear witnesses

36. Diane Brumfitt, neighbor and school counselor

37. Stephen Miles, neighbor who lived 6 blocks away and identified as possible suspect by John Ramsey

Ramsey Case Prosecution

38. Alex Hunter, Boulder District Attorney

39. Andrew "Lou" Smit, Retired detective [deceased 2010]

40. Pete Hofstrom, Assistant District Attorney and alleged Ramsey associate

41. Michael Kane, Deputy Boulder District Attorney

42. Bill Wise, First Assistant District Attorney

43. James Kolar, Investigator for Boulder District Attorney's office [2005-2006], wrote a book about the case and appeared in CBS documentary

44. Judge Robert Lowenbach, allowed release of Grand Jury indictments in October 2013

Boulder Law Enforcement

45. Rick French, Boulder Police Officer and the first policeman to arrive at the scene at approximately 06:00

46. Karl Veitch, Boulder Police Officer and the first policeman to arrive at the scene with French at approximately 06:00

47. Paul Reichenbach, patrol sergeant who searched Burke's room [arrived at 06:45**]

48. Barry Weiss, police officer [arrived at 06:45]

49. Sue Barcklow, police officer [arrived at 06:45]

50. John Eller, commander of the Boulder police detective division

51. Tom Trujillo, Detective sergeant

52. Steve Thomas, Former Boulder Police Department Detective and author

53. Linda Arndt, Former Detective and one of first officers at the scene

54. Fred Patterson, arrived at the scene at the same time as Arndt

55. Mark Beckner, Boulder Police Chief

56. Tom Koby, Retired Boulder Police Chief

57. Tom Wickman, Boulder Police Detective

58. Jane Harmer, Boulder Police Detective

59. Melissa Hickman, Detective dropped from Ramsey case in April 1997

60. Thomas Haney, Boulder Police Detective, conducted June 1998 interrogation of Patsy Ramsey

61. Trip DeMuth, former Boulder prosecutor, conducted June 1998 interrogation of Patsy Ramsey. Left his career at Boulder DA in September 2000 to work for Mike Bynum

Ramsey Lawyers

62. Mike Bynum, Ramsey defense "architect"

63. Patrick J. Burke

64. Hugh Patrick Furman

65. James K. Jenkins, lawyer hired by John Ramsey for his ex-wife Lucinda Pasch

66. Harold Haddon

67. Grady Bryan Morgan

68. Patrick S. Korten, a Washington media consultant, once the

top spokesman for the United States Department of Justice

69. Lin Wood, threatened to sue CBS on 21 September for their allegations against Burke Ramsey in *The Case Of: JonBenét Ramsey*

Miscellaneous

70. Tom Hand, architect in charge of remodeling Ramsey residence
71. David S. Sanderton, a Boulder-based criminal defense and civil rights attorney, Republican candidate for Boulder County District Attorney
72. Dr. Francesco Beuf, JonBenét's pediatrician
73. Brian Scott, gardener
74. Jay Pettipeace, House painter
75. Diane Hallis, former employee at Access Graphics [witnessed John Ramsey's behavior in the office after JonBenét's death]
76. Mervin Pugh, wife of Linda Hoffman Pugh, Ramsey handyman, alcoholic, and identified as possible suspect
77. Linda Hoffman Pugh, Ramsey housekeeper, Mervin's wife, and identified by Patsy as possible suspect
78. Linda Wilcox, Ramsey housekeeper
79. Shirley Brady, Ramsey nanny
80. Susan Savage, Ramsey nanny
81. Kristine Griffin, JonBenét's babysitter
82. Pamela Griffin, JonBenét's costume designer
83. Randy Simons, JonBenét's photographer

84. Jeff Merrick, Former Ramsey friend and employee at Access Graphics, and identified as possible suspect

85. Paula Woodward, Emmy-award winning author featured in A&E documentary

86. Jim Clemente, investigator in CBS documentary

87. Laura Richards, investigator in CBS documentary

88. Beth Karas, former New York prosecutor, appeared in Investigation Discovery documentary

89. Diane Dimond, television journalist and reporter, appeared in Investigation Discovery documentary, covered JonBenét Ramsey case from start to finish

90. John Mark Karr, confessed to the crime in August 2006 [False confession]

91. Charlie Brennan, Daily Camera reporter, filed a lawsuit on behalf of the Reporters Committee for Freedom of the Press for the release of Grand Jury Indictments, and won

*A computer services company and a subsidiary of Lockheed Martin

**Some accounts have Reichenbach arriving at the Ramsey residence at 06:10 on December 26th, 1996.

CHRISTMAS LIGHTS

Obi-Wan Kenobi: *That boy is our last hope.*

Yoda: *No, there is another.* — Star Wars, Empire Strikes Back

Cogne #1

In *The Craven Silence 3* we explored the van Dam case in order to assess the Ramsey case against the template of a real kidnapping and murder. We saw clearly how different the behaviour of the van Dam family, the investigators and the prime suspect [a neighbour] were to the set of circumstances we encountered in Boulder with the Ramseys.

Now we want to assess the Ramsey case according to a new template. What happens when a child is killed inside the home? What does it look like? What sort of behaviour patterns are typical? Is there such a thing as "typical" behaviour?

The so-called Cogne case (known in Italian as caso Cogne) involved the death of three-year-old Samuele Lorenzi on 30 January 2002 while **sleeping in his parents' bed** *in his family home in the mountain village of Cogne, in Aosta Valley, northern Italy.* **The cause of death was found to be a blow to the skull. The murder weapon has never been found.** — Wikipedia

Given the circumstances in Boulder, our first question is whether bedwetting was involved in the Cogne case. Given the child was three this is a possibility, but the more pertinent fact is *where* the child was sleeping.

In July 2004 an Italian court sentenced Samuele's mother Anna Maria Franzoni to 30 years in prison for aggravated murder. However, on 27 April 2007 the Corte d'Assise d'appello in Turin reduced the penalty to Franzoni to 16 years of jail for homicide. Franzoni always refuted the charge, asserting that **an intruder had killed her child in the few minutes she left home to accompany her older son** *Davide, then-six years old to the school bus station.* — Wikipedia

What's curious about this case is the parent uses three "alibis" as an explanation:

1. An intruder is blamed

2. The parent is not at home at the time

3. The surviving older son is effectively part of the alibi

Of these three explanations, how many apply to the Ramsey case?

The Riddle of the "Baseball Bats"

"Don't let the past steal your present. This is the message of Christmas: We are never alone." — Taylor Caldwell

"I'm intimately familiar with every piece of sports equipment my daughter has. I buy it; I make sure she has it with her; I carry it; we play with it. John would know if it's Burke's bat because they played baseball together in the yard, but Lou Smit doesn't want to know if he recognizes that bat, the mystery bat. In fact Smit cuts him off in the middle of his answer..." — FR Brown, an avatar associated with ForumsforJustice.org

In our efforts to investigate the "baseball bat" as a probable murder weapon we've made several unexpected breakthroughs since concluding *The Craven Silence 3*.

We stumbled upon the first slew of insights during a routine pass over the baseball bats. In *The Craven Silence* Trilogy we'd tested whether baseball was a factor as a sport amongst the Ramsey children and we found that it was. However we didn't interrogate much further than that.

For this narrative, part of our due diligence was to sweep slightly beyond that first sweep. In order to widen our search, we directed half a dozen seemingly simple questions at both bats and then attempted to answer them. The results were astonishing.

Below is the list of questions:

1. Who do you belong to?
2. What are you?
3. How many of you are there?
4. What are you made of?
5. What sound do you make?
6. Where were you left?

7. *Why?*

We immediately hit pay dirt on the first question, and then the second, and then the third. It seemed as though the baseballs bats alone were the key to a floodgate of buried secrets.

Before we reveal what we found, we must refer to <u>Burke Ramsey's second appearance on Dr. Phil on September 13th, 2016</u>. Just short of <u>33 minutes into the second episode</u> Burke Ramsey reveals for the first time that *he's the owner* of the black "baseball bat".

The show <u>cuts to Burke volunteering this information</u> – it's not even a response to a question from Dr. Phil.

Burke, usually reticent and difficult to engage, not only volunteers this crucial information ["that was my bat"] he also volunteers his behaviour surrounding it. Burke says:

> *"That was my baseball bat…I would normally like, leave it out on the patio."*

Dr. Phil helpfully adds:

> *"So an intruder could have picked it up on the way in."*

Burke answers:

> *"Yeah."*

Well actually "nah", not "yeah".

This is very faulty reasoning on a bunch of levels. First off, if the intruder picked up the bat *on his way in*, then where we find it, if it's something an intruder used, is where the intruder *left it*.

Secondly, if the intruder exited by stepping onto the blue Samsonite case, up through the broken/open window in the train room, and through the grate, then getting the baseball bat to where it was left would mean a real roundabout route around half the house just to go to the trouble to leave the bat behind. Not only would such a tour *leave behind footprints* all over the grass it would make little sense for an intruder intent on a getaway to circle back around the house [see blue line for possible intruder exit].

Conversely if the intruder headed around the other way, it's an even more circuitous route just to leave behind an incriminating weapon [see green line for possible intruder exit].

What would make a whole lot more sense would be if the intruder exited the house at the point where the bat was apparently dropped, right? This point is also closer to where JonBenét's body is found. This makes sense if we're talking about an intruder except this *isn't what happened.*

There's a flicker across Burke's face when he says this, and we have a good idea why it's there. If one knows the layout of the Ramsey residence, the orientation, the grounds – and we have made a particularly detailed study for this narrative – then it's clear Burke's not quite saying all there is to say not only about the bat, but where it is and why it is where it is.

What we can say without any hesitation is the bat has been left on a ledge near a drainage pipe on the opposite side of the house to supposed entry/exit point in the basement. This is not only a strange place for a kid to leave a bat, given that side of the house was hemmed in by trees and the northern boundary, it's also clearly an odd place for an intruder to go to the trouble to leave there.

It doesn't make sense for an intruder to run around the front door, or the other way - around the garage – and then double-back to deposit the murder weapon beside the drainpipe. We're pretty certain the bat is the murder weapon, but if it doesn't make sense for an intruder to leave it there, and it doesn't make sense for the kids to put the bat there in the course of playing with them either, then why the fuck is the bat there?

It seems to be a mystery, doesn't it?

The mystery becomes less mysterious when we address those seven simple questions. We'll get to them momentarily, but let's get John Ramsey's take on the *where* of the bat first.

From acandyrose.com:

SMIT: *Do you remember specifically ever going out this door, the butler door?*

JOHN: *That morning?*

SMIT: *Yes.*

JOHN: *No, I did not.* **I know I did not.**

SMIT: *Do you remember anyone going out that door?*

JOHN: *I don't. That door, from time to time, I'd find wide open because if* **one of the kids would go out** *they'd leave it open. But in the normal course of activity, I remember going down there. And I think on a couple of occasions I went…And the door was just wide open or unlocked.*

SMIT: *Is it problem with the door or is it a --*

JOHN: *No. I think it's just in our house* **kids would come and go out of every orifice and place and that was one of them**.

Odd choice of words, right? Kids would come and go out of every *orifice*.

Orifice is a highly unusual word that refers to:

- Hole
- Opening
- Cavity
- Maw
- Vent

We'll be touching on Patsy's lexical choices too, for example the word "zonked". Why does she use it? Why does John use the word "orifice" when describing kids entering and exiting the house? Why not use the word door? Or window…

From acandyrose.com:

SMIT: *Okay. Okay I am going to show you some more photographs, and do you remember whether your children played baseball or bats or anything of that nature?*

JOHN: *Used. I mean Burke played baseball. We used to play, have batting practice in <u>the back yard</u>.*

John has an odd stutter or splutter there by the look of things. The detective asks him about children playing with baseball bats and John immediately splutters the word "used". He then seems to cover up the semantic stumble by saying "we used to play". What? Had they retired from playing baseball? Or is John trying [and perhaps trying too hard] to establish that the bat Smit is referring to wasn't new. It was used.

From acandyrose.com:

SMIT: *Do you know if there was one bat, two bats or three bats, do you have any idea?*

JOHN: *Well, I think Burke had a bat, I think there was a little plastic bat JonBenét would use, a small one. Used to use little Whiffle balls. And...*

Pssst. We're going to let our readers in on a little secret. John has the opportunity here to talk family baseball matters and yet...he doesn't. Put this card in the back pocket because we'll be calling for it soon.

From acandyrose.com:

SMIT: *I am going to show you a picture, and again this is photograph number 434*, it's a photograph of a bat and it appears to be in the yard and this is a close-up of the same bat and I would like to show both pictures and it's for photograph 435.*

JOHN: *Well, that sort of looks like Burke's bat. I could probably tell exactly if it was or not, but looks familiar. It wouldn't be unusual for it to be lying out in the yard, because it just kind of just got dropped where it was left.*

The crime scene photos 434 and 435 are not available, but the part of the yard that Smit and John are referring to is the back yard, located on <u>the south side of the home</u>. This second bat was located on the edge of the grass near a small pond and play area.

SMIT: *I am going to show you* **another bat.** *It's <u>photograph number 410</u>. This was found in a different location and I will show you a picture of that bat.*

JOHN: *Um, it's hard for me to tell whether it's similar, but --*

SMIT: *Do you know <u>what area of the house that is</u>?*

JOHN: *Looks like it -- I know what it is. It's -- it is there <u>it is here</u> -- it's probably right in here.*

LOU: <u>*The area of the north window*</u>?

JOHN: *Right.*

(MULTIPLE SPEAKERS.)

JOHN: *Right. This <u>down spout</u> came <u>down right there</u>, right there -- no, over here. Well, yeah, it was here. But that's definitely in this area.*

SMIT: *Do you ever recall seeing a bat there?*

JOHN: *No,* **that doesn't belong there**. **When we played baseball** <u>we played right out here</u>, *because* <u>that's the only place you could hit a ball</u>, *and that* <u>yard kind of stretched back this way</u>. *But you know,* **I don't know why there would be a bat there**.

The <u>light-blue bat that comes up in the Ramsey evidence archive appears to be a children's bat</u>, possibly made of plastic, but the point is it's not from the official crime scene archive. <u>The image seems to have been photographed during summer in 1998</u>, possibly as part of a crime scene reconstruction.

Is the blue bat Burke's or JonBenét's? Does it belong to the Ramseys? It's highly unlikely considering the Ramseys hadn't lived at the home for two years at the time this photo was taken. Which brings us to those seven pertinent questions and the answers and insights we do have.

1. *Who do you belong to?*

We believe Burke Ramsey may have misspoken on Dr. Phil. We don't think the black bat is a baseball bat at all, and what's more, we don't think it belonged to a nine year old either. We believe the bat belonged to Patsy Ramsey.

2. *What are you?*

The black bat is <u>a composite softball bat used in women's league</u> softball.

3. How many of you are there?

It's possible there were as many as three bats. There's some uncertainty about a bat found in bushes. It's unclear whether this bat was subsequently moved and placed <u>on the ledge</u>**, or whether 410 is a bat that was on the ledge all along.

4. What are you made of?

It's likely the bat was a composite, which means it may have been constructed of several materials including aluminium, wood and/plastic. These materials would have given the bat additional elasticity – allowing the hitter to achieve more power than from a more rigid material. These bats are designed to hit a rounded object [a baseball or softball] and deform slightly during impact. The material characteristics of the bat and JonBenét's head wound in our view have not been studied satisfactorily.

<u>The top end of the bat</u> is virtually the same size as the lens end of the Maglite torch found on the kitchen counter, and many have been mistakenly assumed to be the murder weapon. The torch was wiped clean. The baseball bat contained what was first mistaken as blonde hair, and later traced to the fibers of <u>the basement carpet</u>.

5. What sound do you make?

The answer is dealt with in detail in the "Zonked" chapter.

6. Where were you left?

This is a harder question to answer. It's possible that a bat was dropped onto a concrete area beside the house, like the ledge, or onto a walkway and this sound of metal "scraping against concrete" was what a neighbour heard late at night on the morning of December 26th, not long after Melody Stanton heard a child's scream.

7. Why

*Why was the bat left on **the opposite side of the house** to the broken basement window?*

Why did Burke Ramsey claim the bat was his?

We believe one possible reason the bat was intentionally placed where it was, was to direct attention away from the broken window – something we'll elaborate on in another chapter. The idea was to confuse and muddy the scene rather than merely misdirect. We believe it is also important to direct attention away from the actual owner of the bat. We think it is interesting that Burke has taken responsibility for owning a bat which we believe he didn't own.

By the end of this narrative we will explain why this scenario – a bat owned by Patsy, placed outside of the home, and possessed [twenty years after the fact] by Burke fits in perfectly with our psychological assessment of the crime.

If Patsy's bat was the murder weapon it would also explain why Patsy may have felt not merely responsible for her daughter's death, not merely a sense of guilt, but a sense of panic and alarm to conceal her connection – however indirect – to the bludgeoning end JonBenét suffered.

There's potentially more to it all than even this. Just as Patsy's ownership of the murder weapon puts a completely different "swing" on the case, we believe there's another big twist in this case which also changes everything – and does so in a way that adds credence to both our psychological narrative and the actual version of events as they unfolded. We don't think John Ramsey broke the basement window, and what's more, we think it was broken late at night on Christmas day.

And then there's this from romper.com:

A shard of wood found on JonBenét's body also matched a baseball bat found hidden in the bushes outside.

*Unfortunately thus far we haven't been able to locate crime scene photo #434 or #435. We have made contact with Zumapress and Charlie Brenna but thus far we've come up empty-handed.

**The top end of the black bat seems to have small branches and twigs around it, which suggests the black bat may have been retrieved from elsewhere in the garden.

Items 3 GLI and 74 BAB on the Search Warrant

TOM HANEY: *Okay. Not a big baseball, softball fan, player?*

PATSY RAMSEY: *No.* – Interrogation on June 23rd, 1998

For those harbouring doubts about Patsy being the true owner of the black "baseball bat", it's time for some rumor control courtesy of Judith Phillips.

From forumsforjustice.org [October 6, 2005]:

Patsy is not in this photograph. She never really played, but practiced with us a few times. During one early practice, [Patsy] was playing 1st base and I was playing shortstop. The ball was hit to me and I whipped it back to Patsy at 1st base. Patsy missed it and the ball hit her ankle. I felt terrible. It was not so badly bruised and she asked me what the heck I did in high school instead of spending all day at the pool. I responded that I played sports. Different worlds!

What's interesting about the photo where Patsy is absent is who is not. Are you sure you want to hear this?

From forumsforjustice.org:

*Cast of characters: starting on the back row on the right (in between the tree trunk) is **Susan Stine** holding her hat and Roxie Walker holding a can of beer. Next row on the far left is Priscilla and I am right in front of her.*

If Patsy played softball occasionally, what about John?

From forumsforjustice.org:

Husbands would come to the field after practice, including John, and bring all the kids. It was such fun in those days. At real games most of the families would sit on the stands cheering us on. Often times, we'd all go out to dinner following the conclusion of the game.

What's interesting is Burke doesn't mention this, neither does John for that matter, neither does Patsy. We'll deal with Patsy's dodgy commentary on the baseball bat stuff later in this narrative. Meanwhile it's important to note Judith's first-hand experience with the woman who would become Patsy's bestie after JonBenét's murder.

From forumsforjustice.org:

> *The next year (after the murder),* **Susan Stine** *came up to me before a game, in front of everyone, and declared loudly that I was in a lot of trouble and I should watch out. I asked her as calmly as I could what did she mean by that statement and she told me that* ***the lawyers will come after me***. *I was embarrassed and appalled and was ready to deck her right then and there. But I thought it through and left it at that. During the entire game, Susan and Roxie sat on the bench as far away from me as possible. I would switch places at times and try to sit closer to them. What a circus!*

And one of the circus tricks the Ramseys seemed to pull off is making those bats disappear. The true owner shifts, the laws of gravity seemingly shift as the bats float in nowhere around the house. But what we know for sure is the police issued a warrant for two bats on December 27th, 1996. The bats were respectively identified as items 3GLI ["Baseball bat"] which was the item listed first on that search warrant, as well as a second bat further down, listed as 74BAB.

One of the more bizarre pieces of evidence was a red clay brick retrieved from the fireplace in the lounge. Stuck to the edges of the brick were what appeared to be melted pieces of fiber.

Through the course of this narrative we'll return again and again to the source of those same "blonde" fibers. By the end of this narrative we wish to conclusively prove exactly where JonBenét was murdered.

A Hand in the Death of Another
"Desensitisation - the process of reducing sensitivity." —
thefreedictionary.com

In this chapter, and the few that follow after, we will interrogate the psychology of killing itself. Before we deal with that, we must understand what we are dealing with.

But just so we know who and where we are working towards, let me draw your attention to the first minute-and-a-half of Dr. Phil's third and final episode with Burke Ramsey.

Holding up an image of a shoe imprint left in the grit of the wine cellar [in the basement], Dr. Phil asks Burke if he recognises it. For a guy who smiled through 75% or more of the interview surrounding the death of his sister, on this particular point Burke's smile falters.

When Dr. Phil refers to the footprint as "evidence against Burke", Burke's eyes widen and he says effusively:

"It's my house; I went to play in the basement all the time..."

It's a compelling string of words. One gets a sense that the basement is part of Burke's territory – "it's my house". What's also curious is how Burke's words curl as he utters them. When you listen carefully Burke seems to betray some kind of nervous speaking impediment as he speaks those words.

While Burke has something of a lisp, when asked about the basement, his lisp becomes especially pronounced. His words tumble out very quickly, bumping against one another in a stream that is not quite fully formed.

"Ithmyhouth...Iwenthooplayinthebaythmenthallthethime..."

Burke seems to be nervous at the best of time, but that string of barely strung up words suggests there is something in the basement, far more than elsewhere in that 15 room house, that Burke has very good reason to be anxious about.

We'll deal with questions of where later. Now we want to address the psychology of killing. How does it happen? Who is capable of it? In order to do that I'm going to drill down and share an example from personal experience. This is not a story for the fainthearted – it's real, and ultimately, I had a hand in the death of another.

The world is sparkling and turning to gold and <u>a dying bird in my hand</u> has something to do with it. I crunch over hailstones dumped by an early summer storm. I rush through the front door; then open a cupboard. I wrap the mute, frozen creature in a small red towel and put the injured bird inside a red cardboard box. The box has the word **Paradise** *written on it.*

For a brief moment the bird in the red box is left on the kitchen counter. But it's not a good place – not for the bird and not for a fragile peace of mind. So I pick it up and place it on a shelf in a dark windowless closet outside my study. The closet is filled with shelves and the shelves hold up a library of books. I turn the light off, but leave the door open so I can hear signs of life or distress.

I resume my chair in the office next door at around 18:23. It's hard to believe so much has happened in the last twenty minutes; so much destruction. The garden outside is a wreckage of green strips. Large <u>Strelitzia leaves</u> are torn to shreds. Deep purple Bougainvillea leaves lie strew on the lawn's pearl icing like discoloured puddles of blood.

The sky still bubbles with angry clouds in a heavenly light. Birds, those still alive, begin a cacophony of celebration. Frogs soon join the throng.

Instead of continuing with work I contact an ex-girlfriend of mine, a local veterinarian. Does she have anything for pain? That's my first concern. Three minutes later she responds on WhatsApp:

18:26 Hey, I'm stuck right now. Keep it warm and put it in a box, see if it recovers from the shock.

18:31 <u>I've already done both.</u>

18:31 <u>Eyes are swollen which is maybe bleeding on brain.</u>

18:31 Just give it some time.

18:31 <u>Ok. I am.</u>

18:32 If that's the case [bleeding on the brain] there's nothing you can do.

18:32 <u>Yup. When I picked it up feet gripped my hand hard.</u>

18:32 Do you know how to put it down if you need to?

I call my father who's a farmer. Since there's no answer I email him at 18:37.

Hi dad, do you have anything like a painkiller to give a bird? Pigeon here hit by hail, alive but in pain. Not sure if it's gonna make it.

I suspect he might reply to the email within a few hours, which speaks to my initial expectations for the bird's prospects.

18:45 <u>Twist its neck?</u>

18:47 Unpleasant but yes.

18:45 <u>I just can't do that.</u>

18:47 Anyone with you who can?

18:48 <u>No.</u>

I speak to a neighbour on my way back to the drain where I've dropped my lens cap. He's the resident fixer-upper in the complex. I ask him if he's someone who will ring a bird's neck. He looks at me with a flicker of dismay; he says he's not. He says: "Give it a chance." I say I am, and I want to.

I head upstairs and open the door. I can see the creature has started breathing laboriously. I hear the breathing. The bird is still completely inert, its head hanging slightly.

18:49 <u>I just think if it's going to die that's less unpleasant than killing it. It's a head injury so twisting the head is really going to hurt as well.</u>

18:50 Not if you do it right; but if you hesitate it will hurt. See if it makes it through the night.

18:52 <u>Seems to be able to blink eye. Think that's good.</u>

18:53 <u>Breathing fairly hard which isn't. What do you think about how much the one eye*is swollen? Other one is less swollen.</u>

18:55 You're probably right about the bleed on the brain. Breathing hard is from shock.

For the next sixteen minutes I feel flustered. With each passing moment I'm more convinced the bird is in a great deal of distress and it probably should be euthanized. The agitation increases. I feel very reluctant to do it. I guess it's a combination of not wanting to "get my hands dirty" but also not knowing the best way to kill the animal. I've tried to pass the buck to friends and family but it's come down to me. Even so, to be honest I don't really consider any options seriously. But then that changes…

"Yah, I remember the viewing. I remember the casket was small and her eyes were closed. I think one of her eyes was a little droopy or something. I thought that was weird." – <u>Burke Ramsey</u>'s observation of his sister's face at her funeral.

Overcoming the Reluctance to Kill

"Don't kill if you can wound. Don't wound if you can subdue. Don't subdue if you can pacify. Don't raise your hand at all until you've first extended it." — Wonder Woman

When I pass the doorway the bird, having warmed a little under the towel, either startles because of my passing shadow or lunges out against a paroxysm of pain. The box tips over the shelf and the wounded creature lands heavily on the floor. It seems to paddle with its wings, a slow, awkward rowing. Blood smears on the carpet. I realise the bird is lying on its back, its damaged head bumping agonisingly against the floor as it flounders. It's painful to watch.

I turn it on its right side, and feel a horrible spasm taking hold of the creature's form. It seems like it's being torn apart from the inside out.

I see one leg is pushed back at an awkward angle - quivering. These are death throes. This seems less a conscious, co-ordinated creature fighting for its life than some automatic nervous mechanism kicking in. Some survival flare flares brightly somewhere within the pain centres of this creature's reptilian brain.

What can I do?

I pick up the animal and the thought occurs to me to cover its head in a piece of red towel, hold it tightly and then twist....

Less than an hour after discovering the injured bird, less than an hour after beginning the process of rescue I'm determined to kill it. But since I'm not an experienced killer I hesitate. There's no doubt this animal is in distress. Kill it! But *how* does one kill effectively? What has happened to my killer instinct? Aren't I one of the world's deadliest animals?

From greatergood.berkeley.edu:

...it had always been assumed that the average soldier would kill in combat simply because his country and his leaders had told him to

do so, and because it might be essential to defend his own life and the lives of his friends.

Marshall's singularly unexpected discovery was that, of every hundred men along the line of fire during the combat period, an average of only 15 to 20 "would take any part with their weapons." This was consistently true, "whether the action was spread over a day, or two days, or three."

To clarify, even in the military – during a war, on an actual battlefield – most men who have been trained to kill, men who are armed and in imminent peril, do not kill the enemy.

From greatergood.berkeley.edu:

Marshall was a U.S. Army historian in the Pacific theater during World War II and later became the official U.S. historian of the European theater of operations. He had a team of historians working for him, and they based their findings on individual and mass interviews with thousands of soldiers in more than 400 infantry companies immediately after they had been in close combat with German or Japanese troops. The results were consistently the same: Only 15 to 20 percent of the American riflemen in combat during World War II would fire at the enemy.

Were those who wouldn't fire cowards?

From greatergood.berkeley.edu:

*Those who would not fire did not run or hide—in many cases they **were willing to risk greater danger** to rescue comrades, get ammunition, or run messages. **They simply would not fire their weapons at the enemy**, even when faced with repeated waves of banzai charges.*

*Why did these men fail to fire? As a historian, psychologist, and soldier, I examined this question and studied the process of killing in combat. I have realized that there was one major factor missing from the common understanding of this process, a factor that answers this question and more: the simple and demonstrable fact that there is, within most men and women, **an intense resistance to killing other***

people. *A resistance so strong that, in many circumstances, soldiers on the battlefield will die before they can overcome it.*

And this is what happened with the speckled pigeon.

19:11 <u>Ok it's dead.</u>

19:11 <u>Died in my hands.</u>

19:11 <u>Was about to do something but then I saw it had stopped breathing. And then jerked and died.</u>

19:12 That sucks.

19:13 <u>I must add it was in a box and then it fell off the shelf.</u>

19:14 <u>So that probably helped.</u>

19:14 Yeah that would've done the trick.

19:15 <u>I thought there was a slim chance swelling might go down and it would recover when warm.</u>

19:15 Not if it had a bleed on the brain.

19:15 <u>But pain also got worse I think [as it got warmer]. Jeepers I don't know how you do your work. It's traumatic.</u>

19:17 You pretend you don't care.

CAROLS & KILLOGY
"A Christmas Carol is such a fool-proof story you can't louse it up."
— Leonard Maltin

Cogne #2

Right off the bat two major disparities materialise between the Cogne case and the Ramsey case. The first is a surfeit of blood evidence [and blood trauma], the second is Franzoni declaring the emergency immediately.

*Mrs. Franzoni, Samuele's mother, **testified she went out for a while**, at 8 a.m. to accompany the elder son (Davide, aged 6) to the school bus stop, just a few hundred meters from home, leaving alone her youngest son. Back home a few minutes later, Franzoni claimed **she found Samuele lying in the bed, covered by a comforter and gasping in a pool of blood**. The victim, a three-year old child, was sleeping in his parents' bed and **had not attempted to escape**. The woman **ran to the window to attract the attention of a neighbor**, to whom she shouted, "My baby's head has exploded", then called 118 (the Italian emergency telephone number) requesting assistance because "My child has vomited blood and **stopped breathing**." —* Wikipedia

As we know, what makes the Ramsey case tough to prosecute are the 13+ hours that passed clouding not just the time of death, but the circumstances surrounding little JonBenét's untimely exit as well.

But if there are disparities there are also similarities:

1. A phantom intruder

2. Covered by a comforter

3. No [known] attempt [by the victim] to escape

4. A window attracts attention...

5. Cause of death is a euphemism. Stopped breathing/asphyxia sounds a lot less harmless than brain damage

There's a fifth similarity, but since it's more intuitive I haven't added it to the list. Isn't there a similar hysteria and pageantry behind one mother screaming out the window to her neighbors "my baby's head exploded" and Patsy declaring the crime immediately to her friends as a kidnapping?

There's been a kidnapping –

Except there wasn't and in the Cogne case there was no literal explosion [as in a powerful force expanding outwards] inside her three year old son's head.

In this context we ought to observe that Patsy, within moments of discovering the Ransom Note calls police and immediately after rallies her friends in the neighborhood. What's missing? Why doesn't Patsy *call* JonBenét or search the house? It's as if Patsy gets the note, by her own account hardly reads it, and then *based only on the note* raises the alarm.

Wouldn't most people check first, not only JonBenét's bed but the entire property? And wouldn't a mother raise the alarm first with her entire household, recruiting everyone at home, rallying everyone in a search to fully assess what has happened? So why does Patsy get hold of John [who is upstairs, far from the basement] but not Burke who Patsy determines should be allowed to sleep peacefully through an emergency. Despite the safety and security facing the entire household at that moment, Patsy doesn't even check on her son herself.

There's also the question of simply securing the residence for their own safety. Check what's open and what isn't. We don't get a sense that either John or Patsy did this before calling the police. Would anyone really sit and wait for the police arrive to do that, or would this be the first priority – find open doors/windows and lock/close them.

If Patsy, John and Burke had acted in a conventional manner JonBenét would have been discovered seven hours earlier. So why didn't Patsy act in a conventional manner?

Even at 10:00 when the time had come and gone for the kidnapper to call, there was no acknowledgement that the kidnapping was no longer real. This suggests the obvious – that the kidnapping was never real to the Ramseys to begin with. The fact that the cops asked for handwriting samples from John and Patsy from the get go suggests the cops – quite rightly – considered the note to be some sort of ploy, in other words, not a genuine lead.

From forumsforjustice.org:

*Det. Robert Whitson arrived at the Ramsey residence **at approximately 9:30 a.m.** to inform John that the FBI had been notified and were assisting in the investigation. Whitson briefly talked to John about security for the home, and John again stated that he had personally locked up the house on the night of December 25, and that he rechecked that morning and found everything was still locked [although he'd later contradict this.] **Whitson and Patterson then asked John for samples of his handwriting. John went to a counter near the spiral staircase and picked up two letter-size pads of white lined paper. John handed both pads to Det. Patterson explaining that one pad contained prior writings of Patsy and the other his prior writings**. Patterson took the pads and made a notation on the top of each indicating which one belonged to Patsy and which one belonged to John.*

Not even the neighbors who examined the note thought the note was authentic. What was their reaction?

Fleet White and John Fernie were "equally mystified." John Fernie also said it seemed to include "fakey stuff." Nobody could understand the bizarre amount of money being requested. Both Fleet and John felt the author was familiar with John. It was noted that John had little to say about the note that morning. He remained quiet while everybody else was discussing their opinions.

What was most fascinating to me was Patsy's reaction to the note in front of others. After the police made photocopies, they gave a copy to Patsy to further examine while she remained in the sunroom. The copy was a little blurry and all you could see was the black handwriting on the page. Yet, Patsy's observation when looking at the note wasn't about the content – the odd phrasing, or amount of ransom requested - she was focused on something else. She said to one of her friends that the paper looked similar to their pads in the kitchen. If she was the author, why would she do that? Why would both Patsy and John lead the police right to those pads?

If the kidnapping wasn't real, if the Ransom Note wasn't real, then the Ramseys had to salvage some explanation with what was left. In hindsight we know this salvage operation actually worked, because the Ramseys were never indicted. The real question is what incriminating evidence was salvaged and how?

The Day After Christmas

"Killing people is like squashing an ant. I mean, you kill somebody, and it's like, 'All right, let's go get some pizza...I mean, I thought killing somebody would be this life-changing experience. And then I did it, and I was like, 'All right, whatever.'" — 21-year-old West Texas Army Pvt. Steven Green described shooting a man who refused to stop at an Iraqi checkpoint

The moment the bird died in my hands was a moment of horror. I wished I could do something, if not kill it then assuage the pain somehow. But there was no doubt when the creature had perished. It had convulsed, it had struggled to breath and then its head drooped down until it hung morbidly below my hand.

I'm not sure I would say I was "relieved" that it was dead. The tension had simmered down from an intolerable level. But the animal was still dead, so there was hardly anything to be relieved about. If anything the pain and suffering the creature had experienced was now simmering in my consciousness.

In spite of all my attempts to rescue the pigeon, when the pigeon was dead I wanted to get it out of the house. I wanted it as far from me as I could; it was a reminder not only of the reality of death, but the unpleasantness of it, and worse, just how impotent I was in the face of death. Somehow the bird's death was also a reflection on *me*, and to be honest, I no longer wished to entertain focused, full colour reflections on mortality. Yes – neither avian nor my own.

By now it was just before 19:00. Night was falling and the ground was still covered in a thick white carpet of hailstones. I decided I would bury the dead bird in the garden early the next day.

I put the bird back in the box, went outside and… I wasn't sure where to put it. On the ground risked interference with neighborhood cats, and ants. I didn't want that. In the end I placed the box on the top of a boundary wall at the far end of the property. Although out of sight and out of smell and out of the way it was still within reach. In a sense it was still under my protection.

Back indoors I cleaned the blood off the carpet. It didn't clean easy. After an initial clean there was still a dark stain in two areas. I tossed the red rag into the washing machine. As I settled back to work the red box called to me.

I could see it through my window if I wanted to, but I did not want to see it. Even so, I had a strong sense that the creature was still out there, decomposing, vulnerable to the elements and to passing predators. I couldn't shake the sense that the poor creature woke up this morning to a blue sky day like any other. Did it have any idea the day would end this way? Did it realise its slowness to get out of the way when the hail started would mean the end of everything it knew, and would ever know?

Sometime, downstairs, I did steal a glance; just a glance nothing more. Each glance was symptomatic of an amateur unused to the mechanisms of killing and disposal.

I was aware of a brewing underlying psychology. The death of this animal *was somehow my responsibility*. And now, so was its disposal/burial. What was I going to do with it? Where was I going to bury it?

The next morning the dead bird was at the forefront of my mind. I know it sounds silly, but I realised I felt traumatised by a few minutes exposure to an animal's last few minutes on this Earth.

I was dismayed to see the box on the wall had tipped over. I didn't think it was the bird coming back to life. When I recovered the feathery carcass it was hard, and I didn't wish to touch it. <u>A busy line of ants scattered under my touch</u>.

Death is repugnant to us, and it ought to be. Without life, nothing is possible. Without life, everything the organism is or means to be ceases with immediate and permanent effect. It's a devastating realisation.

And as I hithered-and-dithered in search of an adequate grave, this devastating realisation weighed heavily on me. I didn't want to bury the creature somewhere where I would be reminded of this traumatic episode. In the end I decided upon a derelict piece of

Earth up against a hot wall, partially obscured from view by a dead white tree trunk.

Then I placed the bright red box with its unlucky passenger inside. I had to remove the cardboard coffin again to widen the hole. Once done I watched with morbid fascination as I heaped bare earth onto the box and its feathery occupant. Soon it was gone, and only bare earth remained. It was now permanently out of sight, and yet those scavenging ants still danced in my mind.

As I went through the front door, covered in disturbed dirt to dust off and wash off, Dali's painting The Persistence of Memory flickered through my mind. In the bottom-left corner of Dali's artwork an orange timepiece appears to be a fruity carcass feasted on by ants; by death.

As I washed the dirt – the death – from my hands, it was impossible to shake off the knowledge that John and Patsy, and perhaps Burke too [had they known about JonBenét dead in the basement] would have felt a grave and agonising tension with each passing moment. Had they looked in on her as I had glanced – inadequately, uncertainly – at the red box? Would they have wandered about ants and cockroaches, rats and mould taking a hold of her near naked form? I would have. Would they have worried about the smell of it, and the smell of death on their own clothing? I would have.

Once my hands were clean the buried pigeon spoke more eloquently to me than any man. It said:

No matter how good or evil, no matter if you are a man or a mouse, an insect or an elephant, whether rich or poor, happy or sad, no matter how beautiful or ugly, fit or fat, loved or unloved, rich or poor – everyone will end up like I did, in the dirt.

The Psychology of Killing

"I guess I kind of like to avoid conflict...I guess part of me doesn't want to know what's going on." — Burke Ramsey

"For any particular thing, ask What is it in itself? What is its nature?" — Marcus Aurelius, Meditations (c. 175)

I did not murder the bird in the red box. Murder is the wrong word; people cannot murder animals. There is no such crime and no law for it either*. It's only murder when human beings intentionally and maliciously** kill other human beings.

An animal killing another animal is also not murder. And yet something it's hardwired into us not to kill. It was this very impulse that bubbled to the surface when I made the intellectual decision: *I am ready to kill this defenceless bird.*

Of course it died before I could.

But what if I could train myself to kill with impunity the next time it happened? Would being a more effective killer mean I was a more effective person? And what would I need to do to develop this psychological "effectiveness"?

From greatergood.berkeley.edu:

*Since World War II, a new era has quietly dawned in modern warfare: an era of **psychological warfare**, conducted not upon the enemy, **but upon one's own troops**. The triad of methods used to enable men to overcome their innate resistance to killing includes **desensitization, classical and operant conditioning, and denial defense mechanisms**.*

Let's recall that John Ramsey was in the military in the Philippines for three years and was a reservist for eight more years. I have served in the Air Force and during my training a flustered recruit shot his sergeant. The movie Full Metal Jacket brilliantly captures this world of shit masked by the uniform. Making a person into a regimented automaton is one way to desensitise a person to the human condition. <u>Did Patsy do that to her children</u>?

In terms of classical and operant conditioning, Ernest Becker*** states:

"...if the amoeba were the size of a dog we should have to grant it a mind: it does act purposively in relation to various stimuli..."

Becker then lists four levels of mindfulness:

1. *"The simplest organism takes note of its world [and] steers a course through it, and gets what it needs from it, it is "minding" its world."*

2. *"The conditioned reflex...is [about] a real liberation from the environment...[Something] becomes a sign [or symbolic] for something else...he can enrich his world by responding to it....an animal associates the sound of a gun, or a train, with the disappearance of its mate."*

3. *"...the animal sees a relationship between two things in his visual field, and decides to act on it himself. The best example of this is the chimp who uses a stick to knock down a banana, suspended out of reach.*

4. *"...the highest level of reactivity [is] symbolic behaviour. Man coins a designation for an object, and then responds to that arbitrary designation...Mind culminates in the ability to choose what it will react to..."*

In my view true crime tends to operate primarily in the third stage. If this seems overly-simplistic, <u>consider Hannibal Lecter's views</u> on the subject, <u>from imdb.com</u>:

Hannibal Lecter: *First principles, Clarice. Simplicity. Read Marcus Aurelius. Of each particular thing ask: what is it in itself? What is its nature? What does he do, this man you seek?*

Clarice Starling: *He kills women...*

Hannibal Lecter: *No. That is incidental.* **What is the first and principal thing he does?** *What needs does he serve by killing?*

Clarice Starling: *Anger, um, social acceptance, and, huh, sexual frustrations, sir...*

Hannibal Lecter: *No!* **He covets. That is his nature. And how do we begin to covet,** *Clarice? Do we seek out things to covet? Make an effort to answer now.*

Clarice Starling: *No. We just...*

Hannibal Lecter: *No.* **We begin by coveting what we see every day.**

In this particular case, I do think anger, social acceptance and a kind of repressed sexual frustration were factors. But coveting is the central activator. If we consider the killing of JonBenét an "inside job" as John Ramsey put it on December 26th, and if we consider JonBenét's blood relatives as the key "insiders", who best fits the description of:

- Angry

- Socially withdrawn

- Repressed [sexually and otherwise]

More than these, which of the three Ramsey family members was the most covetous? This answer is less simple – or easy – than it seems. But the psychological key to unlocking it lies in Lecter's crucial observation:

We begin by coveting what we see every day.

And which of the three surviving Ramseys was seeing something vital, something transformative, on a daily basis? Who would be the most stirred or consumed by a little girl's meteoric ascendency? The mother who fashioned it? A father who approved of it? Or the older brother who was displaced by it?

---

*As with the killing of slaves in ancient times, in modern society people can be held liable for killing animals in the sense that it may be equivalent to "destruction of property", as in the case of farm animals and certain kinds of valuable pets or endangered animals.

**The legal definition for murder requires that the killing be "unlawful". This suggests that certain intentional killings of human beings can be construed as "lawful"

***The Birth and Death of Meaning

Computer Games - Classical or Operative Conditioning?

"In the 1950s scientists discovered that rats which had been trained to feed themselves by pressing a lever, would press it obsessively if the food was delivered randomly. People have discovered that this works on humans as well. If you give people a lever or a button to press and give them random rewards, they will press it all the time."
— Adrian Hon, Games designer, chief creative officer of SixToStart

The American military has studied man's resistance to killing in an effort to diffuse it. The horror is that this "safe switch" can easily be flipped, and it can be flipped on virtually anyone.

From Wikipedia:

Modern military training was modified to attempt to override this [reluctance to kill] instinct, by:

- *using man-shaped targets instead of bullseye targets in marksmanship practice*
- *practicing and drilling how soldiers would actually fight*
- *dispersing responsibility for the killing throughout the group*
- *displacing responsibility for the killing onto an authority figure, i.e., the commanding officer and the military hierarchy (See the Milgram experiment)*

By the time of the United States involvement in the Vietnam War, says Grossman, 90% of U.S. soldiers would fire their weapons at other people.

That's an impressive six fold increase.

Chris Kyle, America's most effective [read: "lethal"] sniper* played video games when off duty. One might imagine Kyle's off-duty activities had nothing to do with his record as the most lethal sniper in US military history. Psychology tells a different story though – Kyle's "game" mind-set likely had an enormous impact in the real arena, where virtual lessons could be applied as a kind've gaming continuum.

From nypost.com:

"Combat was a daily event," Kyle recalled. "It starts happening, your training takes over. You start telling jokes to each other. Guys are laughing, high-fiving, saying, 'Hey, watch this one.' You're cool under fire. It's when the fire stops and when everything is done that your heartbeat starts to spike."

When he was back in the States, Kyle was subjected **to virtual-reality testing in an attempt to unlock the secrets of his, arguably, irrational calm** *when confronted with such remarkable violence and peril.*

He explained, "They wanted to do this experimental-type stuff **to figure out the mind-set**, *heart rate, and all this other stuff of SEALs.* **They basically put us in this video game**. *It was a virtual thing. . . . It puts you right back into some scenarios you're in."*

In other words, the American military tested Kyle's combat psychology by putting him in a video game. This is an ordinary commercial video game known as a first-person shooter.

From nypost.com:

As it turned out, at that point, **Kyle only felt vulnerable when subjected to virtual combat**. *After his platoon would come back to camp following a number of days in the field, the rest of the guys would immediately crash in bed. The Texan, however, would instead fire up his PC and* **play games long into the night (or day)**.

While typically more a connoisseur of sports titles like "Tiger Woods PGA Tour" or "Madden NFL," he tried his hand at digitized warfare, as well. "The new 'Call of Duty' came out, and we had the *headsets and **we hooked up our whole camp so we could be playing each other from our rooms,*** *Kyle explained. "We were going online with satellites and everything.*

I've also gone through an "addiction" phase to first-person shooter LAN games. Counterstrike is a good example where the weapons function as they do in reality – they sound the same, they're more or less effective as the real-world ordinance, and people die and bleed out gradually or rapidly depending on where they are shot. Headshots are more effective than leg shots.

From nypost.com:

*"I had a headset that one of my guys gave me, and I'm sitting there playing. **And the same kid keeps killing me**, and he was talking mad junk to me. I'm sitting there, and I'm getting pissed. "He's cussing and everything. Come to find out, he's like a 12-year-old kid back in America. He kept killing me, and he's like, 'I'm going to slay you.'*

"Motherf--ker — when I get home, I'm going to sneak into your bedroom and I am taking you out. I'm a Navy SEAL!"

"Whatever. You're in your mama's basement."

Kyle laughed as he considered the surrealism of it all: "Oh, God — I couldn't handle the war games anymore. I just wanted to take that little kid out."

Now we know for a fact that Burke was playing computer games religiously as nine year olds are wont to do. As a kid, I did. So what is the gaming architecture particular to Burke's game – the Nintendo 64 in 1996 - and how did it condition Burke if it conditioned him at all?

From Wikipedia:

*In Super Mario Bros., the player controls Mario and in a two-player game, a second player controls **Mario's brother Luigi** as he travels through the Mushroom Kingdom in order to rescue Princess Toadstool from the antagonist Bowser.*

The typical action of Mario? <u>Bashing his opponent to death</u>.

From <u>Wikipedia</u>:

Mario's primary attack is jumping on top of enemies, though many enemies have differing responses to this. For example, a Goomba will flatten and be defeated, while a Koopa Troopa will temporarily retract into its shell, allowing Mario to use it as a projectile. These shells may be deflected off a wall to destroy other enemies, though they can also bounce back against Mario, which will hurt or kill him. Another attack, for enemies standing overhead, is to jump up and hit beneath the brick that the enemy is standing on. Another is the Fire Flower; when picked up, this item changes the color of Super Mario's outfit and allows him to throw fireballs, or only upgrades Mario to Super Mario if he has not already. A less common item is the Starman, which often appears when Mario hits certain concealed or otherwise invisible blocks. This item makes **Mario temporarily invincible** *to most hazards and capable of defeating enemies on contact...*

In this single paragraph describing the gameplay the word "attack" occurs three times, "hit" occurs twice, and "kill" and "hurt" once each. Other words used to describe the game include "destroy", "defeated", "flatten" and "invincible".

If we're convinced that Burke was involved in his sister's death [and in *The Craven Silence 3* we've suggested a "Burke + 1" theory], then we must also explain – if he did it – how he overcame the reluctance to kill?

From <u>playwithlearning.com</u>:

Behaviourists describe "conditioning" as a universal learning process, dividing it into two types:

- *classical conditioning occurs* **when a natural reflex responds to a stimulus**

- *operant conditioning occurs* **when a response to a stimulus is reinforced**

The key principle of Behaviourism is the reward or punishment of a new behaviour, commonly described as the 'carrot and stick' approach to learning. The theory states that rewarding someone for particular behaviour encourages him to behave in the same way in a similar situation. The reward reinforces behaviour. Conversely, if behaviour is punished, the subject is less likely to repeat it. In Behaviourism, people can learn not to do things as well as to do things.

Irrespective of what was happening in Burke's real world, if he was gaming a lot, we have an insight into the architecture of his psychological world.

From playwithlearning.com:

Computer games are sometimes described as a "Skinner box" because of the way they offer reward or punishment for the player's behaviour. Like the classic experiment, many games **require the performance of a repetitive task to achieve some goal or reward.** *In behaviourist theory, a reward or positive reinforcer is anything that increases the frequency of a behaviour. Conversely, punishment or negative reinforce is something that decreases the frequency of a behaviour. The strict (narrative) structure and scheduling of rewards is classic behaviourism and characterises many games.*

What repetitive tasks occur in the Mario game mythos? Bashing. To proceed up a level and win points, bash your way to the top, and even better, recruit an ally. This psychology is reinforced not only by repeated gameplay but by reinforcers within the game.

From playwithlearning.com:

Traditional positive reinforcers in computer games include:

Points

Power-ups

Bonuses

Unlocks

Negative reinforcers include:

Failure to beat high score

An increase in obstacles or opponents

A decline in health

Multiplayer and social reinforcers include:

Status

Leaderboards

...Game designer, Jon Radoff continues:

"The behaviorist approach to games...channels inquiry away from the harder problems of immersion, cooperation and competition..."

In other words, chronic gaming desensitizes the user to the real world and reinforces negative side-effects such as social awkwardness.

From verywell.com:

Authors such as Gwynne Dyer and Richard Holmes have traced the development of boot camp glorification of killing. They've found it was almost unheard of in World War I, rare in World War II, increasingly present in Korea, and **thoroughly institutionalized in Vietnam**. *"The language used in [marine training camp] Parris Island to describe the joys of killing people," writes Dyer, helps* **"desensitize [marines] to the suffering of an 'enemy,'** *and at the same time they are being indoctrinated in the most explicit fashion (as previous generations were not) with the notion that their purpose is not just to be brave or to fight well; it is to kill people."*

The purpose of the gaming character is also to kill the enemy, and thus the character is – by definition – desensitized to the suffering of the enemy.

From verywell.com:

But desensitization by itself is probably not sufficient to overcome the average individual's deep-seated resistance to killing. Indeed, this desensitization process is almost a smoke screen for conditioning, which is the most important aspect of modern training. Instead of lying prone on a grassy field calmly shooting at a bull's-eye target, for example, the modern soldier spends many hours standing in a foxhole, with full combat equipment draped about his body. At periodic intervals one or two **man-shaped targets will pop up in front of him, and the soldier must shoot the target.**

We are naïve if we think, in the context of the Ramsey scenario, that a small child playing a game where obstacles are bashed away is so far removed from a deadly military assassin drawing inspiration from similar games conducted remotely [as it turns out] with a child.

From verywell.com:

In addition to traditional marksmanship, soldiers are learning to shoot reflexively and instantly, while **mimicking the act of killing.** In behavioral terms, the man shape popping up in the soldier's field of fire is **the "conditioned stimulus."** On special occasions, even more realistic and complex targets are used, many of them filled with red paint or catsup, which **provide instant and positive reinforcement** when the target is hit. In this and other training exercises, **every aspect of killing on the battlefield is rehearsed, visualized, and conditioned.**

*Chris Kyle had 160 confirmed kills.

JonBenét Ramsey murder - thirteen familiar flourishes present in other famous cases

"He who has not Christmas in his heart will never find it under a tree." — Roy L. Smith

The JonBenét case seems to have drowned in a deluge of detail. In the extremely basic anatomy of the JonBenét case we see thirteen familiar flourishes present in other famous cases.

1. There's <u>the covering of the body with a blanket</u> [Amanda Knox]

2. The murder corresponds to some imminent event, celebration or holiday [Amanda Knox – All Souls Day + trip to Gubbio , Oscar Pistorius – Valentine's Day + trip to Brazil, Steven Avery – Halloween + <u>large settlement</u>, Jodi Arias – <u>an imminent trip to Cancún</u>]

3. There's a murder in the "comfort" of the home [Amanda Knox, Jodi Arias, Oscar Pistorius, Steven Avery and arguably O.J. Simpson too]

4. There's contamination of the crime scene [Amanda Knox, Jodi Arias, Oscar Pistorius, Steven Avery]

5. The police/prosecutor are the real culprits [Amanda Knox, Oscar Pistorius, O.J. Simpson, Steven Avery]

6. Close to the time of the murder or just prior to the incident, the main suspect was supposedly asleep or in bed [Amanda Knox, Oscar Pistorius, O.J. Simpson]

7. The murderer is actually the victim [Amanda Knox, Oscar Pistorius, Steven Avery, Jodi Arias, O.J. Simpson]

8. The "real" murderer or the cause leading to the murder is a nameless, faceless intruder/phantom/gangster/resident evil [Amanda Knox, Oscar Pistorius, Jodi Arias, O.J. Simpson]

9. The murderer courts the media, rather than taking the court/police into their confidence [Amanda Knox, Oscar Pistorius, Steven Avery, Jodi Arias, O.J. Simpson]

10. Long period, in excess of 10 hours before discovery of the body [Amanda Knox, Steven Avery, Jodi Arias]

11. The crime involves injury to the neck and/ or strangulation [Amanda Knox, O.J. Simpson, Jodi Arias]

12. The crime involves sex and/or money [Amanda Knox, Oscar Pistorius, O.J. Simpson, Steven Avery, Jodi Arias]

13. The crime is also associated with feces, urine or fecal matter [Amanda Knox]

Which name comes up in all thirteen of these flourishes? Amanda Knox is also the only one alleged to have had an accomplice with her [Raffaele Sollecito] *at the scene of the crime* involving the sexual assault and murder of her British housemate Meredith Kercher*.

Oscar Pistorius is alleged to have had an accomplice who wiped data off his phone [allegedly his brother Carl]. Steven Avery is alleged to have committed the crime with his nephew, Brendon Dassey. O.J. Simpson enjoyed the silence and support of numerous people, including his pal and lawyer, Robert Kardashian.

In all of these examples we see the collusion of family members and friends or both. The collusion of others in a crime clearly makes it more difficult not only to isolate and prosecute the criminal, but also complicates the prosecution of the crime itself. But as we've seen in our interrogations into the Amanda Knox narrative, the strongest link where there is more than one suspect *is also the weakest*.

In the Amanda Knox case we saw both Knox and Sollecito initially support one another, then one withdrew the other's alibi without realising it meant their own alibi was lost at the same time, and then the pair resumed conditional support of one another [although it's far from clear today what either's defence is and how each defence supports the other].

A cursory [and very unscientific] poll on Websleuths shows the most likely suspects for JonBenét's murder:

1. Patsy 38.39%

2. An Intruder 31.24%

3. Burke 21.62%

4. John 8.75%

While the Intruder scores high, in reality the score is:

Ramsey family murder: 68.76% vs Intruder murder: 31.24%

I tend to take the same view broadly because it seems unlikely that a felon would risk breaking into a house, take the time to write a genteel three page ransom note in-between abducting, murdering [but not raping] poor little JonBenét.

There are many more detailed reasons for these aspersions that go to the content of the handwritten note, the lack of footprints in the snow and virtually no signs of breaking and entering. But before we get to all that, let's open the door to one popular theory

From westernslopewatchdog.com:

Try to imagine being a nine-year-old kid growing up in the shadow of a five-year-old beauty queen. He was frustrated, angry, and, in theory, probably just beginning to discover his sexuality.

I'm a vegetarian pacifist, but I remember what it was like [to] be a nine- or ten-year-old. I was cruel then, blowing up grasshoppers in tin cans and shoving firecrackers down fire-ant holes. Cruelty comes with being a nine- or ten-year-old boy.

JonBenét Ramsey was killed by bludgeoning and strangulation. There was no DNA discovered in her vagina, meaning she was not

raped… John and Patsy Ramsey came together after the killing like no married couple has before. Why is this? Most parents of dead children split up.

* Many allege a third perpetrator as well [Rudy Guede, an ethic Ivorian living in Perugia Italy, who was convicted and is doing time].

HOLLY & CANDYSTICKS
"Killing is not so easy as the innocent believe." — J.K. Rowling, Harry Potter and the Half-Blood Prince

Cogne #3

One has the impression that the small mountain village in northern Italy had something else in common with a small mountain enclave in Colorado. The Cogne ~~coroner's report~~ psychiatrist's assessment* seemed to back up the mother's tall tale. Folks standing up to defend their own in small communities is typical.

Shortly after [Franzoni's frantic scream], neighbor psychiatrist Ada Satragni arrived on the scene. **The doctor believed Franzoni** *that the child's skull would have "exploded" [he claimed] a cerebral aneurysm may actually increase the intracranial pressure, causing the explosion of bones.* — Wikipedia

The scientific explanation appears to make some sense.

A few days later, Dr. Satragni released an interview in which she proposed that perhaps Samuele, aware of being home alone, had desperately burst in tears and that "The violent crying might have caused the opening of the head." At the time, Dr. Satragni devoted herself to wash the dying child and then carried him out, in front of the house, despite the cold weather and without any caution to protect his head or neck. — Wikipedia

Here we **get massive contamination of the crime scene**, but what's curious to me is the gender of the doctor. It's a woman defending another woman, and perhaps a mother defending another mother who was also her neighbor. It's all fair to middling except the actual "scientific" assessment – a child cried so hard when it was left alone [for a few minutes] it burst its head/skull.

Another neighbor, Mrs. Daniela Ferrod, noticed that, for the entire time Mrs. Franzoni **remained motionless and silent**, *without saying anything or even trying to touch her son.* — Wikipedia

I also want to deal with two reactions to two aspects of the Ramsey case on that morning and early afternoon after Christmas. First let's look at the reaction of neighbors, and John and Patsy, to the **Ransom Note** and second, the reaction of Patsy to **the appearance of JonBenét's dead body,** when John brought her up from the downstairs basement.

1. If the police were puzzled** by the weirdly specific ransom specified [$118 000 instead of $100 000 or $200 000], John's pals Fleet White and John Fernie were equally weirded out. Why not make it a big round number? Why not make it a bigger number? Why would a foreign faction do all this for chump change? The semantics used indicated an educated murderer, if not an experienced one. And John? The Ransom Note was directed at Mr. Ramsey and then devolved to calling John by name three times, what did John make of all this? What was John's attempt to explain this? John had no comment. As for Patsy, she had no comment on the content of the note. She did make a random remark about the kind of paper the note was written on. Since Patsy was referring to a smeary black and white photocopy of another photocopy, the cops wondered how Patsy could see any textural similarities with her own yellow pad lying in the kitchen.

2. Even more damning was Patsy Ramsey's immediate reaction when John brought JonBenét's corpse, with its outstretched arms, out of the basement just after 13:00. To be unequivocal, Patsy showed no immediate reaction. If anything the first thing Patsy did was to freeze. Both Barbara Fernie and Priscilla White launched out of their seats but Patsy momentarily remained where she was.

Upon arrival of the helicopter that would carry Samuele to the ER, neither Mrs Franzoni nor her husband (Stefano Lorenzi, surveyor, 31 years), who had been informed of the tragedy by phone, followed their child. . — Wikipedia

Did the Ramseys wish to see their child prior to the autopsy? Did they wish to say goodbye to the girl in the privacy of a morgue? Or had they said their farewells much earlier?

*The psychiatrist was a neighbor.

**The Boulder police demonstrated their suspicions surrounding the authorship of the Ransom Note as early as 09:30 on the morning after Christmas, barely three hours after arriving at the Ramsey residence.

Why was Patsy still wearing the same outfit on December 26th?

"One of the most glorious messes in the world is the mess created in the living room on Christmas day. Don't clean it up too quickly." — Andy Rooney

Now that we've addressed the psychology of killing, we need to address the psychology of cover-up.

On the eve of Lifetime's movie, *Who killed JonBenét*, speculation returns to Patsy. Did Patsy kill her daughter? Is Lifetime's movie and the documentary about Patsy [aired directly after the movie] a serious attempt to point a finger at the untouchable Ramseys, or is it dressed up *Apologia*? Is it just another PR campaign for the Ramseys with weeks remaining to the 20 year anniversary of the six year old girl's mysterious murder?

We're less interested in the theory that Patsy did it than the back room stuff going on in setting up these documentaries. Although we will interrogate the Lifetime programs by the end of this narrative.* As far as we're concerned, the contents of the programs are yet another attempt at misdirection.

The real question isn't a simple yes or no answer on whether or not Patsy murdered JonBenét. The real question is *what was the extent of her involvement* in her daughter's death? What was suspicious?

For starters, Patsy wearing the same clothing the next morning as the night before was suspicious. We think there are three possible explanations. The first is that Patsy didn't even think about her clothes. She was flustered and with so much going on, *her own appearance* was the last thing on her mind. The second possibility is that Patsy initially forgot to change in the chaos of that morning, but then later realized it after everyone arrived. She could have theoretically changed at any stage - at 08:00, 09:00, 10:00, 12:00, 14:00, etc. but she didn't because how would she explain that? The third possibility, and the one Nick and I now feel is most likely, is that Patsy intentionally kept the same clothes on as the night before. Why would she do that?

From acandyrose.com, 48 Hour Investigates, October 4, 2002:

BRUCE LEVIN: (from the Atlanta meeting taped Aug 29, 2000 9:34am) (Patsy was smiling through all of this) *we believe the fibers from her jacket were found in the paint tray, found tied into the ligature found on JonBenét's neck, was found on the blanket she was wrapped in, was found on the duct tape and that was found on the mouth. I have no evidence from any scientist that suggests that those fibers are from any source other than your red jacket.*

LIN WOOD: *Well come on, what other sources did they test?*

ERIN MORIARTY: (voiceover) *Patsy's attorney, Lin Wood asked prosecutors to produce the evidence and when they wouldn't he refused to let Patsy go on the record. But she did go on the record with us.*

ERIN MORIARTY: (Talking to Patsy) *What do you think about these fibers?*

PATSY: *After John discovered the body and she was brought to the living room. I laid eyes on her: I knelt down and hugged her. But I was, had my whole body on her body.* **My sweater fibers or whatever I had on that morning are going to transfer to her clothing****.

---

*An analysis of the Lifetime documentary broadcast on November 5th, 2016 is provided in *The Day After Christmas 2.*

Of course they're going to transfer and that's precisely what Patsy likely considered as she prepared for the police to arrive. Later that day Patsy's clothing walked out the front door with Patsy when she and John were ordered to leave the house. But not before she put on her fancy fur coat. I think Patsy thought she'd be free and clear; if police found red fibers they'd simply brush them off as coming from the mom. When Patsy realized this wasn't the case, the Ramsey lawyers sprang into action. According to Steve Thomas*:

A huge legal fight would ensue over the coming months as we sought to retrieve their clothing, particularly Patsy's red turtleneck sweater, her black-and-red-checked blazer, and any fur garments. They would eventually assume tremendous importance.

Something else I find disturbing in addition to withholding her clothing, is how when speaking to Erin Moriarty, Patsy refers to JonBenét as "the body." She doesn't say "JonBenét's body," she doesn't even say "her body," she refers to the freshly dead JonBenét as "the body." That's pretty damn detached.

****JonBenét: Inside the Ramsey Murder Investigation*

Why would you pretend to be asleep when your sister is missing/dead?

Lacy defended her decision to exonerate the family. She also said that part of her belief that an intruder killed JonBenét was formed during a tour of the Ramsey home a few days after the discovery of the girl's body on Dec. 26, 1996. During that tour, <u>Lacy said she saw a "butt-print" in the carpeting around the corner from JonBenét's room</u>. "Whoever did this sat outside of her room and waited until everyone was asleep to kill her," Lacy said, according to the ABC report. — <u>9news.com</u>

Three years and three months after JonBenét's murder, her parents published their book *Death of Innocence*. The title seemed to be more a reflection of their trials and tribulations as "innocent victims" than a tribute to their innocent daughter. What's curious though is that the Ramseys book beat Steve Thomas' book in the race to the bookshelves by as little as two weeks.

Death of Innocence was <u>first published on March 15th 2000</u>, and Steve Thomas' *JonBenét: Inside the Ramsey Murder Investigation* <u>was published April 11th, 2000</u>. As a result of lawsuits against both books, both books were re-released several months later that same year, this time Steve Thomas' book pipped the Ramsey's book to the post by two months. An edited and updated version of *JonBenét: Inside the Ramsey Murder Investigation* was released on November 15, 2000 while the next iteration of *Death of Innocence* appeared on January 1st, 2001.

We'll deal with the books themselves, who sued who and regarding what, in the next narrative. For now we're going to glimpse a short extract in Thomas' book dealing with the immediate aftermath of JonBenét's murder.

We want to deal with the first two questions:

1. Was Burke awake early on December 26th, 1996?

2. How did the Ramseys behave after JonBenét's body was "discovered" in the basement?

Let's start with Burke.

1. Simple question – was Burke awake early on that day after Christmas?

There are two simple answers to this question. The first answer is that Burke was awake when nobody else was, and we know that because that's what he said on Dr. Phil. The question has to be clarified – by early do we mean was Burke awake in the wee hours [close to midnight] on December 25, or was he awake at around 05:30, 05:52 [the time Patsy called 911] on December 26, and in the hour prior to 07:00 when the police and neighbors arrived?

Again the short answer, from Burke himself, was that he was awake on both occasions. The difference between him being awake late at night was that, according to him, no one knew he was awake and downstairs, while the next morning no one knew he was awake ["pretending to be asleep"] upstairs, in his bed.

But we don't really want to stop there, at Burke's answers.

The answer to the question, as we'll see, is less important than the question itself, and the questions surrounding this question.

Why does it matter whether Burke was awake? Well it matters a great deal when Burke was awake and perhaps not in his bed, or not sleeping on the night of his sister's murder. It matters because Burke is potentially a witness [perhaps more] to what happened to his sister on the night of her murder.

One can also anticipate if Burke was somehow involved in his sister's death his parents would explain away his involvement by saying he was sleeping. If a cover-up occurred, the cover-up would have worked best with Burke out of the way in his room, while his parent [or parents] frantically worked through the night to "make things right."

Interestingly, if the parents were aware of fiber evidence, it would make sense for John [if he was involved] to not wear any of his own clothing, and for Patsy to do the same or to remain in the clothing she'd worn all day.

Coming back to Burke, in early versions of this story, the assumption was always that Burke was asleep. One of those who made this assumption was detective Steve Thomas. Thomas pinned the entire crime on Patsy, and one of the ways to make that mistake was to take Patsy's word at face-value on Burke, Patsy's word on Burke's behaviour and Patsy's word on Burke's whereabouts [all according to Patsy].

Time and time again in true crime we see that murderers are also liars. Murderers often murder to conceal or silence, so why would a murderer undo that effort by blowing the whistle on themselves? Why wouldn't they lie about something they did in secret?

In fairness to Thomas, we have the benefit of more than eighteen years of additional hindsight, and more than that, we have the benefit of Burke Ramsey's own words in his first ever television interview in 2016, to go on as well.

Regarding the night of December 25th Burke Ramsey has this to say:

BURKE: *"Yeah, I had some toy that I wanted to put together. I remember being downstairs after everyone was in bed ... wanting to get this thing out."*

And the next morning?

Dr. PHIL: *"Where were you when that phone call was made?"*

BURKE: *"In my bed..."*

Dr. PHIL: *"It was still dark?"*

BURKE: *"Ya, I was just laying there."*

Dr. PHIL: *"How long from the time she came in, before the police came in?"*

BURKE: *"Under an hour."*

Dr. PHIL: *"After she left, what did you do?"*

BURKE: *"I just laid there. **I didn't really know what else to do.**"*

Consider the oddness of this statement. You have a nine year old voluntarily – he claims – staying in his room. In Patsy's 1996 newsletter she describes Burke as "a busy fourth grader". In 1995 Patsy describes her son using exactly the same word:

"Burke is busy in his third grade year...He continues with Boy Scouting and the piano. This winter he is the tallest guy on his basketball team. Summer on Charlevoix was spent taking golf and sailing lessons each day. Burke is quite the sailor!"

But we don't have to take Patsy's word. At Sunday mass in Boulder on January 5, the weekend after JonBenét's funeral, we see a smiling Burke exiting the church. He arrives at the door and drops down the steps of the church ahead of his parents. A friend of Burke's wearing a green jacket* appears just off camera to the right. The friend runs off and Burke tears after him, a bemused look on his face.

Does this seem like a shy and retiring child who didn't know what to do? In our view that statement only makes sense if Burke had been told to stay put. Obviously if he was told to stay in his room, guilty or not, he couldn't do much either way – to help JonBenét or to help his own case.

Dr. PHIL: *"Were you curious?"*

BURKE: *"I'm not the worrying type."*

67

Dr. PHIL: *"So, who came and got you eventually?"*

BURKE: *"I think it was my dad that came in."*

Dr. PHIL: *"You do go downstairs. Describe that scene."*

BURKE: *"I just remember like, I ... **I have an image in my head of the kitchen. And, it was early morning. There were a few people around that I didn't really know.** There might have been a police car, I think. I just kind of remember walking slowly downstairs and everyone was like, "Hey we're going to take you to Fleet's [family friend]."*

Burke's description of the scene is a whole lotta nuthin'. Everything Burke says we know. There's a kitchen. It's early morning. There are people around. There's a police car. He walked downstairs. What's missing of course is what a genuine account would include. Where was mom and dad? How were they? Who was there that you recognized? What Christmas gifts or food or other things were lying around that you remember? Did you see the ransom note or hear someone talking about it?

Of course, incredibly and unbelievably, Burke tells Dr. Phil that [20 years later] he hasn't really read the ransom note, at least not that he can seemingly recollect.

Instead Burke's powers of description appear to be extremely weak. The image in his head is hardly an image at all, is it?

On December 20th, 2008 an Australian posted the following comment on the topix forum, via a Sydney-based avatar named Limaes.

From topix.com:

*One thing I feel certain about is that they [John and Patsy] told him [Burke] to stay in bed and **pretend to be sleeping** if anyone came into his room and when they got him up, they scooted him straight out the door and straight past the police WITHOUT HAVING TO SPEAK TO THEM.*

The dodges continued a few days later when the police wanted to talk to Burke. Bynum, the Ramseys' "interim attorney" informed them that according to Dr. Beuf, Burke Ramsey could not be interviewed. No further explanation was given. Just simply, the good doctor has "determined" Burke is off limits.

We know Burke *was* eventually interviewed on January 8, 1997, but it wasn't by police. He was interviewed by Dr. Bernhard, from the Department of Social Services [DSS]. Kolar asserts the only reason this interview took place was to prevent DSS from taking Burke away from his parents and placing him into protective custody, something that would be standard procedure considering his sister had just been murdered in their home. In other words, this interview took place because it had to take place – not because the Ramseys were being cooperative. It would be two additional years before police got to speak with Burke.

It's important to put a very fine point on this idea. Was it Burke's idea to "pretend to be sleeping"? Why on Earth would he pretend to be asleep if his sister was in danger and his parents were looking for her? Why, with his parents calling 911 [which he claimed to hear on Dr. Phil], would Burke not head on downstairs and find out what the hell was going on? And if John and Patsy were frantically looking for JonBenét, why wouldn't they ask Burke if he'd seen her, why wouldn't go through the house calling out her name?

From crimefeed.com:

*Many experts have said that they hear three distinct voices on the 911 tape, and claim that Burke's voice can be heard saying "What did you find?" at the end. Burke denied speaking those words or being present when the call took place, but added a qualifier: "I definitely don't remember that **unless someone erased my memory** or something," he said.*

Burke said he remembered a policeman coming into the room, and shining a flashlight. "I remember her [Patsy] saying, 'Where's my baby? Where's my baby?'" he said. "I just laid there and didn't really know what else to do."

We've been through this territory before, and we know this part is contentious too, because Patsy denies ever going to be Burke's room, or even talking with him that morning. So why can't Burke or Patsy agree on who was where and who said what?

From crimefeed.com:

*Dr. Phil pointed out that people may find it odd that he stayed in bed when a police officer came in with a flashlight. Burke responded: "To be fair, I didn't know that it was a police officer. I guess I kind of like to avoid conflict. I guess **I just felt safer there**."*

Talk is cheap, isn't it? First of all, why would one child feel safer in his bedroom and in bed [alone it must be stressed] when his sister has [according to Burke and his family] been abducted from bedroom and her bed on the same floor of the house? There's only one thing more ludicrous than Burke feeling safe when JonBenét was missing [and dead as it turned out], and that's John and Patsy allowing him out of their sight knowing "there's a killer on the loose". Of course if Burke had something to do with JonBenét's demise sending him to his room, to be out of the way – not out of harm's way but out of the way of prying investigators – makes perfect sense.

In terms of Burke's own version of events - that he decided of his own volition to hang around in bed while pandemonium was breaking out elsewhere in the house - what are we to make of Burke's contention?

Is Burke really the kind of kid who liked to avoid conflict? Burke's description of himself sounds "mild-mannered" except we know that at age nine, Burke was anything but a normal, balanced child. He was smearing his own shit throughout his home, including on his baby sister's Christmas gift. Smearing shit on someone else's stuff, including a Christmas gift, putting a grapefruit sized piece of one's own rolled up dung into someone else's bed – does that sound like someone trying to avoid conflict, or does it sound like someone trying to foment one?

When Steve Thomas references the "peculiar scene" of young Burke being "awakened by his father and Fleet White" we're all too aware that Burke recently said he *wasn't* sleeping. The longer answer to the question is that late at night and very early in the morning of JonBenét's murder Burke wasn't sleeping. We also know from his own words that he was in bed pretending to be asleep. If Burke wasn't asleep why did the police – including Thomas – think he was sleeping? Burke hasn't spoken for twenty years so he's going to be an unlikely source about his own sleeping habits for the past twenty years. So who is the source?

Let's examine what Patsy told the Boulder police on June 23rd, 1998.

From acandyrose.com:

PATSY: *There weren't a bunch of people...there in the house yet. I was talking to the 911 person. So I don't know what conversation.*

HANEY: *Were only your family in the house at that time?*

PATSY: *Correct. Burke was upstairs asleep. John was here on the floor in his underwear looking at the note, I was on the floor calling 911.*

Could Patsy have misspoken? Any chance she forgot about it; forgot what really happened? Let's go to Patsy's very first detailed statement made four months after JonBenét's death to the Boulder police on April 30th, 1997.

From forumsforjustice.org:

TRUJILLO: *When did you check on Burke during all this? You talked about John going to check on Burke.*

PATSY: *Yeah. I think he ran and [checked] on him when I was up, up there uh, you know, it just all happened so fast. I said, 'Oh, my God. What about Burke?' And I think he ran in and checked him while I was running back downstairs **or something**.*

TRUJILLO: *Okay.*

PATSY: *But I remember he, you know, I think he ran and checked on him and, and he told me he was okay **or whatever**.*

TRUJILLO: *Okay.* **Was Burke still in the same bed? He hadn't moved beds or anything** *like that?*

PATSY: *I don't know. I didn't go in there and look.*

According to Burke, Patsy did go in and look. Even in a fictitious scenario one would imagine the little girl's mother checking for JonBenét in Burke's room, and also checking to see if Burke is okay. That during the entire morning Patsy didn't have time to get to Burke beggars belief.

From <u>forumsforjustice.org</u>:

TRUJILLO: *Okay. John talked about that with all the commotion and you guys yelling and stuff, did that wake up Burke at all?*

PATSY: *No, it didn't.*

TRUJILLO: *Okay.*

PATSY: *He didn't get up for a while.*

TRUJILLO: *Cause we talked, John went up later on and, and* **woke up Burke***...*

PATSY: *Right.*

TRUJILLO: *...and...*

PATSY: *Yeah. Brought him down.*

TRUJILLO: *Okay. Uh...*

PATSY: *Got him dressed and...*

TRUJILLO: *Okay. So you're on the phone call 911. John's reading the note. What happened then?*

PATSY: *Uh, that woman on 911 or whoever I was talking to...*

TRUJILLO: *Um hum.*

PATSY: *it just seemed like she took forever, you know. I said, I mean, she just kept saying well what is it, you know, and I said our little girl has been kidnapped, you know, and I gave her the address and, I mean, she just, I mean, just, she, I just said sent somebody fast, you know. Uh, it just seemed like she was just, I'm sure she had things she had to go through...*

There's also a whole lotta nuthin' from Patsy. She seems to be suggesting Kimberly Archuleta was remiss in some way. Actually, of course, Patsy is the one who hangs up and is not particularly helpful – she doesn't even provide JonBenét's name.

From forumsforjustice.org:

TRUJILLO: *Um hum.*

PATSY: *but oh. And John just was reading that note and, and then uh, and he went up and got dressed sometime before the policeman got there he had gotten dressed . . .*

TRUJILLO: *Um hum.*

PATSY: *and uh, the Whites and the Fernies came over. . .*

TRUJILLO: *Okay. Do, who called the, who called the Whites and Fernies?*

PATSY: *I did. I did.*

TRUJILLO: *Okay. Do you remember which ones you called first? Who called? Who did you call first?*

PATSY: *I, I don't exactly. I think I called the Whites first, but I can't remember exactly.*

TRUJILLO: *Who did you talk to at the White's house?*

PATSY: *Pricilla, I think.*

TRUJILLO: *Okay. Do you remember what you told her about what was going on?*

PR: **Not**, *I mean, I was just hysterical. I think I, I probably told her that she had been, JonBenét had been kidnapped. And uh, to come over and . . .*

This is a little slip. The answer to whether you remember what you told someone, is either you do or you don't. The answer to whether you told someone JonBenét had been murdered is either you did or you did **not**.

From forumsforjustice.org:

TRUJILLO: *Then you called the Fernies.*

PATSY: *Fernies.*

TRUJILLO: *And who did you talk to at the Fernie house?*

PATSY: *Uh, I think I talked to John. I think I talked to John.*

TRUJILLO: *Okay.*

PATSY: *(Inaudible) I don't remember. I don't remember. I think John Fernie got there first, before Barbara, but I don't remember who answered the phone really.*

It's a pity Trujillo doesn't quiz Patsy about the Stines. Why weren't they called? They were the neighbors closest to the Ramseys, and besides location, the Stines were the last to see the Ramseys on Christmas night. Could JonBenét not be there – just 0.4 miles up the road? That would be 2 minutes by bicycle. Why not check whether or not JonBenét went out on her new bike? Why not call and fucking find out? But Trujillo misses the opportunity to nail down this detail, and moves on.

From forumsforjustice.org:

TRUJILLO: *Okay. So John runs upstairs, gets dressed. You're already dressed. Who's the first person that comes in the front door? Who's the first person that makes it over to your house?*

PATSY: *Uh, well. The policeman.*

TRUJILLO: *Okay. The policeman arrives.*

TRUJILLO: *Who, who all was, where was John at the time that the officer arrived?*

PATSY: *Oh, I don't I don't know. I remember I, I don't know where he was. I walked out onto the front step there and I was just, I was just kind of out of it. I was hysterical.*

In the Bonita papers, drawn from various police documents, Patsy was described by friends as being so hysterical that she was "incoherent." She was loudly praying to God and screaming to Jesus. In Schiller's book, he reports Priscilla White helping Patsy while she was "vomiting and hyperventilating."

At this point in the morning, Patsy allegedly doesn't know what's happened to JonBenét. If the situation were sincere, I can certainly understand a mother being upset and crying, but vomiting and incoherent? Wouldn't a mother who's determined to find her daughter also have some semblance of coherence? Wouldn't they be actively working with the police on what to do next rather than flailing hysterically on the ground?

From forumsforjustice.org:

TRUJILLO: *Um hum.*

PATSY: *I said that there was a note and that our daughter had been kidnapped and we were trying to get the money and I don't, I don't remember.*

TRUJILLO: *Okay. So you met the officer when he came into, or came up to the front door.*

PATSY: *Right.*

TRUJILLO: *You're the one that opened the door for him.*

PATSY: *Right.*

TRUJILLO: *Okay. Um, the officer kind of herded you into that, the sunroom area?*

PATSY: *Right.*

TRUJILLO: *And then, the way I understand it, then the Whites and the Fernies got there?*

PATSY: *I believe that's right, yeah.*

TRUJILLO: *Do you remember who came in first, the Whites or the Fernies?*

PATSY: *I think I think it was the Whites, but I can't remember.*

TRUJILLO: *Okay. Uh. . .*

PATSY: *It seemed like they got there pretty quick.*

TRUJILLO: *Fleet and Pricilla arrived?*

PATSY: *Yeah.*

TRUJILLO: *Okay. About what time did John go upstairs and wake up Burke to have him leave, cause I know that was after the Whites got there. Is that right?*

PATSY: *I don't know what time that was, but it was more, it was more daylightish. I mean that was after every, a lot of people were there by then.*

Sunrise in Boulder was at 07:22 on the day after Christmas. While it's likely Burke was secreted out of the home when more people were around, what's less likely is that it happened look after sunrise. Linda Arndt arrived at 08:10 and didn't report seeing Burke.

If the Whites arrived close to 06:30 it's likely Burke left soon after, close to 07:00 [and thus before sunrise, in the dim murk of a glacial mid-winter dawn.]

From forumsforjustice.org:

TRUJILLO: *Okay.*

PATSY: *Uh, and there was some discussion about what to do about Burke and I think Fleet said he could come over to their house and play or something.*

TRUJILLO: *Um hum. What, what kind of discussion, I mean, other than Fleet saying he can come over to my house and play.*

What to do with Burke?

PATSY: *Well . . .*

TRUJILLO: *(Inaudible)*

PATSY: *just you know,* **we just thought it was best that he not be around.** *It was, it was just bedlam, you know, and I was a mess and, you know the police trying to do their job and all and . . .*

TRUJILLO: *Um hum.*

PATSY: *you know.*

TRUJILLO: *Was it uh, was Linda [Arndt] there by the time uh, when Burke was leaving?*

PATSY: *Um....*

TRUJILLO: *Do you remember that?*

PATSY: *I don't remember exactly. She was, she was there pretty soon, but it seemed like, I remember sitting in the sunroom and it was, more daylightish when she got there.*

TRUJILLO: *Okay.*

PATSY: *So I don't know, I don't know what time it was really.*

TRUJILLO: *Okay. Who called Father Rol and let him know what was going on?*

PATSY: *I think Barbara [Fernie] said she did.*

TRUJILLO: *Okay. Do you have any idea about what time Father Rol got there?*

PATSY: **I don't know what time anything happened.** *I was just, I was just frantic.*

TRUJILLO: *Okay. Kind of maybe, make your own timeline here.*

PATSY: *Um.*

TRUJILLO: *Um, do you remember if Burke left the house before or after Father Rol arrived?*

PATSY: *No I don't, I don't remember.*

TRUJILLO: *Okay. Um, again, who,* **who took Burke out of the house? Did John, John and Fleet do that or did just Fleet drive him away?**

PATSY: *Uh, I don't believe John left. I think that John brought him downstairs and uh, he came over to me and told, really couldn't (inaudible) or anything and he had tears in his eyes, I think, I think we just said you can go over and play at the Whites. I don't remember exactly who took him out of there.*

So we have Patsy who can't remember the time, she can't remember who she called, she can't remember who was in the home when Burke left, but she can remember seeing tears in poor little Burke's eyes, and kind've remembers what she said to him. Oddly, with her little girl missing – kidnapped apparently – Patsy doesn't seem to know who takes Burke away and by inference, where. Think about that for a second. One child is missing, presumed kidnapped, you don't check on the other, you don't talk to him and you don't know who has taken him somewhere else?

Patsy, <u>do you really think you can save your boy</u> from the fiery dragon?

From forumsforjustice.org:

TRUJILLO: *I know it's a difficult time and these are some hard questions we have to talk about. Um, Patsy, and again it's more just hard to understand sometimes and I just want to make sure the secretary can understand . . .*

PATSY: *Yeah.*

TRUJILLO: *so John brings Burke downstairs and then, is that, that's when you told him that JonB ...was missing. JonBenét was missing.*

PATSY: *Yeah, I think Burke, Burke, I think John had talked to him some upstairs. I don't know.*

This is ludicrous. Patsy can't confirm when Burke found out about JonBenét. Do we believe her when she says she doesn't know when Burke found out about it? Because the inference is that not only did Patsy not tell Burke, but that Burke might have not known why he was being dressed and taken away from his parents. Really Patsy? You wouldn't have told him? You wouldn't have asked your son about your daughter?

From forumsforjustice.org:

TRUJILLO: *Okay.*

PATSY: *(Inaudible) came in and, you know, hugged him before he left.*

TRUJILLO: *Did he say anything to you before he left?*

PATSY: *(Response inaudible.)*

TRUJILLO: *And then you a, then somebody took him over to the White's house.*

PATSY: *Correct.*

When Mary Lacy observed that *"Whoever did this sat outside of her room and waited until everyone was asleep to kill her"* she also made a vital inference. Who would sit in a house while people are awake, sit outside JonBenét's door and *wait for them to go to sleep?* Which is the most obvious candidate?

*Doug Stine?

Under the Christmas Tree
"Christmas is a time when everybody wants his past forgotten and his present remembered." — Phyllis Diller

Before we deal with the second question from the previous chapter, let's revisit Steve Thomas' version of events between 07:33 and 08:03.

According to Thomas at 07:33 a K9 unit was placed on standby. Even if JonBenét was kidnapped, it hardly makes sense that the unit wasn't used to at least sniffle out an entry and exit route. Was the reasoning not to use the unit to appease kidnappers who were spying on the Ramseys from a distance? Well wouldn't two families, the cops and a reverend, be of greater concern than one sniffer dog?

Of course had this formality been undertaken JonBenét's corpse would have been discovered six hours sooner, and not under the auspices – or control – of John Ramsey. The entire case could have turned on just this.

Thomas is vague about when exactly Burke left the Ramsey residence. What he does report is the first officer on the scene, Rick French, noticing Burke leaving the house and going over to talk to Burke.

Now what happens next is interesting. <u>Are you sure you want to hear this</u>?

*"[When he saw] Burke being taken away [French] went over to talk to the boy. But John Ramsey intervened. The father told the policeman that **Burke didn't know anything and had slept through it all**, and he hustled the boy to a waiting vehicle.* — Steve Thomas, JonBenét: Inside the Ramsey Murder Investigation

Think about that. How could John "know" that Burke knew nothing? According to John's account, he never asked Burke a thing.

John Ramsey "intervening" is a nice safe lawsuit-avoiding way of saying that John interfered with the police. Were the Ramseys cooperating with the cops? Didn't they want Burke to share what he knew, if he knew anything, if that could help JonBenét? Evidently John knew better, and John didn't want Burke talking to the police.

It was one of the poignant moments of the morning. [Burke's] sister was thought to be the victim of a terrorist kidnapping, but Burke was exiled...to **an unprotected location***, where he could be watched over by friends instead of police..."* — Steve Thomas, JonBenét: Inside the Ramsey Murder Investigation

Of course "unprotected" depends on your point of view, doesn't it? If Burke murdered his sister, and if John and Patsy were covering it up, and if their friends were voluntarily or unwittingly helping them, then Burke going to the White's would be the best protection for Burke and incidentally, the Ramseys too.

Furthermore, the right friends could theoretically maintain a barrier, even one of civil politeness, against necessary police enquiry.

On the other hand, if JonBenét had been attacked and murdered by an intruder with evil intent, if this was a case where a "child killer was still out there", then sending Burke away made no fucking sense. Compounding the fucked-up reasoning is the possibility of a botched kidnapping. The kidnapper – an organised foreign faction familiar with police countermeasures – failed to abduct JonBenét, and thus failed to secure a ransom. And now you're going to let Burke run around and give them, criminals who have clearly targeted the Ramseys, another chance?

If this seems farfetched it's not. In the film *Ransom* the kidnapper strikes twice. Politically motivated kidnapping, especially in the Middle East, tends to focus on repeating the same formula. Kidnap a high profile Westerner – a journalist or similar – and then demand either a king's ransom or the setting free of particular prisoners.

From tandfonline.com:

Kidnappers are more likely to be convicted of another kidnapping offence than be convicted of the more serious offences of rape of a

female or homicide. ...five out of every 100 kidnapping offenders convicted of first-time kidnapping will be reconvicted for this offence within 20 years.

It's time to let go of phantom kidnappers and Burke and turn our attention back to the Ramseys. Our focus will boomerang back to JonBenét's awkward older brother later in this narrative. What we want to do now is deal with the second question.

2. How did the Ramseys behave after JonBenét's body was "discovered" in the basement?

Early in the day, just after 08:10 patrolman French was relieved of his ground floor vigil thanks to the arrival of Arndt and Patterson. French then reconnoitred the garage and downstairs area, checking for entry points. French found the wine cellar door in the basement not only closed but visibly secured on the inside. Thomas does not mention the train room, but this room was also "secured" with <u>a small chair</u> propped against the door.

As such, for a cop innocently looking for a genuine access point, neither of these doorways made sense to go through. What's unfortunate is French was walking around the house with the "kidnap" narrative headlining underneath his forehead. As such he was looking for entry and exit points, no more. Had French been simply looking for a little girl who lived in that house he would have found her.

When French emerged from the basement stairs he saw Patsy staring oddly at him through her fingers. He described Patsy covering her face with both hands, yet "eyeballing" him at the same time.

If Patsy knew JonBenét was in the basement, then surely this was the moment she'd been dreading. Was French about to announce "I've found her"? Patsy searched his face, and he gave her an odd look…that seemed…to last…forever…and then French sauntered down the hall and out of sight.

If Patsy knew where JonBenét was, she would have been flabbergasted by this. He went down there and didn't see anything?

How could he not see her?

If Patsy was flabbergasted by the cops, so were the cops – by her.

Thomas notes that Patsy had contradicted herself early on – first saying to French she had checked JonBenét's room on the way to finding the note, and then switching the two around. Finding the note and then rushing to find JonBenét missing from her bed. The second explanation – as told to Arndt – did have a better ring to it than the first, didn't it?

Thomas points out that John Ramsey told French, Arndt and Whitson that he had personally checked all doors and windows the night before. Later John denied saying this at all. Perhaps the denial was intended to "open the door" or "open the window" so to speak for the intruder theory. If John had made sure the house was secure, then it was John's own version that it was secure and thus less likely that a phantom intruder had entered anywhere. If that was the case, suspicion would naturally fall on the Ramseys. Oops.

Something else Thomas highlights is John's claim that he read bedtime stories to both kids before tucking them in. Well, not according to Burke, and later not according to John either.

Also weird was Patsy's claim that JonBenét went to sleep wearing a red turtle-neck top. It's weird because JonBenét's dead body wasn't wearing a turtle-neck of any kind. Instead JonBenét was dressed in white. Curiously, red fibers were found on the inside of the duct tape pulled across the little girl's mouth. The fibers matched Patsy's outfit, not JonBenét's turtleneck and yes, the fibers were red.

What stands out most to me isn't necessarily Patsy's behaviour or John's per se, it's how different John's bearing was to his wife's. Ironically Thomas uses the same word Arndt does to describe John: *cordial*. Patsy meanwhile is described as: *overwrought*.

Let's match them up and see how they differ.

> *Cordial is pleasant, affable, affectionate, warm, jovial*

John is mostly composed, and even makes the odd joke.

Overwrought is tense, stressed, emotional, nervous, overexcited

Patsy on the other end seems overanxious. She has two friends consoling her, and repeatedly asks, "Why didn't I hear my baby?" It's difficult to say giving how murky it's gotten around the Ramseys, but it's possible this was a genuine feeling of regret expressed by Patsy.

Think of the irony of it though:

Why didn't I hear *my baby?*

The Craven Silence

Perhaps Patsy did hear and wasn't saying. Or perhaps Patsy heard too late, covered up and then wasn't saying. After all, whatever happened to JonBenét in the beginning wasn't her fault – not directly.

Well, it might have been your fault Patsy.

In my opinion it was natural for John to cover up his real feelings with genteel politeness. If John was purposefully trying to deceive, I get the sense that his default setting to misdirect would be to fake calm composure. In the same way, wouldn't it be natural for Patsy to conceal her true emotions by overacting? By showboating? Patsy's feelings are hidden beneath the pageantry of excess showiness. Burke referred to this "hysteria" as his mother "going psycho".

Both displays work provided they're demonstrated separately. It makes less sense for one parent to be composed while the other is hysterical. Someone's behaviour is off when there's such a strong mismatch.

Curiously the police officers themselves noted that John and Patsy were not only worlds apart in terms of their emotions, they were actually apart physically within the confines of the house. Lisa and I suspect this division had partly to do with the knowledge of an affair and general unhappiness in their marriage.

If either of JonBenét's parents was committing adultery, we feel John is the more likely candidate, but it's also possible they were both cheating, Patsy to "even the score" rather than from ordinary philandering. If this is true, if one or both parents were busy with infidelities on the day of their daughter's death, they would feel a far deeper sense of guilt towards JonBenét, Burke and each other. Guilt in this sense can be a source of solidarity, especially if Burke, John and Patsy each had something [or someone] to feel guilty about.

In *The Craven Silence 3* we suggested a scenario where John left the family home at midday for three to four hours. If John was cheating on Patsy while she was stuck entertaining a house full of kids on Christmas, Patsy might have gone out after visiting the Stines later that night to get her revenge on John. Now he could be stuck looking after the kids. If this happened, and if John went out to find her and bring her home, then that would have meant the house was left unattended even for a short period. And if that happened it could account for the Grand Jury wanting to indict both parents on charges of felonious child neglect leading to the death of a child.

With noon approaching, *for about an hour*, Arndt didn't know where John Ramsey was.

When she saw him again he was in the kitchen casually rifling through his mail. Arndt then noted a change in the cordial Mr. Ramsey. He sat alone at the table, concentrating intensely, his one leg bouncing across his knee in sync with his mental agitation.

Was John worried about how long it was going to take to find JonBenét? And the longer it took the more her little body would begin to spoil on the floor? Was he worried who Burke was talking to? Was he worried that time was running out for them to fly out and regroup? Was he worried about Access Graphics? Was he worried about legal representation? Was he worried about media-fallout and containment?

Fortunately for John the tension he exuded soon infected Linda Arndt. To diffuse the tension she thought she'd get John to do something – keep him preoccupied. Arndt suggested John search the house from top to bottom in search of anything significant. Despite Arndt's suggestion that John start at the top, he went down to the bottom – the basement – instead.

When Fleet White ran up the stairs from the basement, Patsy knew – we believe – with *absolute certainty* that John was bringing their little girl back to the surface. That hands-over-face feeling of horror was hard to hide. Priscilla White and Barbara Fernie, who had been tending to Patsy, sprang forward instinctively, wanting to know why Fleet was panicking, what could they do, what was happening, how could they help?

At the same time Patsy remained ominously inert on the couch.

When John emerged he was carrying JonBenét at her waist. Instead of cradling her or carrying her against his shoulder, he carried her like a smelly doll, his arms outstretched just as her little arms were in the rigors of death.

Arndt ordered John to put the small corpse down, and told Fleet White to guard the basement door. Fleet charged off, but instead of doing as he was told, he snatched the tape John had torn off JonBenét's mouth and examined it.

We won't deal with the contamination now, we'll simply home in on the behaviour of both parents at this crucial juncture:

JOHN

Immediately after being told by Arndt that JonBenét's was dead, because apparently John didn't know, John groaned, then confided to Arndt: "It has to be an inside job."*

After sharing this useless morsel Arndt told John to call 911 and go comfort his wife [Patsy had started wailing from a distance].

Two minutes later John was back and threw a blanket over JonBenét's body.

John then proceeded to express his grief.

John knelt beside his dead child and stroked her hair.

He lay down and put his arm around her.

Arndt thought he seemed to be crying, but saw no tears.

Then John kneeled, hugged her, and called her his "angel".

If John's behaviour was insincere, if it was pageantry, he had completed a show for the benefit of police. He'd shown himself to be a loving, caring, considerate father. He'd shown himself to be sad – and more importantly surprised – about his daughter's death. A sudden outpouring of emotion supported the notion of not knowing JonBenét's status for all those unfathomable hours in their home until just then. Now it was Patsy's turn.

PATSY

Before Patsy saw JonBenét, she uttered a "guttural wail" from the far side of the house.

Patsy fell across her daughter where she lay on the floor.

One of Patsy's friends tugged at JonBenét's arm, pleading that she not leave them...

Hoverstock then led the hysterical retinue in prayer.

Patsy, on her knees, raised both hands to the Lord.

Patsy cried: "Jesus, you raised Lazarus from the dead, raise my baby from the dead**."

If the Lord was there, he did not listen to Patsy's prayer, and if the Lord didn't, why should we?

---

*In the Oscar Pistorius trial we find that Oscar, from the –get-go, informs everyone "I thought she was a burglar." Instead of mourning Reeva Steenkamp his priority is to explain why he shot Reeva Steenkamp.

**Like Patsy Oscar also turned the death of a loved one into a church spectacle, loudly proclaiming he would dedicate his life to God and Reeva's life if God would only save her.

Baseball Bats, Footprints and Tracks in the Snow
"Christmas isn't a season. It's a feeling." — Edna Ferber

If <u>The Craven Silence</u> Trilogy has provided clarity of the *why* and to some extent the *who* of the murder, in this narrative and the two following we want to address *where* and then *what*.

The JonBenét Ramsey case is unusually complex in part because of the crime scene itself. In theory it is a four floor 15-room labyrinth, and if one includes the outdoor terrain as well, it becomes a truly confusing rabbit hole of considerable scale to fall through.

What we've demonstrated in the previous Trilogy is how the psychology of misdirection plaguing this case actually shines and illuminates away from the spaces we need to be looking at. In a real sense the misdirection give us plenty of guidance not only at what to look at, but also where not to look.

In this narrative we will attempt to finally answer not just where this crime was executed, but *exactly* where JonBenét was murdered. In order to reach that point, we have to address the intruder narrative. This time we're not interrogating the intruder narrative in order to prove it false. This time we want to find zones we can safely exclude as we pass over the crime scene with a view to nailing down the where and the "then what".

Before we begin, let me clarify what I mean by "then what". Once we've reached a particular insight either on the day after Christmas, or a year or more after the Christmas of 1996, we want to see where a certain course of action led. Did it lead to someone or away from someone? If a certain decision was made, a certain course of action taken, we want to see where it went – in terms of the District Attorneys, the lawyers, the cops, neighbors and of course the Ramseys themselves. If they decides X then what? What we're trying to do is figure out the strategy behind X, rather than X itself. What did X lead to, what did X lead away from, and by following the "then whats" we'll be able to track our way back – hopefully to something material.

In this narrative one of the key "then what" issues surrounds the broken basement window. We are going to make a shocking claim regarding that window – firstly that an intruder didn't break it, secondly that John didn't break it and thirdly that it was broken on the night of the murder.

But we're getting ahead of ourselves. Before we even get to the broken window we need to test whether the misdirection leads us away from the window or toward it. We're in something of a quandary here because this is in fact a rare instance where *we have both*.

Let me explain.

The misdirection away from the broken window in a certain sense involves the iron grate and the "no snow" narrative. Let's be absolutely clear what the point is of the "no snow" theory. It's out there to make it possible for an intruder to approach the Ramsey home without leaving footprints. In other words, the "no snow" theory is a sort of free pass to the intruder to say: "hey, you got to the house without leaving a footprint".

The broken window is a separate narrative saying this is where the intruder got out. If so, did he go in the same way? If he did, did he know there were windows down there? Did he know the doors in the basement wouldn't be locked or that they would trip an alarm? Or did the intruder go in via another entry point – <u>the open Butler door</u>? We're trying to follow the misdirection narrative, and we a vital clue that we feel points us away from the supposed entry and exit point. The baseball bat.

Interestingly the black bat is found on the cold, shaded North side of the house. This was an area with less lawn and paving, and a sort of dishevelled and dark terrain one wouldn't expect kids to play in. The Ramseys confirm this in their questioning with police.

One might imagine a burglar approaching the Ramsey residence at night from its darker and more abandoned side. This assumes the neighbours on that side have no line of sight, because the north side is pressed fairly close to the boundary compared to the remainder of the residence.

We should also note, when detectives pointed out the bat found in this area, Patsy confirmed that she thought it was strange for it to be there at all because the kids didn't usually play on "that side of the house."

We've covered this territory before, but this time keep the antenna up for aspersions of "a second boy" surrounding the baseball bat discussion.

We're going to detective Tom Haney's useful June 23rd 1998 interrogation from acandyrose.com:

HANEY: *Do you know how many bats [Burke] might have had? Would he have had more than one?*

PATSY: *I don't think so. I mean, I think that looks metal. Metal bats are pretty -- I mean, they are not cheap. So I can't imagine -- I don't think he had more than one, if he had one.*

HANEY: *But he did have one?*

PATSY: *It seems like he had one, but I can't say for sure it was that one.*

We've dealt with the WTF nature of Patsy's answers in this area, but let's be frank on the basic issue here. Patsy knew her son played little league, she mentioned it in her newsletter, so Burke absolutely had to have a baseball bat to play with.

Patsy saying "it seems like he had one" is crazy talk. Obviously he had a bat. And there's not just one bat lying around outside but two, maybe even three. Are these bats left behind by other neighborhood kids, abandoned in a derelict quadrant of the residence – in the shade, on the cement, up against the wall?

A whole lot of giant red flags have hoisted around this particular point, and here the misdirection is away from Burke owning a bat, and also from owning this particular bat. It's in the Ramsey's side yard, actually on the ledge of their house, but it's not Burke's bat?

From acandyrose.com:

PATSY: *Like I said, [Burke] would know. I'm sure he would know. He might know if they ever played over there, but that bat seems weird to me; yeah, very strange. And I can't imagine -- what is this? Like a bench or something?* **Where is this?**

PATRICK BURKE: *It looks a little side --*

HANEY: *I think it is sort of the edging of the house.*

PATSY: *When they quit playing they throw it on the ground. I can't imagine anybody would be neat enough to lay it up on anything like that if they were over there. That just -- that just doesn't --* **that is something.**

DEMUTH: **Who played baseball with Burke in your yard?**

PATSY: *Evan. Mostly Evan. (inaudible). The guy from next door that was occasionally over there, Scott, on our side or their side, I don't know.*

What's interesting here is Patsy fingering Evan. Out of a host of kids – she could have mentioned Fleet White's son, or the Stine's boy [Burke's classmate] – Patsy points out Evan. And she's not the only one. John does too, as he explains in an interrogation with detective Lou Smit which happened at the same time* Haney was grilling Patsy in 1998.

From acandyrose.com:

SMIT: *After the children opened their gifts, do you know what they did that day, your children?*

JOHN: *Well they played around the house. There were some kids in and out, I think. Because I wasn't there for several hours.*

SMIT: *And* **where were these kids from?**

JOHN: *Only, I think based -- well I'm pretty sure* **I saw Evan and Kile**, *I forget their last name.*

SMIT: *Colby?*

JOHN: *Colby. They were there.* ***I don't remember specifically knowing that.*** *But I think Patsy, I heard her saying neighbors and girls from up the street.*

SMIT: *Do you know their names?*

JOHN: *I don't. I don't.*

SMIT: *We were trying to determine who all JonBenét or Burke had had any contact [with.] And later on we'll kind of get into those reasons. But right now we have to find out any contact with the children.*

JOHN: *Yeah, I know. Well, there were a number of kids there that day.* ***Our house was always kind of, kids were in and out of there all the time*** *and it was usually the Colby boys. There was a family that lived not immediately next door, but the house over, that had moved in recently after the Whites had left the house. I didn't know them. I think there were a couple of girls in the house that had come down to play.*

Again, note who John doesn't mention. He doesn't mention his own friends who have kids that are <u>friends with his kids</u> – yes, the Whites and the Stines. And one of the reasons stated by the parents why they didn't go to the Fernie's on Christmas night was they thought Burke would get out and start playing with Luke and so they wouldn't be able to make a quick stop.

From <u>acandyrose.com</u>:

SMIT: *How about the children like to the south of you?*

JOHN: *Let's see, south. That's --*

SMIT: *(INAUDIBLE).*

JOHN: *Yeah. It's possible. But I don't remember seeing them there. But they were there occasionally. The boy, the son, this is on the house next to us, towards [Baseline street]. Their son, who seemed like a very nice kid, was always attentive to JonBenét in a nice way; a brotherly way, I thought.*

SMIT: *Do you know his name?*

JOHN: *I don't.*

SMIT: *Is it Luke?*

JOHN: *Luke? That rings a bell, yeah. That's right.*

SMIT: *Do you know of anybody from the family who always lived next door to the north?*

JOHN: *Not a lot. They had a child and they were divorced after that. He had children from another marriage; two boys, I think. All nice kids.*

SMIT: *And were they around them that day?*

JOHN: *I don't remember for sure. Patsy probably would remember that.*

At this point the detective realises he has a whole lotta nuthin'. So he gently nudges John.

From <u>acandyrose.com</u>:

SMIT: *See, we're trying to determine the gap of anybody who could have contact, and usually the neighbors and people close and we would just like to have their names.*

JOHN: *Again, Patsy would have more information on that.*

Not very helpful is he, in assisting with his daughter's murder investigation. How hard is it to try to write down a complete list of all your neighbours? Draw a diagram, assign names. John would rather have Patsy do it.

From <u>acandyrose.com</u>:

SMIT: **Or maybe Burke would have some information on that, I'm not sure. (INAUDIBLE).**

This prod from Smit doesn't work. John speaks a little more directly about a little girl living diagonally across from them, next door to the Barnhills, the old folks who had a key to their home and babysat their dog [and JonBenét's Christmas bike].

Let's skip through the waffle of vanilla flags until we find a red one, even a small one will do. And here we go.

From acandyrose.com:

SMIT: *How about across the alley from you,* ***I have always been interested in those houses back there***. *Were you ever acquainted with anybody back there?*

JOHN: *No. I talked to this lady once in that house there.*

SMIT: *That's 756?*

JOHN: *Yeah, she was a British lady. We did meet these people, David and Ann.* ***The Cobies were weird as hell****, frankly. Their house was a pig sty. I mean it was, I had never been in it but Patsy had, and she just described it was, you know, a mattress on the floor for the kids,* ***the kids always dressed themselves****, they looked like they just dressed themselves in the morning and were I felt **very uncared for**. He was very weird.*

John seems to be directing the attention away from the neighborhood kids – to the parents – which is interesting in and of itself. But he gives up quite a lot here. We're told these people are pigs. They don't dress their children. They neglect their kids [a charge the Ramsey parents narrowly escaped facing themselves] and worst of all they're *weird*.

From acandyrose.com:

SMIT: *Who is he?*

JOHN: *The husband, or the father. He told me once that he was teaching his kids how to ride a bike and he would knock them over so they would learn how to fall off a bike.*

Whatever you make of this statement, the point is, John is

admitting that bikes were a big deal. Both of the neighbor's kids had bikes, and so did the Ramsey kids. While we're on the topic, notice anything strange about the photograph of the cops and the snow in front of the Ramsey home <u>on the morning of December 27th</u>? Look <u>closer</u>. <u>Closer</u>.

John, you were saying?

From <u>acandyrose.com</u>:

JOHN: *One day Burke took over a little gun, a plastic gun and he just went crazy, he didn't want any guns in the house.*

SMIT: *Do you know what the man's name is?*

But for all John's intimate knowledge of this guy, he can't even remember his name.

From <u>acandyrose.com</u>:

JOHN: *Ruth and -- Patsy would know. He worked for the state. I think. He used to take the bus down to Denver every day. Just, their daughter who was at that time maybe early teenager, would spend hours and hours and hours out on the swing in the backyard, just swinging and swinging, it was like a rope swing. And somebody said gee, that must be -- there must be something wrong with her. We said no, maybe she just doesn't want to be in the house.*

Now let's move on to a bigger red flag. It's beside the point that these are false flags, they're nevertheless leading us away from something, and we need to know where we're being led astray so we know where to go.

We're finally back to Burke's playmates – and more specifically Evan, the kid Patsy ID'd immediately when Haney asked who Burke played baseball with. Like Patsy, John has a thing or two to say about this kid.

From <u>acandyrose.com</u>:

JOHN: *That's probably right. Evan was a strange little kid. He was --*

SMIT: *(MULTIPLE SPEAKERS.)*

JOHN: *I just didn't care for him. He was, one time JonBenét was out in the driveway and she had a -- this was several years ago, she had a dress on that didn't have underwear on because it gotten taken off or what and Evan was down, you know, trying to look under her dress and here he was probably at that time a 7 or 8-year-old. I said Evan, cut that out.*

SMIT: *Now didn't they have an older one there too?*

JOHN RAMSEY: *Kai** was there, they had a daughter, two daughters. Ruth was the mom, and the daughter was older than the boys, you know. But --*

There's something bizarre about John extracting a memory from "several years ago". The interview was conducted in 1998 and JonBenét was murdered in late 1996, almost 1997, basically a year earlier. Three years prior to the interrogation is 1995. Further than that would make JonBenét an infant. A small boy looking at a half-naked baby and possibly laughing seems like very wishy-washy stuff. Unfortunately super sleuth Lou Smit doesn't get clarity on this detail.

Now to summarise the Evan stuff from <u>topix.com</u>:

Evan was ~a year older than Burke and had a brother who was a couple of years older than that. His name was variously written as Kai, Kile, or Kyle. John Ramsey didn't think highly of the Colby family.

Back to Patsy and the baseball bats.

From <u>acandyrose.com</u>:

DEMUTH: *Did they have their own baseball stuff they brought over?*

PATSY: *I don't know. I didn't pay that much attention.*

HANEY: *Okay.*

Given what John has just said – there's a poor family next door with nothing but a mattress for furniture, the kids don't dress themselves and dad [gasp] catches a bus to work, we might have a case here for one of the Colby boys coming over, playing baseball and leaving their bat lying around.

There's only one glaring problem, and it suggests some other kind of "lying around" is taking place. Do you see it? Patsy has admitted the aluminium baseball bats are so expensive not even they, the affluent Ramseys, could afford them. And John has described the poor pigs next door as not only untidy but also not wealthy.

I've mentioned this before but it's important to hoist this flag highest of them all. Patsy tends to answer briefly and unhelpfully in general, occasionally providing a lot of fluff when pressed. What Patsy doesn't do is ask questions, unless it is to communicate that she couldn't possibly know something. For example, later in this narrative we'll show how Patsy actually asks the detectives whether or not the basement window was broken***.

Before we deal with that, let's address the big red flag raised by this question right here.

From acandyrose.com:

PATSY: *Did anybody take hand prints off of that, do you know?*

Patsy wants to know if handprints were taken of the baseball bat. Why would it matter? Why would it matter to Patsy? Meanwhile Haney's answer is understandably cagey.

From acandyrose.com:

HANEY: *I believe it was recovered.*

DEMUTH: *We have that, yeah.*

PATSY: *Because that looks -- that just doesn't --*

HANEY: *That was 410.*

Unfortunately Haney cuts her off, and the conversation then

wanders down another warren of rabbit holes covered wet with vanilla icing and false flags.

*John Ramsey was interrogated by Lou Smit and Mike Kane on June 23rd, 24th and 25th 1998.

**Also identified variously as Kile and Kyle in various documents.

***"Was it [the window] not fixed?"

Into and Out of Intruder Territory

"Christmas... is not an external event at all, but a piece of one's home that one carries in one's heart." — Freya Stark

We've started the work on bats and who they belonged to. Now we want to address why the bats were left where they were left. We must also be quite clear who the bats didn't belong to. That's an easy answer – they didn't belong to the Colby's.

For the rest of our analysis we need to look at sights and sounds. Footprints in snow are visual cues. We'll be using actual video image to show the inside and outside of the premises, as well as blueprints to precisely locate where the bats were left. This is an important exercise for another reason as well. We need to know where the bats were left in order to have an idea where in the house they were dropped from, and that might give us an idea not just *who* dropped them or where they were finally found but whether they could have been heard at all.

SOUNDS – metal bat or metal grate?

Let's start with sounds; were there any? Does it seem presumptuous to suggest the bats – or a single bat - were dropped at all? Perhaps. An aluminium or composite bat falling against the concrete paving from one story would account for the neighbour Luther Stanton* hearing the sound of metal *scraping* against concrete paving.

From pbworks.com:

"Stanton's husband had heard **a crashing sound** *– the sound of metal on concrete – sometime after the scream" (Schiller 1999a:531-532).*

Interestingly on the pbworks site the subheading dedicated to this snippet of information is titled **Metal Scraping Sound.** That happens to be how I've thought of it too. But "scraping" isn't the word Stanton's husband actually uses. So was it scraping or crashing and is it important to make the distinction?

Is it conceivable the the metal grate and the aluminium bat could both produce the same sort of metallic noise. I'd hazard a guess that a metal bat landing on concrete would making a more "ringing" type noise [think xylophone] than a heavy hollow grate landing on a custom-frame. A heavy grate landing on a frame set against the earth might sound more like a bang, and not a bang of metal on concrete, just a bang.

Intuitively I have a feeling the noise was more approximately a "clanging" noise. A clanging noise would account for the materials involved, whereas a bang would not. Would a metallic scraping provide the same cues? Perhaps, but then is the word "scraping" a better description of the process or the sound? Scraping suggests *something moving against something else*, either because it is dropped or shifted, possibly both.

I think the solution to our problem is this: for a scraping sound to be heard from a distance of 150 feet [45 metres] it would need to be a fairly loud "scraping". Filing one's nails, or scraping a metal nail on brick wouldn't cut it. Scraping a car's hubcap would do it. Would scraping a baseball bat along a concrete surface be loud enough? Possibly. But <u>a bat that has been dropped</u> and which then bounces and rolls against concrete and stone, perhaps knocking against the vertical brickwork of the house or the concrete drain – that ought to do it.

There is credibility in a counterargument too. A slow opening grate or slow closing grate might scrape loudly against concrete, especially if it were rusted **and not opened in a long time.** The question is *how loudly* are we talking about?

The answer is straightforward, and it's the same test we apply to the sound of a clanging bat. The sound would need to carry for 150 feet [45 metres] and into a bedroom, which is where the Ramsey's neighbors - Luther and Melody Stanton – were situated. Facing south, the sound – whatever it was – carried through the crystal clear silence of Boulder's cold, rarefied air. So <u>what sound was it, and where on the Ramsey property did it originate from</u>?

If we decide the sound originated from the grate, on <u>the south side</u>

of the house, the acoustics are good and it supports an intruder theory. On the other hand, if the sound occurred just around the corner of the front door, on the north side, the acoustics [in terms of sound travelling] are poorer, although the terrain necessary to create a loud clanging [or crashing] noise is perfectly suitable. The other point to stress is that Burke's bedroom is directly above both the front door area [East elevation] and has a window overlooking precisely the area where the baseball bat [410 was found].

So we're at something of an impasse. From a purely acoustic perspective, both sound sources work. If the grate doesn't necessarily produce the right sound, it's located better for that sound to be heard. If the baseball bat produces the right sound, it's located on the wrong side of the case, although an argument can be made that the sound would be more than sufficient to penetrate the jutting corner of the Ramsey home. What we can say with confidence about the location of a possible baseball bat clanging – had the bat been dropped closer to the centre of the north Elevation – say directly outside the Butler Pantry door – the acoustics would dramatically decrease at least for the Stanton's to be able to hear it.

We must also address the scream – where could it have been made in order to be heard by the Stanton's [or not heard]. And we will do so before the conclusion of this narrative.

If the sounds lead us in a direction, to be fair, we must acknowledge they lend credence to both theories – the intruder and "Burke did it" theories. In order to find out which is the more likely, we must find evidence to reinforce the one theory, and an argument to disprove the other.

Let's move on to visual cues.

SIGHT – footprints and ergonomics

Why is the incriminating bat found on the north side? We feel this is to misdirect away from the south side area, including the train room basement area but more crucially, it is to draw attention *to the outside of the house*.

Both the bat and the broken window/suitcase setup take us out of the Ramsey home and into Intruder Territory and its flocks of wild geese and the wild goose chases that were, and still are, the result. We won't be doing any of that in this narrative; not directly.

In our view the broken window is *an inconvenient truth* for the Ramseys. Although it fits in with an intruder narrative – certainly as a theoretical point of access as Smit discovered – in our view the Ramseys didn't see the grate/window as an access point. If the Ramseys were involved, we still don't think their initial cover up was to suggest a burglar or intruder had broken in through the basement.

Instead there seemed to be an effort to suggest a burglar had wandered in [and out] through the open butler pantry door, and as it happens, the Ransom Note and torch on the kitchen counter were also situated here. The baseball bat, if intentionally placed where it was, also directs attention away from the basement. In fact it asks the onlooker to consider *the north side of the house* rather than the south, and the butler pantry door and front door, as possible entry points. Furthermore a basement window on the north side, rather than the broken window on the south side seems to be where attention is being redirected.

Even if this line of reasoning is incorrect the reader is entitled to ponder: what the fuck is so important about the basement window? In retrospect, knowing what investigators have discovered, the reader is entitled to some circumspection in this regard.

As we know, on the other side of the broken window is the blue Samsonite suitcase propped directly beneath it. We believe this suitcase – like the bat – is intended to draw the viewers mind into the house but still *away from the window*.

It's not perfectly clear whether the suitcase was a ploy, and if it was, how effective and how much effort went into it or not, simply because the way it appears in crime scene photos *isn't the way it was found*. Fleet White says he discovered the suitcase square against the wall. *He* then moved the suitcase to inspect the ground area for glass [from the window], then left it where he'd moved it.

Besides that, there are zero footprints and/or garden/snow debris forming a trail either from <u>the outside through the window</u>, over the suitcase and into the basement or vice versa.

Whatever we may say about the suitcase, what's generally clear is <u>its prominent role in the JonBenét Ramsey crime scene mythos</u>. The suitcase leads us into the Ramsey home to its owner, John Andrew, and thus, indirectly leads us out of or at least away from the Mama, Papa and Brotha Ramsey.

If there is substance to our theory, that there is misdirection both <u>towards the window</u> [in the sense of someone climbing through it when no one did] and away from it [in the sense of someone climbing out via this window when no one did] this must mean the broken window has more to it than meets the eye. But to test the merits of the window we must first test the misdirection leading both to and from it. Let's begin from the outside. This is theoretically where the Ramseys want us, sniffing and snooping around <u>the outside of the house</u>, hunting for clues in the garden just as Lou Smit did. We won't be inspecting the grate or interrogating <u>spiders and their webs</u>. Instead we'll look at the "footprints in the snow" or lack of.

The Ramsey case is chock full with ironies. If pageantry preceded this crime [and we know it did], if there is pageantry in the execution of this crime [and we believe there is a great deal] then surely it follows there should be pageantry in the aftermath as well.

There is a murder victim with pageantry tied up in the murder weapon, there are record length ransom notes, and then there are psychological clues flapping in the Christmas Chinook.

Isn't it ironic that surrounding this idea of pageantry, this veneer smeared over everything and the smarmy commentary by the suspects surrounding a murder over Christmas, behind all this is an idea of expensive gifts wrapped up but where <u>the wrapping is torn back</u>...? The veneer is exposed. The greed is exposed. The pageantry is uncovered for what it really is.

In the same way there is a sort of symbolic irony in this idea of footprints both appearing and disappearing in snow. The very idea conjures snow into and out of existence seemingly at will. Footsteps miraculously are scripted back into a story, however where actual shoeprints are discovered, those shoes and boots are scripted into oblivion.

The point really isn't how this happens, although the next narrative is devoted to the science of snow and ice, and an attempt at fully and finally dismantling the "no snow" theory. Nor is the point that it happens. The point is *why* does it happen? Why *must* there be footprints? Why *must* there be no snow? It's to setup up a corresponding psychology, isn't it? It's so that there *can be* an intruder. Someone needs to come from the outside in.

To reiterate, we really don't think the Ramseys initially wanted police to think the intruder got in through the broken basement window. If they did, John would have mentioned it from the get go. If they did, John would not have blockaded the entrance to both the train room and the wine cellar [something an intruder would not do, nor could he if he'd exited the house through the basement window.

There really does seem to be a strong sense that John, Patsy and Burke *don't really want us in the basement to begin with.* Instead they want us in the kitchen, in the garden and examining baseball bats, one that isn't really a baseball bat at all [and who have suddenly been dispossessed by the Ramsey family, no one knows who they belong to].

If you take away the broken window – what are you left with? Bats perhaps – but how did they get there? Someone either brought them there or someone who lived in the house dropped them there or someone found them in the house and dropped them there on their way out.

But why would they drop them in unusual places? Why would that aspect be odd of all things? Why would where baseball bats are lying be the strangest thing? Why would Patsy not recognise the bats? All this pageantry around bats is to feed the idea not merely of an intruder lurking about, but *where* the intruder is lurking.

Guess what – the bat toting bat dropping intruder is not lurking *anywhere near* the broken basement window. And besides that John apparently, according to him, broke the window *not* the intruder.

To settle matters we must return to the Ramsey residence on December 26th at the same time Rick French arrived [05:59] and then Reichenbach [0:6:10]. We must see what they saw, step where they stepped and see where that leaves us.

If trace amounts of snow that fell on Christmas night could theoretically "rain" on the Ramsey's intruder parade by creating an inviolate surface of pristine snow and frost, the Ramseys needed a way to muddy this incriminating scintillating moat.

What could they do to muddy the entry and exit point? They could invite a small army of foot traffic. This would contaminate not merely the inside of the house but perhaps more importantly, the outside too. And thus it was important for the Ramseys friends to arrive at about the same time as police – early. And of course, that's exactly what happened.

From acandyrose.com**:

John Fernie was angry when he read Charlie Brennan's story about footprints. Like many media stories, this one came from an unnamed source and made the Ramseys look guilty.

Schiller insinuates that reckless and spurious leaks from the cops were driving rumors and gossip intended to maliciously implicate the Ramseys.

The fact is an unprecedented number of local cops were assigned to the Ramsey case – 30 had been assigned just four days after JonBenét's body was found. This was the largest law enforcement investment in one case in four years for Boulder PD. One would imagine with so many officers running rampant, loose lips would sink ships, right? Well, on December 29th the media expressed their frustration in an article with the words "details still elusive in slaying". The day before the press quoted the police as saying the case was "still a very delicate and sensitive issue" and as such, no one had been identified as suspects.

The article on the 29th that notes what is *not known* includes:

- No suspects had been identified [though the police continued to search the Ramsey residence day and night over a period of days, then weeks]

- Police would not comment on which family member found JonBenét's body

- No details were provided for an estimated time of death

- No details were provided for the manner in which JonBenét was strangled.

As for the connection of the "kidnapping" to the murder, police did say:

"Right now, we are focused on the homicide aspects of the case." — John Eller, commander of the Boulder police detective division

But if that sounded astute and encouraging, this didn't:

"The ransom note was a typical - if there is such a thing - kidnapping ransom note, the kind you'd find in any movie." — John Eller

Besides deciding very quickly that the kidnapping scenario was bogus [and thus the Ransom Note], this article clearly contradicts Schiller's position that the cops were "trying to make the Ramsey's look guilty". What we must acknowledge is for the past 20 years the Ramseys have pointed a finger of blame at the clueless cops. The Ramseys and their apologists also allege that the cops leaked fake information, thus creating a media driven conspiracy.

Well, at the time of the murder the police weren't giving up much, and the first real "press release" didn't come from the cops, but from the Ramseys direct to the media, sidestepping the cops completely. If anyone had loose lips about the case and about killers on the loose, it wasn't coming from the cops, the media, or even the neighbors.

But not everything reported in the Ramsey's favour was necessarily a fair reflection of the facts either.

From dailycamera.com:

*"They're cooperating with the police," said city spokeswoman Leslie Aaholm...But family friends say **discussing the death with police and loved ones has devastated the family**.*

"[JonBenét] was killed after she went to bed, so they never got a chance to say goodbye, and it's terribly difficult for them," said a close family friend.

Could that close family friend be Susan Stine? And if so, how would Susan know when JonBenét died when not even the coroner knew, not even the cops knew, and we're still not 100% clear 20 years later?

The bottom-line is the police, while their investigation wasn't perfect, and Linda Arndt had blundered worse than most, was nevertheless broadly a professional and well-resourced operation.

From dailycamera.com:

Police remained tight-lipped about other elements of the crime. They would not comment *on the clothing JonBenét was wearing when she died, the condition of her body, the instructions in the ransom note, or possible contact the kidnapper may have had with police or the family.* **Authorities also did not reveal information** *about the Ramseys' domestic staff and which members had access to the house.*

As investigators search for clues, **the family remains secluded in a friend's home under police protection, family friends said.**

There's an irony there too – 1) secluded 2) in a friend's home) under police protection. Let's go back to something one of those friends said, specifically about snow.

From acandyrose.com

John Fernie was angry when he read Charlie Brennan's story about footprints. *Like many media stories,* **this one came from an unnamed source** *and made the Ramseys look guilty.* **Fernie wondered if the source had provided the reporter with all the facts.**

It should be noted that Brennan's article about there being no snow was published on March 11, 1997 by the Rocky Mountain News. In other words, almost three months had passed before the first "leak" occurred? The leak was the spectacularly revelatory point about "no footprints" in snow.

One might call this a "leak" if the idea was for police to remain permanently tight-lipped about the case. On the other hand, is it a leak if the Ramseys are giving press conferences, hiring lawyers and PR people? Well, only if the powers that be running the cop shop have warned the cops working the case to shut the fuck up about the case. Why? Because failure to abide might mean someone losing their job or the department facing a lawsuit. Strings were being pulled all over town thanks to affluent influence.

Frustration with the "no progress of the case" [including the Ramseys' failure to submit themselves voluntarily and unconditionally to questioning] probably gave rise to "leaks", and rather than being malicious, they seemed more strategic. In any case, one month after Brennan's story was "leaked" the Ramseys pitched up in Boulder under various conditions and submitted to their first thorough interrogation by detectives.

But if the police were up against it with the Ramseys, in their own department, they also had Team Ramsey to deal with.

From acandyrose.com:

[Fernie] knew that his own footprints were there in the snow that morning. He had driven up the back alley to the Ramsey's house *just after 6:00 A.M. in response to Patsy's frantic call that terrible morning. He remembered walking* along the brick sidewalk to the patio door, looking through the glass panel, *and* reading a line or two of the ransom note, which was lying on the floor just inside the door.

Let's be clear, John Fernie is referring to the bricked walkway on the south side [the Stanton side] of the Ramsey residence. What's interesting is <u>Fernie helpfully indicates he can actually see the Ransom Note through the window</u>, and what's more, it's close enough to read a few lines.

From <u>acandyrose.com</u>

*Then [Fernie] ran through the snow-covered grass, around <u>the south side of the house, to the front door</u>. If the cops had been looking**, <u>they would have found his footprints</u>**. A year and a half after JonBenét's death, Fernie told a reporter that the police still had not checked the shoes he wore that day, though a shoe imprint had been discovered next to JonBenét's body.*

The craziest part of Fernie's testimony – besides the fact that the Ransom Note seems to have levitated from one side of the house to the other – is that by inference Fernie confirms that there were no other footprints that *he saw* besides those he left. Obviously the police did not need to check his shoes if they arrived on the scene before he did, and we know French and Reichenbach both arrived right around 06:00.

Besides these curious slights aimed at the police, Fernie also claims not merely that he left his own footprints in the snow, but that there was snow to leave them in.

*The Stanton's resided at <u>738 Fifteenth Street, diagonally across the road in a southerly direction</u>, from the Ramseys

**From PMPT Page 236

A War of Words Part 1

"It's harder to heal than it is to kill." — Tamora Pierce

One could dedicate a very thick bible simply to the war of words involved in this case. For the purposes of this narrative we'll stick to the war of words as it applied to the "snow-no snow" theory.

If John Fernie's testimony included an allegation of a Ransom Note with magic powers, able to levitate across the Ramsey residence, then there's a curious parallel with the snow stories, and the inferences drawn from there. In no time, the salivating media – starved of some real meat to chew on regarding this story – saw an intruder who would need to levitate across the Ramsey garden in order to break in. Naturally enough after committing the crime, the phantom intruder would need to perform the same magic trick upon exiting the mansion. Well, such was the rhetoric in the media in the first quarter of 1997.

Let's go to the particulars of those discussions right now.

From <u>acandyrose.com</u>:

On March 10, 1997, Charlie Brennan, a 15-year veteran of the Denver Rocky Mountain News, was sitting at his desk in the newsroom when a colleague tapped him on the shoulder and gave him a tip about the JonBenét Ramsey case. It sounded like a good one, so Brennan, 44, followed up by calling a man Brennan characterizes as a "law-enforcement source."

*The source confirmed the information Brennan's colleague had passed along: The police noted **in their initial report that there were no footprints in the snow outside the Ramsey home the morning after the murder.** This made it unlikely that an intruder had entered the home.*

We know in retrospect that the counter narrative that emerged was that the walk ways were free of snow. I will deal with that narrative exhaustively in the next book, but suffice it to say it's doubtful police would report no footprints in snow if the entire residence were not surrounded by snow when they arrived. If just a few small islands of snow had survived on the lawn, the thought of "no footprints" would not likely have surfaced. Just as "no footprints in mud" would not likely occur to someone arriving at a home where no mud was visible or necessary to negotiate.

From acandyrose.com:

Brennan scribbled down notes, made a few more calls, and hunkered down to write his page 4 report:

Police who went to JonBenét Ramsey's home the morning she was reported missing found no footprints in the snow surrounding the house, sources said Monday.

That is one of the earliest details that caused investigators to focus their attention on the slain girl's family, police sources said. Although there was no significant storm just before police went to the house the morning after Christmas, it had snowed lightly several times from Dec. 23 to 25, weather records show.

If anything, the weather records certainly tipped the scales in Brennan's favour.

From acandyrose.com:

Brennan's scoop was as close to a smoking gun as anything publicly known at the time. Until that point, a broken basement window on the south side of their home meant an intruder could have gotten into the house and killed John and Patsy Ramsey's daughter. Now a lack of footprints in the snow indicated otherwise.

Now despite the pageantry involved – the bats, the notes, and the elaborately garrotted child – the crime basically came down to a face-off between two unlikely candidates. It was pure undriven, untrammelled snow versus a broken basement window. To be simplistic:

Unbroken Snow vs Broken Window

Of course, thanks to the tight-lipped situation with the cops, and due to unseen strings tying up leads hither and thither, when this lead finally popped, it gushed into print like champagne over a wedding dress.

From acandyrose.com:

Brennan's findings made national headlines, appearing in publications such as the Milwaukee Journal Sentinel, the Chicago Tribune, the Atlanta Journal-Constitution, and the San Francisco Examiner. Even The New York Times reported Brennan's findings. (Those papers' combined readership is 2,519,501.) In all, 23 publications and news programs picked up the report, according to a search on the Lexis-Nexis database.

One might imagine whoever was sewing up the case had essentially succeeded. The Ramseys would go on with their lives unaffected, and so would Boulder – it was simply an abomination that was better forgotten than acknowledged. Brennan's no snow lead broke through the frosty veneer and the muddy bullshit beneath began its stinky journey through the ether.

From acandyrose.com:

*His **No Footprints In The Snow** scoop solidified Brennan as an important force on the Ramsey beat. When journalists from national publications began parachuting into Boulder to get their share of the action-such as Vanity Fair's Ann Louise Bardach, and Lawrence Schiller, who had been commissioned by The New Yorker to cover the Ramsey murder-Brennan was the man they called. In fact, when Schiller decided to expand his New Yorker article into a book, he hired Brennan to help with the reporting. (Brennan won't say how much money he made from collaborating on Perfect Murder, Perfect Town...)*

The shock waves around the Ramsey case reverberated beyond the New York Times. CNN picked up on it too – yes, the same station that had broadcast the Ramsey's first appeal to Americans on 1 January 1997. Now the chicken had come home to roost.

From acandyrose.com:

Although Brennan was beginning to enjoy the national exposure-

The New York Times was reporting his discovery, Larry King Live was calling-his scoop would soon quietly fall apart.

When Daniel Glick heard about Brennan's No Footprints headliner, he thought it was a bombshell. Glick, a former Washington correspondent for Newsweek who now writes for the magazine from Boulder County, even went so far as to say on Larry King Live that if the Ramseys' claims of an intruder were to be believed, the killer must have had the power to "levitate."

But in mid-June 1997, Glick and his writing partner, Sherry Keene-Osborn, both began to question the story's accuracy. Keene-Osborn said she got a call from an "impeccable source" who warned her that much of what ran in the newspapers and magazines (including Newsweek) were flat wrong. Glick says he raised an eyebrow when, while visiting the Ramseys' Boulder house, he noticed that flagstone surrounded its south side.

This is pure speculation, but we think Lou Smit was that "impeccable source". And history would show that twenty years on, Smit's impeccable detective work would lead everyone following his trial to sweet fuck all. But the counter narrative had succeeded. The momentum Brennan had generated now began to backfire and then implode. Well, not exactly. If Brennan's story lost a little momentum as critics second-guessed it [and they did], it didn't lose much, and we think for good reason.

From acandyrose.com:

*[The media started] re-reporting Brennan's scoop. Glick says he found a meteorologist at the National Oceanic and Atmospheric Administration who told him that there was little snowfall and that the temperature had been mostly above freezing in the week prior to the murder. Glick says he then deduced that because there were no leaves on the trees to block the sunshine from reaching **the flagstone patio outside the broken window**, there probably wasn't any snow on the ground outside the broken window-even though there were patches of snow on the lawn.*

Glick's pontifications sound very "expertish", but for all his expertise, the bottom-line is snow only had to be seen very early in the morning, not throughout the day. It's easy to establish whether temperatures would have allowed snow and frost to develop in mid-winter in one of America's snowiest cities, and when the cops arrived just before 06:00, it was very definitely below freezing. Reichenbach who arrived after French [between 06:10 and 06:30] noted the temperature as 9 °F [-12.7 °C] on his way to the crime scene.

Naturally some called these numbers into question, suggesting Reichenbach had reported 9°C rather than 9 °F. Of course given that the maximum that day only reached 7°C according to official weather records, the entire line of argument is misleading, and what's more, erroneous.

From acandyrose.com:

To confirm, Glick says, he contacted a "frost expert" who told him that scientifically one couldn't even determine whether or when frost would have been on the ground outside the window. In other words, the police notation of "no footprints" was meaningless; it certainly did not rule out the entrance of an intruder.

Glick had contacted a weather man and frost expert who were able to "make the snow" disappear. And so suddenly what the police reported seeing was "officially" unseen.

From acandyrose.com:

Glick and Keene-Osborn wrote a story that questioned Brennan's reporting. **The article was largely ignored by other print outlets**, *though Geraldo Rivera mentioned Newsweek's report on Rivera Live and Glick discussed his findings on two episodes of Larry King Live. Given the relatively little play by the media outlets that had so quickly picked up Brennan's No Footprints piece, Glick and Keene-Osborn's piece* **hardly made a dent** *in what John and Patsy Ramsey's attorney now calls "the greatest urban legend of the case." In fact, five months after Newsweek disputed Brennan's story, The Washington Post reported that "from the start, circumstances surrounding the crime focused suspicion on the parents....There* were no conclusive signs of forced entry at the home and no footprints in the snow that fell that night."

If anyone would know the likelihood of snow in Boulder it would be Boulderites. So to contend that one of the snowiest cities in America either had no snow, or that it had melted before dawn...well, it wasn't going to be easy to get converts, certainly none with fewer than two brain cells to rub together.

From acandyrose.com:

*The importance of the No Footprints story, Brennan contends, is not whether there actually were footprints or not. Rather, he says, **his report showed the direction in which the police investigation was heading**: By noting a lack of footprints (wrongly or rightly), the police were clearly considering the potential guilt of the Ramseys. "What I reported was that police noted in their reports an absence of footprints," says Brennan. "That's not Charlie Brennan saying, 'Hey, there was an absence of footprints.' I'm saying, 'Hey, the police put it in their reports.' And they did! They did! That was never wrong."*

Of course there's the other side to the story too. Months had passed after JonBenét's murder and no suspects had been identified. *A Craven Silence* had set in, and some publications were determined to blow the lid off it.

From acandyrose.com:

[So] when The New York Times ran its story about Brennan's No Footprints article, the paper didn't play up the aspect of the direction of the police investigation. The Times's headline was "No Sign Of An Intruder At Home Of A Slain Child."

Let's stay with Brennan for a moment. Let's reflect on how the Ramsey case started for him, and his initial impressions.

From guardian.com:

'I'll always remember that day. Shortly after dinner I got a call from my office saying that there was this kidnapping situation at a

home in Boulder, nearby, and could I get over there.'

Charlie...a reporter for the Rocky Mountain News... was the first journalist to arrive at the Ramsey home on 26 December, and he is perhaps the only one who has followed the story consistently for the past 10 years. In 1997, Brennan teamed up with Lawrence Schiller...

*'Before I left home I called one source I had at the DA's office, and I was told that yes, **it's a kidnapping, and the child is inside the home**. And I thought, these facts do not belong in the same sentence. **It sounded like the craziest kidnapping I'd ever heard of**, and my source agreed, and said it did not add up.'*

*Statistically speaking, in cases where a child's body is found in the family home, the culprit is almost always a 'family member perpetrator'. Early on the morning of the 26th, when the Ramsey case was thought to be a kidnapping in a wealthy neighbourhood, the Ramseys were treated as victims. As soon as the body was found, they became prime suspects. Except that **they were never exactly declared to be suspects** - the foggy phrase 'under the umbrella of suspicion' was used...*

Twenty years later the Ramseys still have never been declared suspects, not exactly. Although there are television documentaries like the one that aired last night* that appear to question the Ramsey's innocence, they ultimately turn out to be *Apologia* <u>dressed up as genuine investigations</u>. Any investigations that make more aggressive aspersions face lawsuits.

From <u>guardian.com</u>:

*Charlie Brennan arrived to find a macabre scene. Patsy Ramsey's over-the-top Christmas decorations were still in place - red and white striped candy canes dotted along the walkway, white lights around the doorframe, an illuminated Santa in a sled **on the snow-strewn front lawn**. And all around the house, crime scene investigation tape, investigators' vans, police cars. There was only one other reporter there that night and Brennan thought: 'Where is everyone?' When the body was brought out, he remembers thinking, 'that's the most bizarre name. And I thought: this is going to be an* *unusual case.'*

Eventually, other details emerged which competed with the original picture. Though there was no sign of forced entry, there was that small broken window into the basement that had been left open...

We're back to the broken window. But first, let's wrap up the reporting and counter-reporting around issues of snow, and no snow.

From <u>acandyrose.com</u>:

To Glick, Brennan's piece unfairly threw a dark shadow on the Ramseys and forever cast them as the homicidal parents. Again, Brennan disagrees: "The public opinion train was way out of the station by the time that story broke," he asserts.

For many reporters, getting the story out ultimately became more important than getting it right. And context was hardly the only element missing. Tabloids such as the Globe, which kept JonBenét on the front page for three years (and counting), fabricated stories outright, says <u>Jeffrey Shapiro, a freelancer who exclusively reported for the Globe</u> from February 28, 1997, to February 11, 1999.

We'll assess Shapiro's involvement in *The Day After Christmas 2*. But in sum, certainly around the first few weeks and months after JonBenét's death, we have to wonder: were the police and/or the powers that be protecting the Ramseys?

Conversely – were the Ramseys protecting the police? <u>The answer to the latter question appears to be "no"</u>**. Not only were the Ramseys not looking out for the police, they were hiring their own investigators and experts. Were these experts meant to assist the police or counter the cop narrative?

From <u>nytimes.com</u> [10 January 1997]:

...in recent days the Ramseys have declined police requests for formal, videotaped interviews. Last week, the parents hired separate legal counsel, two locally prominent criminal defense lawyers. They also hired Patrick S. Korten, a Washington media consultant who

once was the top spokesman for the United States Department of Justice, to handle the press attention. Mr. Korten did not respond to telephone messages left with his office this week.

Ultimately the Ramseys were issued an apology from the District Attorney. Ultimately they were not prosecuted due to "lack of evidence". Ultimately they were allowed to come and go, in and out of Boulder as they pleased. Ultimately they were allowed to set conditions for their own police interrogations, and their lawyers were able to secure postponements while they prepared for these depositions.

As for Charlie Brennan leaking bogus information from disreputable sources in law enforcement:

"That's how journalism works. You report the spin that your best sources feed you and that's how you keep them as sources."
—Chuck Green, a 32-year veteran of The Denver Post

If that's a journalist's approach to a crime involving a third party, what is John Ramsey's approach to investigating the murder of his own daughter?

"I don't know for sure what happened, and I don't want to know, really." — John Ramsey to abcnews.com

*JonBenét's Mother: Victim or Killer

John Ramsey as quoted by the dailycamera.com: *"Our biggest concern as a family has always been that the Boulder Police Department has **little experience or training in homicide cases.... The law in the hands of the **unskilled and the unknowing** is a terrifying thing...I have been unwilling to submit my family to what seems to be **little more than a lynch mob hiding behind the authority of police badges**. It is not true that you can buy justice in this country, but sadly, it does take money to protect your rights against **abuse of the law** by those charged with its application. My experience has made me wonder how many innocent victims of **police misconduct** there are who were not able or did not know how to protect their basic rights as citizens. **Our fight with the Boulder Police** started when they refused to release JonBenét's body to us for burial until we complied with their demands. It has continued ever since."*

Did Burke Break the Basement Window?

"Was it not fixed?" — Patsy Ramsey, when asked why the basement window that John broke wasn't fixed.

If the presence of a second boy in the Ramsey residence was the most shocking revelation in <u>The Craven Silence</u> Trilogy, what we're about to reveal may be our biggest breakthrough yet.

We might as well get it over with:

1. We don't think John Ramsey broke the basement window

2. We don't think an intruder broke the basement window

3. We believe the basement window was broken on Christmas night shortly before JonBenét's murder

4. We believe Burke [or a young "accomplice"] smashed the window

5. We believe the window was smashed with ~~Burke's~~ Patsy's black softball bat

6. We believe the same bat – Patsy's bat – was used to smash JonBenét over the head

7. We believe the entire paintbrush-garrotte may have been used to muddy potentially incriminating evidence from Patsy's bat. Hint: <u>The paintbrush exterior was dark</u>, ditto the bat.

Absolutely central to answering this question is another question:

Just how security conscious were the Ramseys?

Are we to believe a window broken around the perimeter of the family home would have been left not merely unrepaired, but forgotten? Not likely, but "not likely" is not good enough.

In order to address security concerns we need to closely observe Patsy's comments on the subject. We ought to be aware that on February 21st 2001 John surprised a burglar in his new home in northwest Atlanta. We ought to be aware that the Ramseys had tight security before moving to Boulder and "state of the art" security after moving away from Boulder. Besides all this, the Ramsey residence certainly appeared to be kitted out in a high-tech alarm system, with keypads on several floors including the Ramsey parent's third floor bedroom.

But before we interrogate the Ramseys security systems, before elaborating on the above points we must finalise the observations made about snow.

In the previous chapter we provided a basic algorithm:

Unbroken Snow vs Broken Window

In this chapter instead of considering weather data or debunking additional counter-evidence [we've already provided a few samples of these from Fernie and Glick] we simply want to demonstrate at this point that our hypothesis is *possible*. We'll get to probable in due course.

Unlike in the previous chapters, we don't have our work cut out for us, not on issues of snow or absent footprints. All this has already been done and dusted courtesy of the Boulder Police Department. All we really want to do here is review their evidence.

From forumsforjustice.com:

French did a quick inspection of the interior of the house and found all the doors locked, including the door leading from JonBenét's bedroom to the second floor balcony. There were no signs of the missing child. French inspected the basement during this search, **but was not able to open one room in the basement on the south end of the house because of** *a top latch. John told Officer French that too had personally checked for unlocked doors and windows – John said he found the house locked up as it had been left the night before.*

To be clear, John basically reassured French that **he'd also checked** the house and found nothing untoward in terms of doors and windows.

From forumsforjustice.com:

*When asked about the security alarm system, John told French that **it had not been engaged for several years.***

If true, this makes it likely that if John did break the basement window sometime in the past [as he would later claim] then the lax security attitude would explain why the exterior window was still broken when JonBenét was found murdered. That may satisfy some pundits but I'm going to call bullshit on this statement because we see clear evidence of an alarm system at the front door as well as in the Ramsey's own bedroom.

But as you well know, appearances can be deceiving. The narratives conjured up by John and Patsy convey the impression of a laissez-faire approach – where the home is a sort of revolving door through which children come and go, run amok and enjoy wonderful and innocent adventures. The untidy home we see in the crime scene photos seems to back up this impression, however when we examine the home and its inhabitants more closely, a far different impression emerges.

    1.   We're told John Ramsey does not like to be disturbed by noise.

    2.   Patsy does not like dogs [and didn't like Jacques]

    3.   The Ramsey house originally built in 1927 was extensively remodelled in 1991, 1993 and 1994 and included numerous features including:

        A.   An intercom system

        B.   Central air conditioning

        C.   A home security system [which included a fire response]

D. Was vacant in the summer of 1996 while the family vacationed in Michigan

Any large home left entirely vacant for weeks at a time is going to not only need top notch built-in security, but a working alarm system to alert the owners or some sort of security response outfit about a break-in. Furthermore, it's common knowledge now that "in the months before the murder" approximately <u>100 burglaries had occurred in the neighborhood</u>.

The psychology of a dude who likes remodelling and retrofitting and customising a home to be "just right" sounds like someone who likes to control his world. It sounds like someone who wants things just the way he wants them, and once one had that, one needs to maintain it, right? Once you've kitted out your house with radiant heat inside to warm your toes in winter and a sprinkler system outside to take care of the garden in summer, one also needs to protect these investments. That's security.

Besides this, there's the testimony of Tom Hand. Hand was an architect in charge of remodeling the Ramsey home. Hand has previously described as "very security conscious".

Also worth noting, in the summer of 1997, when the Boulder Police Department needed access to the residence [they wanted to test Fleet White's story that the wine cellar was <u>too dark to see into</u> with the light off] instead of applying for a search warrant, the D.A.'s office unexpectedly announced the "co-operation" of the Ramseys.

The Ramseys had simply consented to the cops having the run of the house to do their detective work. If it seemed too good to be true, it was. In short order the cops discovered the house was basically bugged with recording devices and motion detectors. Much, if not all of this equipment, was rigged in the basement area.

When the door enclosing this "security system" was forcibly kicked in, the sergeant in charge* found a VHS recorder which was recording four interior rooms of the Ramsey home. Interestingly the recorder *had to be manually activated.* Ramsey investigators later admitted they had set up the devices due to concerns around possible break-ins.

We've skipped ahead to July 1997, let's jump back to December 26, 1996 and French's observations just after 06:00.

From forumsforjustice.com:

After his cursory inspection of the house, French took a statement from John regarding the events of the prior evening. John related that the family had arrived home around 9:00 p.m., that Burke and Patsy had gone immediately to bed, and that he had read to JonBenét for a few minutes before he went to bed. Apparently the morning's stress had also confused John, as the sequence of events he related to French about the prior evening would differ at his later official statement.

Arriving almost immediately after the first officers on scene were John and Barbara Fernie, *close friends of both John and Patsy.*

The key point to note of course is that John Fernie arrived after French and Reichenbach**, and perhaps after Veitch as well, so his whining about why his footprints weren't checked or his shoes examined seems overstated.

From forumsforjustice.com:

They were soon joined by Fleet and Priscilla White...Bill and Heather Cox, guests staying at the Whites' home, also appeared. Barbara Fernie called the Ramsey's pastor, Rev. Rol Hoverstock from St. John's Presbyterian Church, and asked him to come.

At one point Patsy screamed at John, "You have to give them the money and get our baby back." John, attempting to comfort his wife, responded, "We'll get her back. She'll be okay."

If John seemed sufficiently composed [cordial] to reassure Patsy, Fleet White was less relaxed.

From forumsforjustice.com:

Within minutes of arriving at the Ramsey home, Fleet decided to look around the house... Fleet was hoping that JonBenét...was just hiding somewhere in the house. Since everyone had been told by the police officers not to go upstairs, Fleet went <u>down to the basement</u>. He noticed that the lights were on. He found a small piece of glass from a broken window in a <u>room used for model trains</u>. In checking the latch for the window he discovered that it was unlocked, <u>but closed</u>. Fleet also noticed a blue suitcase was sitting underneath the window. He continued with his search by opening every cupboard and door. He opened the door to the wine cellar, reached inside, but could not find the light switch and could not see inside the room. <u>The wine cellar</u> is completely <u>formed by cement</u> and has no windows. Finding no evidence of anyone entering or leaving from the basement area and no trace of JonBenét, Fleet went <u>back upstairs</u>.

This is incredibly valuable first-hand observation from Fleet, and it seems – since he knew the basement area – he did a better job of investigating the scene than French had a few minutes earlier.

What's useful from Fleet's observation, besides the strangeness of the basement lights being on – perhaps left on by French - it really boils down to a seemingly throwaway contradiction.

He found a small piece of glass in a room used for model trains – He discovered the window was closed.

What's interesting in virtually all crime scene images is that <u>the window is open</u>. It's been broken, we're told, in order <u>to open it</u> and <u>get in</u> or <u>out</u>. **So why does Fleet find it closed?** Did the window blow itself closed? Well, consider where this window is – <u>it's below ground level</u>, protected by a metal grate, and in the basement area of the house – typically one of the least drafty areas of the home. On top of this it's just about dawn, perhaps the time of day that's the most windless***. Even if a slight wind was blowing, the area of the grate is sheltered on two sides – the East and the South. If a wind was coming from the North West, perhaps a strong wind would push into the grate. <u>As it happens a mild wind that day was blowing ESE</u> – basically into the front door area of the house.

When crime scene video was shot that evening, a spider web over the window can be seen fluttering slightly in the breeze.

Even if Ramsey apologists would be so bold to suggest the wind had blown through an open basement window, perhaps through the vent in the boiler room [facing East] and somehow funnelled its way through a maze, and through a closed door, the problem would be that the window could not be blown *open* – because the basement window in the train room opens to the inside. So given the direction of the wind and the orientation of the Ramsey home, and sunken position of the window itself, the window could not have been blown open, and further would not have been blown closed.

This means unless an intruder closed the window behind him, the window was actually closed throughout December 25th and 26th. It is our contention that this is precisely the case – that the window was broken, but not broken to open or close it, not broken for entry or any other kind of access and not to "stage a break-in". We believe the window was smashed through the course of "horse-play" in the basement on Christmas night.

From acandyrose.com:

Each window had four panes, and Fleet White, having been down there earlier, pointed out [to John when they were down there together at 1:00pm] **the baseball-sized hole** *in the upper left pane of the middle window.*

Now let's review Reichenbach's observations.

From forumsforjustice.com:

Patrol Sgt. Reichenbach, responding to the call to go to the 15th Street address, passed a time and temperature sign in a mall parking lot on his way to the Ramsey home. The temperature in Boulder that morning was 9 degrees [Fahrenheit]. A light dusting of snow lay sprinkled on the ground, mostly visible on the neighborhood lawns. **Upon his arrival at the residence Reichenbach conducted a brief inspection of the outside of the premises.** *In addition to the newly fallen snow, portions of the yard were covered with* **one or two inches of crusty snow** *from a prior snowfall. He noted that* **no** *footprints were visible in the new snow that adhered to the grass and pavement areas* surrounding the house nor in the old snow still remaining.

So now we know who the source is of the no footprints observation. And somehow that information trickled through law enforcement and eventually onto Charlie Brennan's desk almost three months later.

Now let's examine what those in charge of the crime scene discovered.

From forumsforjustice.com:

Det. Michael Everett, the Lead Crime Scene investigator Boulder police department, was also told to report to the Ramsey residence to assist in the crime scene search with Det. Sgt. Tom Wickman, the supervisor in charge of the crime scene. When they arrived they too inspected the outside of the residence. They discovered a basement level window with a broken pane. As they were inspecting the window well for any evidence of entry, they noticed that **the grate placed over the window well was covered with a spider web which appeared undisturbed**, *making it unlikely that anyone had entered through that window.*

So what do we have? We have John not reporting either an open window or broken window. We have one officer confirming no footprints in snow, another confirming the basement was secure [entry doorways were secure and windows closed]. On top of this we have the steel grate – a possible source of a scraping noise – ruled out because of an undisturbed spider web spread over and around it. Besides unbroken snow we have an unbroken spider web, and as CBS demonstrated, even the fragments of spider web remaining in the corner of the window ought not to have been there had someone climbed either in or out.

From forumsforjustice.com:

According to John and Patsy, Burke had remained asleep during Patsy's morning screams and commotion of people coming and going from the residence.

Given that Burke's room and windows directly <u>overlook the front area</u> of the Ramsey house, including the road, and given it was dark when police first arrived, it's difficult to imagine a child remaining inert in bed with flashing lights throbbing against his window. If Burke was involved in his sister's death, having seen him on Dr. Phil smiling while demonstrating how he hit JonBenét, one wonders whether he was thrilled at this enormous reaction – the whole world had seemingly come to his bedroom. And perhaps he was the master of all the mayhem he'd unleashed.

From <u>forumsforjustice.com</u>:

*At approximately 7:00 a.m., John decided it was time to wake Burke. It had already been decided that Burke would be taken to the White's residence where relatives were still staying for the holidays. John, **accompanied by Fleet**, went up to Burke's room. John woke his sleeping son, "Why don't you get up, buddy. You're going over to White's house to see Fleet, Jr." Burke's only reaction to the disturbance of his sleep was, "Okay." Burke put his clothes on,* **grabbed his Nintendo and a couple of Christmas toys** *to take on his visit to his friend's house, and followed his father and Fleet downstairs. Fleet immediately took Burke outside to his vehicle and drove away.*

Never once did Burke ask why policemen were at his house. The only conversation that passed between the two during the ride was occasional mention of Burke's Nintendo he got for Christmas which he had brought with him.

It's interesting that Fleet accompanies John to the basement and to Burke's room. Fleet would eventually pay dearly for being at his friend's side during these crucial hours – he would be investigated and also suspected of being a child molester. We'll deal with some of those spurious charges in the next narrative. Meanwhile, as Burke enjoys his jaunt to the White's, we have a window to figure out.

If the police reports are solid then we can rule out an intruder breaking the window. If an intruder didn't break it, one of the Ramseys probably did. Is mild-mannered John really the sort of guy who would gain access to his home by climbing through a subterranean basement window?

There were 104 windows on the Ramsey home; 100 of them allowed access from the outside. There are also several doors, many made of glass, like the butler pantry door and the side door to the garage and other doors on the south side where John could have easily broken out a pane and gained entry. So which entry point does John choose when reportedly locked out? Basically the most difficult damn window in the entire 7,000+ square foot home. The best part of this break-in story though, is that John claims he did it half-naked.

From acandyrose.com, the 1997 police interview:

JOHN: *Yeah, well, as I recall, I did it at night and I had a suit on, and **I took my suit off and did it in my underwear**. But, it's not easy, I mean, you can get in that way, you get dirty, but...*

TRUJILLO: *It's not a graceful way to get in?*

JOHN: *No, no.*

THOMAS: *Tom, let me just ask John this. Do you sit down and slide through, buttocks first if you will, through a window like that or, do you recall how you went through the actual window, John?*

JOHN: *I don't...remember. Seems like, I mean, I don't remember, but I think **I would probably have gone in feet first.***

THOMAS: ***Feet first, backwards?***

JOHN: *Yeah*

THOMAS: *And when you went through in your underwear, were you wearing shoes?*

JOHN: *I still had my shoes on, yeah.*

Thanks for that visual, John.

Here's some food for thought before we move on. One of the window panes is broken. There are shards of glass still in the window. Now see <u>how a body would go through that window</u>. And John stuffed his nearly naked body through that hole, risking serious injury, for what purpose? To spare dirtying his suit? He couldn't afford a dry cleaner?

Surely he'd just call a locksmith, or smash in a window and open a door? If it wasn't John it was Burke, but how do we narrow it down?

One way is the indirect approach – by poking around this idea of "security concerns". We know Patsy had security concerns, but what about John?

From <u>forumsforjustice.org</u>:

TRUJILLO: *Okay. And let me back you up just a little bit. Do you guys ever use the alarm system I that house at all?*

PATSY: *No, we didn't use it in years.*

TRUJILLO: *Okay. Do you remember about when the last time you used the alarm system was?*

PATSY: *Well, I remember when JonBenét was probably two or three, it was, the house was still under construction. She was probably two.*

TRUJILLO: *Um hum.*

PATSY: *And I didn't even know the alarm system was activated yet, because we had had so many people in and out of there. She drug that little, this little bench we had back by the garage door, drug it over and I think she was trying to hit the garage door opener, but she hit, you know, boom, boom, boom on that . . .*

TRUJILLO: *The keypad.*

PATSY: *keypad and I mean it just, it's an interior alarm. It's got the speakers or whatever they are inside the house and it is just deafening. And uh, John, we ran back to the keypad, cause I had never really heard it go off and she was standing there, you know, like, and uh, I mean, I didn't even know how to shut the dumb thing off cause I didn't even know it was activated and pretty soon I,* ***I was trying to call Safe Systems*** *or whoever it was that I thought had been working on it and uh, I mean, you just couldn't stay in the house it was so awful, so loud. And uh, I remember grabbing John's cellular phone, because I couldn't dial it inside the house it was too . . .*

It's a very long answer isn't it, and oddly enough, if there is a record of the call to the security company, it's not from the home phone. Typically though, people who set their own alarms off do so for two reasons:

    1.   The alarm is on because of security concerns.

    2.   The alarm is installed for the same reason.

    3.   Ergo there would be no alarm in place if there were no concerns about security.

Is Trujillo buying Patsy's bunkum?

From forumsforjustice.org:

TRUJILLO: *Um hum.*

PATSY: *loud and pretty soon I heard these sirens and apparently* **she had hit the button that, you know, don't ask questions, just sent help.**

TRUJILLO: *Um hum. So everybody came.*

PATSY: *Everybody came and, and, you know, they were saying well, you know, if this is your house why don't you turn it off? And I was like we don't know the code, you know, so that was the last,* **so we didn't use it because of that, cause, <u>cause like every time that we ever used the alarm system</u> it would go off erratically and* . . .

See the contradiction? They never used the alarm system because they didn't know the code, but each time they used it the alarm would go off…?

From forumsforjustice.org:

TRUJILLO: *Had problems with it? So it hasn't,* **you hadn't use it or it has it not been hooked up to an alarm company at all?**

PATSY: **I believe it was hooked up to a, um, I don't know if you call it an alarm company or whatever, but for fire . . .**

TRUJILLO: *Um hum.*

Of course Patsy has just mentioned the alarm system a weak moments earlier – Safe Systems. But now suddenly she can't remember. Unfortunately though, Trujillo seems to miss this. Let's see if Haney does better.

From acandyrose.com:

HANEY: *What changes have you seen in yourself since the death, outside of taking away the TV and the newspaper?*

PATSY: I think the biggest change that I have had personally, um, when I had cancer, I was afraid to die because I had two children and a husband and I didn't want to leave them. And now, I am not afraid, because JonBenét had to go there. If I get cancer again, and you know, I can see her on that side. And then God willing, if I stay healthy, I have my son to enjoy here. And (INAUDIBLE). So I am not -- I am just not afraid anymore.

Not be indelicate, but this is classic Patsy. Her daughter has been murdered, and Patsy basically suggests if she gets cancer again [which she did] that would be okay. And if she didn't die [she died in 2006], then she'd have her son to enjoy. It seems a fairly dreary way of looking at things, almost as though cancer and JonBenét is first prize, Burke is second and John isn't even mentioned.

From acandyrose.com:

HANEY: *How about changes in John since this happened?*

PATSY: I think we both regret not being as security conscious as we should have. I think when you live in a major metropolitan place like Atlanta **we always used to have an alarm, we always locked our doors.**

In Atlanta the Ramseys "always" had an alarm and "always" locked their doors, but not in Boulder?

From acandyrose.com:

PATSY: *We moved to Boulder and it just seemed so safe and small town, you know,* **next door kids, and I think we just let down our guard.** *And I think we will forever be regretting that, you know, I mean we have since gotten a dog. I am not real crazy about dogs. Dogs have (INAUDIBLE) and burglars don't like noise. We have lights that come on, motion lights. We have cameras. We have a security alarm, of course, that we use. I know exactly who has every key, you know, and we just -- you know, were too lax.*

There seems to be a hint of sincerity in this, doesn't there. Let's play it back again:

"I think we just let down our guard. And I think we will forever be regretting that..."

I don't think Patsy is referring to "her guard" in terms of security. I think that was in place. I think she let down her guard in terms of her kids, specifically Burke. And there's regret there, possibly with good reason.

From acandyrose.com:

HANEY: *The alarm that you had at the Boulder house here, when was the last time that you had used it?*

PATSY: *When JonBenét was probably about two years old, we were still doing a lot of construction, and I mean there were* **people in and out of that house all the time, fixing things** *and* **I didn't know what they were working on.** *I knew they were working on the alarm system. But I didn't really think that it worked yet. Because we had had a lot of doors and windows taken out and put back in, so I thought it was kind of in the works. Well, one evening, John and I just sat down with a glass of wine and, you know, boom, boom, boom, you know, all things. And we went running back to the key pad, which was back there by the garage door, and JonBenét had pulled her little chair over next to the door and I think she was trying* *to reach the garage door button, garage door open button, which was just above it. And she pushed you know, two, three, four buttons on that alarm key pad, and it all -- everything broke loose. I mean it was deafening.* **And here came the squad cars and the ambulance and the fire truck,** *you know, the whole thing. Whole nine yards. And -- and so we never really used it. They were asking me: what's your code? I said I didn't know I had a code because I didn't know the thing was working yet.*

It's interesting that Patsy refers to people in and out all the time "fixing things". Things were always being fixed. Also, the alarm goes off and a bunch of paid for services show up – ambulance, firetruck, squad cars. You don't just have an alarm system, or have one and not use it – you subscribe to a service. You pay for a service. Why would the Ramseys have a service and pay for it if they weren't using it?

From acandyrose.com:

HANEY: *So you never --*

PATSY: *We never had used it. But we had it, it was in the house when we bought it and we -- we did whatever you do to activate the fire alarm, you know, tied into that.* **Smoke detectors and all.** *If it went off, it can call the fire people like that,* **but we never, you know, set it.** *Because it was always going, it seemed like it went off erratically, more than it was worth. You know. And like I said, we kind of had been lulled into the, you know,* **complacent feeling of security.** *So –*

Are the Ramseys complacent people? Were they complacent on the day their daughter turned up dead? Is the hiring of lawyers the same day [December 26th] a sign of complacency? Is going on CNN before the week is out complacency? Is a three page Ransom Note a languid wishy washy attempt at covering up one's tracks?

From acandyrose.com:

HANEY: *You say you got a dog. You had a dog up here, right?*

PATSY: *We have a dog in Boulder that we bought.*

HANEY: *And what -- what happened, I guess the dog was somewhere else?*

PATSY: *He -- he had to have a Bichons Frise.*

HANEY: *I am sorry?*

I'm sorry too. What the hell is Patsy talking about? Who had to have what? And this isn't even coming close to answering Haney's question – where was the dog when JonBenét was murdered? It was their dog, it could have or should have barked if someone had broken in so…did it? And if it didn't, why didn't it? Perhaps because there were no footprints in the snow…?

From acandyrose.com:

PATSY: *A little Bichons thing, white-haired, puffy, fluffy dog. Not a hound dog. It's a little -- I mean, JonBenét -- we went to the puppy shop one day and she said, "Oh, that one." And, you know, they put this little white fluffy thing in her arms and, you know, I said wrap it up. Yes, we will take one of everything that goes with it. I mean, it's just putty. It was a darling little dog…*

Wow! It actually seems like Patsy loves dogs but…not according to Linda Wilcox another Ramsey insider.

From tripod.com:

LINDA WILCOX: *Well, first of all, Patsy didn't want a dog. And, she didn't want JonBenét to have a dog. This particular dog didn't get the potty training thing down very well, he tended to leave puddles.* **He was pretty much relegated to the wood floor at the bottom of the spiral staircase and out the side door off the patio**. *However, they had, John told Patsy to get JonBenét a dog. It was John's decision to get a dog and* **Patsy chose a Bichon**. *She got it from a pet store, and I came there one day, his name was Jacques, a little guy, cute little fur ball. Well, one day the dog went to the vet and came back. But the dog that went to the vet was smaller than the dog that left. I had said something to Patsy, the next week I walked in and I asked Patsy what happened to Jacques. She's like, "What?" And I said, this isn't Jacques. And she's like, SHHHH, don't tell* *anyone, no one else knows. Turns out the first dog had something wrong like some kind of liver disease or something and it was dying.* **It was a bad dog**, *so she called the pet store and made a switch before anyone knew.*

We've been through this stuff before, but we're reeling it in simply to expose Patsy on her drooling doggy talk. If Patsy is this disingenuous about the family dog, how much more so is she about "security concerns?"

From tripod.com:

LINDA WILCOX: *One more thing...I think the first summer, the summer of '94, they took the dog with them to Michigan. See Patsy took care of the dog, John took no responsibility for it whatsoever. He tolerated it at best. And, if it got anything of his, heaven forbid. I don't know this, but I think they got rid of the dog because when they were in Michigan, they were busy with pageants. They were doing other things and there was no one to look after the dog. I think they gave it to the neighbors when they left for the summer because they didn't want to hassle with the dog. Life was good for them until it was inconvenient.*

Like, JonBenét, for example. She got no affection at all when she was little except maybe from their nanny. Until she started to perform or produce, she was basically ignored. At one point, John was complaining because he had to get her dressed one morning because Suzanne had been out of town. He couldn't find any clothes that matched. The reason was, she was wearing cast-offs from Burke because she didn't have any clothes of her own... Suzanne told me (garbled) I mean this kid was 3 1/2, she was in Nursery school in the morning. The poor kid was so busy every afternoon she was only 3 years old...

Coming back to dogs as a security measure, Margaret Dillon to the West of the Ramsey's across the alley reported that her dogs – who barked at anyone and everyone in the alley – "made no noise on Wednesday night..."

If the alarm was off, was Jacques off too, and Margaret Dillon's mutts set to slumber? When DeMuth grills Patsy on Jacques, Patsy gets a little tripped up.

From acandyrose.com:

DeMUTH: *Where was he usually?*

PATSY: *He was usually at our house. I mean it was 50-50, you know. He just --*

DeMUTH: *Now explain that1 50-50 to me. I mean is that kind of -- would he stay overnight at Barnhills or was it just 50 percent of the day?*

PATSY: *No. Some nights he would spend the night over there. And, you know, if I was going to be gone all day, maybe two -- rather than leave him in the house alone, they liked to have him over there and they played with him all the time. So I would say Betty Ann, I am going to Denver, I won't be back until 5 o'clock or something, do you want Jacques? Oh, yes. And then the kids usually went over and get him and (INAUDIBLE). So it was kind of --*

DeMUTH: *50 percent of the time he was not spending the night in your house?*

PATSY: *Right. Maybe not quite 50 percent, maybe 40 percent.*

DeMUTH: *And would he bark when strangers came around?*

PATSY: **He didn't bark a lot, but he would, yeah. Uh-hum. He could bark, yeah.** *I think, I think when -- you know, he just was so good with the kids and the kids were romping all over, you know, playing with him, I think when he sensed danger, probably would have.*

Would have what? Barked?

From yourpurebredpuppy.com:

The three most common behavioural issues with the Bichon Frise are: 1) housebreaking: Bichons are usually difficult to housebreak; 2) separation anxiety: most Bichons are so sociable and dependent on human companionship that they don't do well when left for long periods of time; and 3) **some Bichons are barky** -- and some have a high-pitched bark that can set your teeth on edge.

If you want a dog who...

Is small but sturdy

*Makes **an alert watchdog**, but is not aggressive*

Is good with other pets

A Bichon Frise may be right for you.

If you don't want to deal with...

Notorious housebreaking difficulties

*"Separation anxiety" (destructiveness **and barking**) when left alone too much*

Potential for excessive barking

In terms of the intruder theory we now have:

- Unbroken snow
- Unbroken spider webs
- Unopened broken windows
- Inactivated house alarms
- Unbarking neighborhood dogs

The bottom-line to all this is that no intruder and no one else opened the basement window. It was never opened, it was simply broken. And because it was broken on the south side of the Ramsey house, the sound of the broken glass was not sufficiently loud enough to carry all the way to the Stanton's.

Having dealt fully [if not completely] with the snow narrative, the security narrative and the chronic canine laryngitis sweeping Boulder during the Christmas of 1996, it's time to return to the thing that's neither open or closed, neither here nor there, neither broken nor fixed.

Let's deal with the broken window via the 1998 police interview.

From acandyrose.com:

DeMUTH: *What did you do after the window was broken, did you have some involvement with that at all?*

PATSY: *Well, yes. When I came back, you know, from the lake, I mean **there was glass everywhere all over the floor**, and I cleaned out -- picked up pieces of glass, you know. He never cleaned it up, obviously, and cleaned it up, and **I had Linda sweep down there because the kids, the boys would** sometimes play in here.*

DeMUTH: *Did you clear the area out then? Was it cleared of stuff?*

PATSY: *Well, you know, kind of pushed back, but the **boys would go down there and play** like **they are building airplanes**.*

Burke's wallpaper in his room is filled with airplanes, but it's still curious that she's jumped from cleaning up a broken window to Burke building flying objects one supposes in the basement. Patsy also refers to unflushed excrement left by boys using the basement toilet. Then Patsy brings up the airplanes thing again. Trip Demuth tries to bring Patsy back on point.

From acandyrose.com:

DeMUTH: *Do you know why the window wasn't fixed?*

PATSY: *No, I don't. **Was it not fixed?***

DeMUTH: *Well, what do you know about that window, the condition of that window on Christmas of '96, have you --*

PATSY: *I just remember a little to do list that Linda Hoffman had included fixing that pane in that window. Whether he got to it or not, I don't know because he wasn't able to fix the play room doors, you know, so he didn't get to everything.*

John claims the window had been broken for months after he broke it. Patsy is saying she foisted the clean-up and repair on Linda and her husband. As we'll see in a moment, John foists the clean-up onto Patsy. Seems the Ramseys didn't really mind what was broken in their home, did they? Or did they?

Let's go to Patsy's 1997 police interview with her arch nemesis Steve Thomas.

From acandyrose.com:

THOMAS: *Tom has some questions for you about when John had to break in that basement window . . .*

PATSY: *Right.*

THOMAS: *but was there any reason you couldn't or John could not have retrieve the key from the Barnhills at that time to get in rather than breaking the window?*

PATSY [caught off guard]: *He, he may not have [known] they had a key.*

WTF they have your dog, the kids are going to and from the Barnhills all the time – of course they know about the key! Joe is babysitting JonBenét's bike for shit sakes.

From acandyrose.com:

TRUJILLO: *When did John break that window in the basement?*

PATSY: *He, I don't know exactly when he did it, but I think it was last summer sometime when we, the kids and I were at the lake.*

Now let's get John's take on the basement window. Remember, what we're suggesting is that John didn't break it, and what's more, it was broken the night of JonBenét's murder.

From acandyrose.com:

THOMAS: *OK. When you had previously broken that basement window to gain entry to the home when you had been locked out, can* you approximate what month that was?

JOHN: *Well, I think it was last summer. Because Patsy was up at Lake (inaudible) all summer, and it would have been July or August probably, somewhere in that time frame.*

THOMAS: *Did you remove that grate and get down into the window well?*

JOHN: *Uh-huh.*

THOMAS: *And what did you use to break the pane?*

JOHN: *Ah, I don't remember. Might have been my foot, I don't know.*

THOMAS: *OK. You reach in, I'm assuming, unlatched it and gain entry through that small window.*

JOHN: *Yeah.*

THOMAS: *Did you then replace the grate onto that window well?*

JOHN: *Oh I probably would have done it that night. I'm sure I didn't the next morning or, you know, or thereafter.*

THOMAS: *Did you remove that whole grate off onto the, off the well, to jump down there and get in?*

JOHN: *Ah, probably. I don't remember.*

THOMAS: **Is there any reason that window went unrepaired?**

JOHN: *No. I mean it's,* **Patsy usually took care of those things***, and I just rarely went to the basement, so it just, I guess, got overlooked. Although she did think that* **she asked the cleaning lady's husband to fix it over Thanksgiving** *when they were doing some repair work there, but I don't know if that's ever been confirmed whether he fixed it or not.*

John has done his homework, I suspect, at least on this area. Both John and Patsy concur that "the cleaning lady" gosh-darn it was supposed to clean up and fix the window. Well great, they both confirm the same thing – that fixing the window wasn't something on their radar.

From acandyrose.com:

THOMAS: *And you mentioned when you went down in the morning, the 26th, and it was unlatched,* ***did that strike you as odd or did you bring that to anybody's attention?***

Great question Steve!

From acandyrose.com:

JOHN [stutters a little]: *I, I don't know. I mean when I was, I think, yeah,* ***I think it probably struck me as a little odd****, but it wasn't, I* ***mean sometimes that window would be open because the basement got hot****, or one of those windows would be opened. So it wasn't…*

Note John doesn't answer this question:

did you bring the [unlatched/broken] window to anybody's attention?

Also note that John makes a ludicrous claim. He suggests that it was normal to have the window open because it sometimes got hot in the basement. Really? When it was 9°F and snowing lightly outside? In mid-winter, at night, while committing murder it got hot in the basement?

Although John doesn't answer the question about informing police about the open/broken window when grilled by the cops, look at how he answers the same question when Larry King asks him.

This is the Ramseys on CNN in March 2000.

From acandyrose.com:

KING: *In the book, you write about the suitcase and the open basement window, but the police say you never told them about it.*

JOHN: *That's false.*

PATSY: *False.*

JOHN: *I told Linda Arndt that I found the window open and I found a suitcase under the window. They have photos of this in their crime scene photos.*

Hmmm. I wonder whether Linda Arndt ever confirmed this?

What's more important though is whether the Ramsey housekeeper confirms their claims about being told to fix a broken window and clean up the glass. Does Linda know about the broken window? The window was broken for three or four months, and Linda came to clean the house three times a week?

Well, the housekeeper contradicts the Ramsey's statement in an interview with the Star, June 20, 2000.

From acandyrose.com:

Another thing that made me think Patsy had staged the whole crime was the broken window in the basement. I used to clean their house three times a week. If something was broken, Patsy had me clean it up. On the morning of the murder, police found a broken window in the basement, just a few feet from the room where JonBenét's body was found. **John Ramsey told the police that he had broken the window to get into the house months before when he was accidentally locked out. But I think that is a lie.**

Linda would know wouldn't she? So what we're getting here is the housekeeper literally calling John and Patsy out on the same "lie". What are the chances Linda was given the order to clean, to fix and she ignored the order for three or four months? What are the chances Linda simply didn't notice the broken window in the lead-up to Christmas [including hauling Christmas trees out from the basement, decorating them and tidying up the kids' play area]. Any chance the house proud appearance conscious Ramseys would hold a house party in a home with a broken exterior window?

From acandyrose.com:

*If there had been broken glass in the basement, Patsy would have told me to clean it up. Another thing didn't make sense. John claimed he was locked out on that day when he supposedly broke the window. But **he never used a key to come in the front or side door of the house. He always opened the garage door from his car with his remote and came in through the garage entrance**. I think Patsy broke that window herself **on the night she killed JonBenét to make the police think there had been an intruder**, and John concocted the story about breaking the window.*

It's incredible getting this admission from the housekeeper:

I think [someone] broke that window…on the night …JonBenét [was killed]…

We do too. But if John and Patsy wanted the police to think the intruder had come in through the window, why hadn't they explicitly mentioned it to the police? Follow the line of reasoning to its logical conclusion – John and Patsy claim they knew about the broken unrepaired window for months. And yet when police arrive and sweep the house looking for signs where an intruder might have gained entry, there's no helpful suggestion. There's no:

OH BY THE WAY I BROKE A WINDOW IN THE BASEMENT, YOU SHOULD REALLY CHECK THAT, NO HANG ON; LET ME CHECK THAT…

Of course if the Ramseys were truly innocent in this matter, one might imagine both John and Patsy running down into the basement immediately following a breathless appraisal of the Ransom Note. Oh shit, the broken window that we shoulda coulda woulda gotten fixed? Could they have gotten in here? Could the foreign faction have taken her out of here?

And yet that's also *not* what the Ramseys say they did. While Burke sleeps in what's left of Christmases' embrace, John and Patsy simply called friends. They didn't search the house; they didn't so much as set foot outside. Why not? We think because they knew where JonBenét was all along.

And then they weren't sure what to do except pray, be cordial, call their pilot and start the <u>eeny meeny miny moe</u> of selecting legal counsel.

Yes, we think Burke could very well have broken the window. Let's pull up those seven pointers again and see whether our arguments on this side of the chapter make sense:

    1.   We don't think John Ramsey broke the basement window – neither does Linda

    2.   We don't think an intruder broke the basement window – neither does Linda

    3.   We believe the basement window was broken on Christmas night shortly before JonBenét's murder – Linda agrees the window was broken on Christmas night

    4.   We believe Burke [or a young "accomplice"] smashed the window

    5.   We believe the window was smashed with ~~Burke's~~ Patsy's black softball bat, or a ball hit with that bat

    6.   We believe the same bat – Patsy's bat – was used to smash JonBenét over the head

    7.   We believe the entire paintbrush-garrotte was used to muddy potentially incriminating evidence from Patsy's bat. Hint: <u>The paintbrush exterior was dark</u>, ditto the bat.

And all of this brings us to another revelation. Where exactly did the crime take place? We'll reveal our hand on this vital question in the final chapter.

*Wickman

From pbworks.com: *After 5:59 AM Officer Veitch Arrived. BPD officer* **Karl Veitch arrived before Fernies *(Ramsey & Ramsey 1999a: 14)*. "*Contrary to normal protocol, the police did not seal off the defendants' home, with the sole exception being the interior of JonBenét's bedroom. In other words, any person in* *the Ramsey house could, and often did, move freely throughout the home. (SMF P 21; PSMF P 22.)" (Carnes 2003:13).*

***Wind speed was reported as 8mph ESE at 07:00 in Denver on the morning of December 26th, 2016.

BELLS & BAUBLES
"Christmas is a season not only of rejoicing but of reflection." —
Winston Churchill

Cogne #4

It's a curious fact of this case that in the seven hours between the arrival of the police and the discovery of their daughter's body, JonBenét's parents hardly breathed a word to one another. We have virtually zero documented dialogue of the two having said anything to one another, ditto dialogue between both parents and Burke.

When JonBenét's corpse is brought upstairs, Linda Arndt actually had to instruct John to go to his wife [because she hadn't yet moved to look at her own child*]. John returned to JonBenét's dead body within about two minutes, at which time he covered her in a blanket**.

A few minutes later, the couple was told that the baby had died before reaching the hospital. At this point, **Mr. Lorenzi fell to the ground in panic, sobbing and screaming**, *while his wife began to ask him: "Shall we have another baby? Will you help me to conceive another one? Then we will go away from here...." Witnesses claimed that* **Mr. Lorenzi appeared annoyed and upset and did not answer.**

We get three tell-tale giveaways in this paragraph all of them related to inappropriate emotion"

    1. At the time Lorenzi is sobbing his wife doesn't console him, rather she seems to offer him a solution.

    2. There's a mismatch in emotion: Franzoni herself seems composed while her husband is not.

    3. Lorenzi appears upset...with his wife?

How many of these can we apply to the Ramsey case? Well John is cordial while Patsy is at turns inert and then melodramatic. Not only do the Ramsey parents' emotions not match the situation, crucially they do not match one another and neither do the couple make any effort consoling the other.

Doors and windows were closed and did not seem to be forced.

Nothing valuable was missing and there were no traces of strangers. *Traces of blood were concentrated only in the master bedroom where the murder took place and there were none elsewhere.* ***Neighbours did not notice anything unusual.*** *The following day, the couple was summoned by the police in Cogne and here* ***Mrs. Franzoni started saying some bizarre words.*** *Franzoni said to a policeman who tried to console her, "There are even mothers who kill their children, yes, there are ..." and shortly after, she said "You know, sir I do hope that [my son] has been killed." The policeman asked to explain such an odd statement, but she quickly digressed.* — Wikipedia

On the 28th of December when Patsy was fingerprinted did she say anything unusual? Well, as it turned out she did. Besides what Patsy said, almost everything about the procedure was weird. Firstly, the Ramseys weren't "processed" for hair, blood and fingerprints [Thomas refers to this collectively as "non-testimonial evidence"]. Instead they were processed in the Criminal Justice Center, which meant since the mountain wouldn't come to the detective, the tools for taking these samples had to be taken to Mount Ramsey.

Thomas recounted that he expected to find a "grief-stricken" family demanding news of their investigation. Instead the detective found the affluent couple and their son surrounded by a phalanx of high-powered lawyers. Besides the strange retinue of representation, the Ramseys were resolute in their reticence. Thomas described John at the time as "nervous" and not making a peep unless prodded:

*"...He uttered not one unsolicited word...*****

When it was Burke's turn, Thomas describes John as shepherding the boy, whispering in his ear, almost "smothering" him with hugs and fatherly supervision. The crucial moment came when it was Patsy's turn to be fingerprinted. Glancing at her ink-blackened fingers Patsy said: *"I didn't kill my baby."* Thomas leaned forward to inquire what Patsy had said. This time Patsy told Thomas directly: *"I didn't kill my baby."*

Immediately her lawyer took hold of Patsy's shoulder and hissed "emphatically" in her ear. Thomas reports that Patsy didn't utter another word for the rest of the processing, but what she had said spoke volumes. Thomas was right to observe that if Patsy was protesting that she was innocent, what spoke volumes in the lingering, deafening silence was the unasked question.

*From pbworks.com: *After 1:05 PM JBR Carried Upstairs "He then carried her body upstairs. (SMF*** P 39; PSMF**** P 39.)" (Carnes 2003:17).* "Ramsey ripped the duct tape off JonBenét's mouth and carried her up the stairs, setting her down on the floor. Though it's unclear why, Arndt then picked up the body again and moved it to the living room near the Christmas tree where Ramsey knelt beside her, repeating "My little angel," over and over. **Friends carried Patsy, too stunned to walk, over to the body**. Police reports describe her throwing herself over JonBenét." (Glick et al. 1998).

Various authors describe JonBenét's dead body covered by a quilt, a divan cover and a blanket. In the Lifetime movie JonBenét appears to be covered in a mat/carpet of some sort. According to Steve Thomas***: *John was back within two minutes, grabbed a blanket from a chair, and tossed it over the body before Arndt could react. Arndt compounded the error by adjusting the quilt...someone else spread a gray Colorado Avalanche sweatshirt over the exposed feet a few minutes later...*

Note: It was **after JonBenét was covered with the blanket/sweatshirt** that Patsy came out of the solarium and threw herself on top of her daughter.

***SMF - Statement of Material Fact

****PSMF - Plaintiff's Statement of Material Fact

***** JonBenét: Inside the Ramsey Murder Investigation

Pam Paugh and the Attack of the Cardboard Boxes

GRETA: *Do you know who killed JonBenét?*

PAM: *Yes*

GRETA: *Have you told the police?*

PAM: *Yes… Alex Hunter… he is committed to JonBenét… he will do exactly what he said.*

GRETA: *Do you know who wrote the ransom note?*

PAM: *Yes, the killer… I don't know specifically which person.*

GRETA: *Who is it?*

PAM: *She knew them well enough to go with them… my loyalty is to JonBenét…I will not answer that question.*

GRETA: *Do you know them by name?*

PAM: *I would rather not say* — Pam Paugh speaking with Greta van Sustern in 1998, from Websleuths.com

On the afternoon of December 28th, the same afternoon the Ramseys submitted to providing compulsory DNA samples, their lawyers also communicated that they would not give interviews to police. At precisely the same time the Boulder Police were tippy-toeing around the Ramseys trying to collect samples, Patsy's sister Pam was mounting a siege of the Ramsey residence.

Pam was armed not only with permission to enter the residence and take stuff [ostensibly clothing], she also had guile and incentive on her side. Her sister was facing a shitstorm with the cops and it was up to Pam to do damage control.

When the cats away the mouse will play…

Before we deal with Pam's cardboard assault of 755 15 street I want to make the context of what we're dealing with here absolutely fucking clear. It's important to stress that the Ramseys had officially lawyered up before noon that day, and also before providing the forensic samples at a "neutral" location.

Of course the previous day, Friday December 27th, the Ramseys *already had a lawyer* looking out for them. But since their pal Mike Bynum was no longer a criminal attorney he called the most powerful attorney in ~~Boulder~~ Denver, Bryan Morgan of Haddon, Morgan & Foreman. Morgan's firm was one of the most powerful and connected not merely in Colorado but in the U.S.A. And the instructions that issued from Haddon, Morgan and Foreman that day appeared to be three unmitigated instructions:

- Submit to the forensic shit just not at the cop shop
- Shut the fuck up
- Get someone in the house to get your shit

It's either pure coincidence or it's an interesting strategic move that at the exact moment the Ramseys gave the cops something, they took stuff from under the cops' noses as well. Before we deal with the latter, let's find out who we're actually dealing with. This will give us some idea whether strategic directives were issued from the Ivory Tower of a particularly powerful law firm looming in neighboring Denver.

From crimemagazine.com:

*Within hours of finding JonBenét's body, John Ramsey had contacted local attorney and close friend Mike Bynum for assistance. By the end of the next day Ramsey had retained G. Bryan Morgan, of Haddon Morgan & Foreman, the foremost criminal defense firm in Colorado to represent him, and Patrick Burke, **a former assistant state attorney general** to represent Patsy. Burke had successfully defended Richard Scutari, who in 1987 was charged, along with three other white supremacists, with violating the civil rights of Denver talk-show host Alan Berg by murdering him.*

In other words Patsy had her very own big hitter to defend her, and John's counsel in Bryan Morgan/Hal Haddon was bigger still.

From crimemagazine.com:

*The law firm of Haddon Morgan & Foreman also represented President Clinton, from 1981 forward, as was revealed in the Whitewater investigation. Members of the law firm are also **politically powerful in Colorado**. The police investigators were stunned by how quickly John Ramsey had moved to retain separate defense counsel for both his wife and himself. With the law firm came private investigators who, without notifying the Boulder police, began conducting their own investigation of the crime on Dec. 27 by interviewing both the Whites and the Fernies. The results of these interviews were not shared with the police.*

In short order Haddon Morgan & Foreman would find clever ways to undermine whatever the Boulder cops came up with. The cops tried to pull their own strings, but tended to be clumsier at playing hardball with law professionals.

From crimemagazine.com:

The perception that things had deteriorated quickly between the Ramseys and the police was fed by a leak that police had asked the coroner to hold JonBenét's body until the parents agreed to be formally interrogated by police. Det. Thomas steadfastly denies there was any such demand.

Well, there might have been something. The police might have threatened to hold the body and the defense lawyers would then have seized upon this and waved the flag for all to see – look at the horrible, unreasonable police, holding a poor family's daughter's body… It doesn't really matter if it's true or not, what matters is it does point to the cops who are badly on the back foot. Imagine just the idea of the police feeling so helpless to make progress, all they really have to "trade" with is the Ramsey's daughter's body?

From crimemagazine.com:

John Ramsey's attorney, Hal Haddon, later wrote to the prosecutor that: "Boulder police refused to release JonBenét's body for burial unless the Ramseys agreed to come to the police station and submit to a hostile interrogation."

Ramsey and his attorneys have cited this incident as the turning

point that led to an adversarial relationship between the Ramseys and the Boulder police. This is somewhat belied, however, by Ramsey's statement on CNN five days after JonBenét's murder:

Mrs. Ramsey, how do you stand it that your daughter is dead and you are a possible suspect? How do you cope with it?

John Ramsey interjected this response.

JOHN: *"Well, it's - you know at first we were shocked, and then outraged, and then we understood statistically that it's a sad state of affairs...that that's apparently the majority of cases like this in our country family members or parents are ultimately involved so **we accepted being suspects**. But what concerned us and certainly still does concern us, at least up until yesterday, is that any time spent looking at us is time that's wasted, and that in part, is why we brought in an investigative team to immediately look in other... know there are other directions being looked at (sic)."*

Is this John Ramsey playing lexical dodgems? Obviously just a week after JonBenét's death it would make sense to allow the police to simply complete their processes. Let them take samples, take fingerprints, ask what they need to ask. For fuck sakes, the crime happened in the Ramsey home, aren't you going to tell the police basic things like time, things seen and heard, make statements about that broken window, talk about suspicious folks and/or observations? It's your house and *you're not going to help police* figure out what's out of place? The police are trying to find your daughter's murderer, and you're going to be *adversarial* towards them? <u>Are you out of your fucking mind</u>?

What must also be noted is despite the clarion call cheerleading the cops as oafs cynically and heartlessly holding JonBenét's corpse for ransom, JonBenét's funeral took place exactly as scheduled on December 31, just five days after her death. So exactly how long did the police refuse to let the Ramseys have her body back?

Remember an autopsy was performed, a memorial service was held, and the parents jetted out of Boulder, and they were still able to get the funeral service done in Atlanta, and appear on CNN the next day – New Year's Day, 1997.

From crimemagazine.com:

Understanding that the police needed to eliminate them as suspects before going on to other possibilities, the Ramseys still refused to cooperate.

One dude who was more miffed than most was John's buddy Fleet – the same guy who had been there when John had "found" JonBenét's body in the basement. Fleet was also the only person on record who went through the house calling JonBenét's name out about fifteen minutes after arriving at the residence. Fleet also happened to notice John seeming to not want him to go into the one basement room because it was "painted" shut. When Fleet discovered John was not talking to the cops and later talking to the media [which John blamed on Fleet, saying it was Fleet's idea that he go public], Fleet angrily told John the next time he saw him he hoped it would be in a courtroom.

We'll deal with Fleet White in more detail in the next narrative in this series.

From crimemagazine.com:

The Ramseys had agreed, early on, to provide handwriting samples, and did cooperate initially (on Dec. 26th and 27th), but **they refused to go to police headquarters** *[on December 28th] for questioning. From the first stages of the investigation they wanted to be questioned together, rather than separately – something police refused to agree to. Later, the Ramseys would insist that police submit their questions in writing...While initially vowing they would do everything in their power to cooperate with police so the killer of JonBenét could be caught,* **the Ramseys erected barriers that would stifle the investigation** *to this day. They made arrangements to move back to Atlanta, Ga., which would preclude their professed determination to spend the rest of their lives catching the killer, smacking heavily of O.J. Simpson's vow that he, too, would devote the rest of his life to solving his ex-wife's murder. And, like Simpson, they offered a reward for information leading to the killer of*

JonBenét.

Such was the determination to surround the Ramseys with lawyers, even family in Atlanta got their own counsel as early as the end of 1996, just days of JonBenét's death. Think about it – even John's ex-wife in a different city has a lawyer dealing with police inquiries.

From crimemagazine.com:

When police flew to Atlanta, to interview the grown son and daughter of John Ramsey by a previous marriage, **John Ramsey hired an Atlanta attorney to represent his son and daughter as well as his ex-wife** *...[and]...once they had hired criminal lawyers to represent each of them, everything that followed became standard procedure. No good criminal lawyer is going to permit the police to interrogate his or her client. That is normally not in the client's best interest (particularly if they are guilty). And any criminal lawyer would like to see the police investigative file, which is normally not possible until after someone is charged.*

In Schiller's account* Bynum tells Detective Arndt that "the Ramseys would not give any more testimonial evidence without a criminal attorney present". This happens at noon according to Schiller and "by Saturday evening" Morgan is hired. I find Schiller's timeline highly doubtful especially given that the Ramseys were being fingerprinted that afternoon. I doubt they would have been lawyer-less – as Schiller claims – over this crucial period. I think Morgan was hired much earlier, the legal baton was probably handed over at noon if not earlier.

In any event, while the Ramseys were the focus of the Boulder police, something else was going on down the road in Boulder. Was this "something else" just an innocent errand by a conscientious relative or was "something more" going on? Given the above context can one really believe there wasn't a strategic intent in laying siege to detritus of the Ramsey home while the cops swarmed around fingerprints and hair follicles a few miles away?

One might have an opinion either way, and one might not think much of an opinion either way. But if you're wondering why this case is unsolved more than two decades later, here's exhibit B. If A is the massive contamination of JonBenét's body B is the strategic theft of crime scene evidence on December 28th. Here's how it happened:

1. Patrol officer Angie Chromiak was ordered to chaperone Pam Paugh [Patsy's sister] to 755 15 street to collect "some of the Ramseys clothing".

2. The clothing was ostensibly for use at the funeral, and so conceivably should have been one set of formal clothing for John, Patsy and Burke. [Irrespective the reason for removing the clothing, no objects whatsoever should have been removed from the crime scene].

3. Curiously, despite orders from "police headquarters" that Pam was authorised to remove clothing, Pam Paugh was dressed up in a police officer's uniform ["donned a Boulder Police jacket" as Thomas puts it], including a badge and requisite police patches. The official reason for this ruse? It was meant to disguise Paugh's identity from the media. Well, what more than that? I think we must at least acknowledge the possibility that Pam's police disguise may also have fooled other officers on the scene, and besides this, the need to fool the media was perhaps more necessarily to protect Team Ramsey and the powers plucking at police strings than anyone else. Either way, a relative going into a crime scene under false pretences where another relative is a prime suspect is extremely sinister, isn't it?

4. Paugh is accompanied through the house by Detective Mike Everett. After an hour rummaging through the home, Paugh emerged with a single large cardboard box [not a suitcase] which Thomas describes as "full to the brim". That would be bad enough but *goddamit that's not all*.

5. Paugh then spent *several more hours* making additional trips through the house collecting suitcases, bags, boxes and loose items. Chromiak began to get antsy as Paugh continued to

pillage the contents of the house. When Chromiak noted her objection to the detective, Everett told her to butt out on account that "the detectives already know who did it." If there's any rationale that ought to have convinced a junior officer, this was it. "Don't worry, we've got this, we've got all the evidence anyway…" And the flip side of the coin could conceivably be a situation where "Officer Paugh" has been instructed to offer a hand in getting the Ramsey's clothes [but if you can get away with it, take the whole arm!]

6. Paugh's last trip was to the bedroom of the murdered child. As if in obeisance to orders from Heaven itself, Paugh drove herself to get the job done repeating to herself "You can do this!"

7. Everett noted the items Paugh removed, but in general terms. Even so the smorgasbord of stuff Paugh had seized was astonishing and alarming: bills, credit cards, tiaras, a black cashmere coat, bathrobes, a cell phone, bank records, even the Ramseys passports. So much for funeral clothes!**

8. With Paugh in the front seat clutching a bunch of stuffed toys, and the rest of the car stuffed to its gills, Chromiak drove off. Paugh screeched into her ear to remove the latex gloves she was wearing, and then barked at the officer to get her a Diet Pepsi at the nearest McDonalds.

9. While Chromiak indulged Officer Paugh [including paying the bill, Paugh regaled Chromiak with a tall tale about making her first million in her early thirties and not knowing how to spend the money. [Thomas points out that at the time Patsy's sister worked in a department store selling cosmetics.]

With the guts of the Ramsey residence en route to a safe house, Team Ramsey had just scored a massive coup with the cops. Perhaps emboldened by this, the cops were informed the Ramseys now had legal counsel, and they would address the D.A.'s office rather than investigators. At the same time it was made explicit that Burke Ramsey would not be interviewed at all, and that Patsy was not well enough to be interrogated.

Isn't it odd that Patsy, per Dr. Beuf, is supposedly "too medicated" to speak with the police in an effort to find her daughter's murderer, yet she's able to communicate just fine to sister Pam about all the stuff she needs hijacked out of her home? Not so surprisingly, John's accounting of how the trip went down is slightly different, to put it mildly, than how Chromiak reported it.

In Death of Innocence, John writes the following:

*Eventually, arrangements were made for Pam Paugh, Patsy's younger sister, to go back to the house under police supervision and **get a few things we needed**. She [Pam] would be allowed to stand at the door of a room and point at the items. Then the police would carefully catalog these possessions and deliver them to her.*

Hmmm. As for "things we needed"… not quite sure how a Nordstrom card and emerald necklace qualify. John doesn't mention those, but he does say Patsy mostly wanted keepsakes from a cabinet in their room. You know, stuff like baby shoes and rattles. He also mentions **Patsy specifically wanted Pam to retrieve JonBenét's My Twinn doll** from under the Christmas tree. The same tree that JonBenét's dead body was lying under two days earlier. If you'll recall from *The Craven Silence*, this is the doll that was made to look exactly like JonBenét. When JonBenét opened it on Christmas morning and took one look at it, she tossed it aside for another toy. Patsy looked at John with disappointment. All considered, it makes me wonder, why did Patsy care so much about that doll?***

Four long months would drag on before the Ramseys finally deigned to return to Boulder to speak to the police. That was more than enough time for Haddon Morgan & Foreman to have the case sewn up on behalf of their clients. Four months was plenty to ferret out the best legal loopholes money could buy.

---

*Perfect Murder Perfect Town

**According to Schiller's account of the event, Pam also made away with: an oil painting, several American Girl dolls and a portfolio of JonBenét's pageant photos.

*** From acandyrose.com: August 29, 2002 – Anonymous Email to ACandyRose from a former employee of the Pleasant Company, makers of the American Doll: *"The dolls heads are attached with a string that gets in the way when the clothes are changed or the hair is brushed. I was trained to tell parents to use **a piece of duct tape** to tack it down. If you do that and pull it off the stuffing comes out on the tape. They have a huggable body and vinyl limbs and arms attached with bungie cords."*

Gentlemen Prefer Blondes

"Because horror on Earth is real and it is every day. It is like a flower or like the sun; it cannot be contained." — Alice Sebold, The Lovely Bones

"Politicians are not born, they are excreted." — Cicero

In *The Craven Silence 3* we introduced what might seem a bold allegation: was John having an affair around Christmas 1996? Why did John leave the family home on Christmas day of all days for all of three to four hours?

In this narrative and those that follow we'll attempt to bolster these allegations. To do that we must look before and beyond Christmas 1996 to get a general sense of John and his "good southern common sense". Of course there's another more obvious way to address these questions around John's infidelity: we look at Patsy.

If there was smoke or fire, we'll find it with Patsy and when we begin to sniff around it's not long before we find a few sparks. From here on out we will be chasing a potential mistress or too – it's up to the reader to decide whether this is valuable skirt chasing that backs up our psychological basis, or whether it's another wild goose chase.

From forumsforjustice.org:

A dying Patsy Ramsey risked her life in a desperate attempt to save her marriage - coming face-to-face in a dramatic confrontation with a woman she feared was having an affair with her husband John.

That stunning turn of events has triggered hope among investigators that the marriage will explode in a nasty divorce battle and that Patsy and John would rat out each other -- blowing the five-year-old JonBenét murder case wide open.

The above excerpt was published around 2002 in the National

Enquirer. People were hoping "trouble in paradise" would erupt between the Ramseys and any schism would allow some truths to slip through that were – for the moment – sealed shut and hidden from view.

From forumsforjustice.org:

Patsy was undergoing experimental treatment for stage two liver cancer when she risked a fatal infection by leaving her intensive treatment program in Maryland and flying home to Atlanta.

What prompted that trip was a chilling warning from her sister Paulette [Polly] that her 58-year-old husband John was carrying on with a blonde family friend, an insider told the ENQUIRER...

....Paulette's suspicions about John and his dimpled blonde friend shook 45-year-old Patsy while she was undergoing treatment...at the National Institutes of Health hospital in Bethesda, MD.

The point to establish here is merely a hypothesis. If we assume these events to be true [and they might not be], we may also assume when Patsy was first diagnosed with ovarian cancer in her late thirties [in 1993] John might have sought "comfort" elsewhere [although he might not have].

From forumsforjustice.org:

Physicians recommend that patients do not leave the area until the treatment's completion. A cocktail of chemo drugs is so aggressive it can break down a patient's immune system, making them susceptible to any infection.

"Traveling home by plane or car was out of the question," divulged the insider......Paulette warned (Patsy) about a family friend getting too close to John, and the handsome executive was even helping her with her gardening.

Paulette told Patsy, 'You'd better watch out for John and that girl,' revealed the insider.

An attractive married mom, the friend admits she is a frequent visitor to the Ramsey house and even got a gift from John of plants from his property, which she replanted at her home.

"He lent me his truck to take the plants back to my house," she told The ENQUIRER.

While the blonde woman's identity is not revealed, what she does reveal is "I am a close friend of John and Patsy." Furthermore, if we assume that Patsy felt she had to be around to douse John's indiscretions despite being ill, it provides some perspective on the tensions Patsy was under in 1996, and perhaps explains why she did finally succumb to cancer ten years after JonBenét's death.

From forumsforjustice.org:

As for Paulette's accusations, [the blonde family friend] says, "They are just allegations." She believes that Paulette's concern for her ailing sister may have spurred the accusations that preceded Patsy's dash to Atlanta.

"When Patsy decided to come home so unexpectedly, her only explanation to friends was a grim, "I need to get my ducks in a row," said the insider. "It quickly became obvious that the head duck was John."

"[Patsy] suddenly told the doctors she was going home after the first round of chemo was completed." The tense drama rapidly escalated after Patsy, a wig covering her bald head, arrived in Atlanta.

"Paulette invited John Ramsey's blonde female friend to lunch," said the insider. "She asked her point-blank, 'Are you having an affair with John. My sister is fighting cancer -- are you trying to take her man?'

"The friend protested her innocence -- then she went straight to Patsy and told her, "Believe me, there's nothing going on."

The two women dealt with the situation in a dramatic face-to-face meeting.

It seems more like much ado about nothing, but even if it was, Patsy's behaviour here is telling. We know when Patsy met John he was divorced and had ended a two-year affair with Gloria Williams, a secretary. John says that relationship had a *Fatal Attraction* element to it, and ended in the late 70's. John and Patsy were married in November 1980. That's potentially cutting it fine between the first wife*, a mistress and the second, isn't it?

From forumsforjustice.org:

"It was a real showdown, but Patsy finally accepted her explanation," said the insider. "There's no question that **Patsy risked her life** *to go home because she thought her marriage was in danger."*

But despite her emergency mission, **Patsy could not extinguish all the flash points** *in the relationship. "Some family members have* **felt for a long time there were problems in the marriage**. *One of the sources of friction between Patsy and John is* **that he looks at other women all the time**,*" said the insider.*

Whatever we make of that comment, actions speak louder than words. We know John married a much younger Patsy when she was just 23 and he was 37. To date John has had three marriages, five children and at least one mistress. This article isn't confirmation that there was another mistress besides Gloria Williams; instead is suggests the sort of impact *even the idea* of a mistress might have had on Patsy. With John frequently away from home, it's not difficult for suspicions to run wild.

From forumsforjustice.org:

"One time, a woman visited them wearing very short shorts -- and John's eyeballs were glued to her all the time she was there. Patsy was furious with him."

After her sudden trip home, the former Miss America finalist returned to Bethesda to continue her therapy. She recently finished that therapy and is radiating confidence. But grim statistics show it's nearly impossible for Patsy to win this battle. And her pals fear the end is approaching.

It's not clear whether this battle refers to the battle Patsy was fighting against other women or cancer. Ultimately when Patsy lost one of those battles she also lost the other.

*John Ramsey divorced Lucinda Pasch in 1978 for reasons that were never made public.

Who is Kim Ballard? Part 1
"No adultery is bloodless." — Natalia Ginzburg

On May 12 and May 14 1997, just four and a half months after JonBenét's murder, a blonde woman from Tucson, Arizona appeared on the Geraldo* television talk show. Her name was Kimberly Ballard, and she claimed she'd had an affair with John Ramsey. There appeared some basis to this claim because three weeks earlier the Globe had run a story that the Boulder Police Department were investigating Ballard for the same reason.

How did they meet? According to Ballard she placed a personal ad in the USA Today newspaper.

From acandyrose.com:

BALLARD (Claims Affair with John Ramsey): *The ad said, 'Southern belle, blonde, petite.' He was someone to fill a void in a period of my life when I was alone, and I think I was doing the same for him, filling some sort of a need. Stayed in nice hotels, we had-- went to nice restaurants. He bought me nice clothes.*

REPORTER: *Cash, too?*

BALLARD: *Gave me cash, yes.*

REPORTER: *Hundreds? Thousands?*

BALLARD: *Maybe $ 1,000.*

GERALDO: *News on two fronts in the JonBenét Ramsey case today. We'll talk to the woman who claimed she had an affair with John Ramsey in just a moment. She's on the telephone.*

The other night we played you some video and audio excerpts of interviews that Kim Ballard has been giving, the lady from Tucson, Arizona, who claimed the affair with John Ramsey back in '94 and '95 as Patsy Ramsey was recovering from cancer surgery. And, Ms. Ballard, I'm happy to say, joins us right now on the telephone.

Hi, Kim. Are you there?

BALLARD: *I'm here, but I can barely hear you.*

RIVERA: *OK. I'll—I'll speak up. We can hear you--we can hear you fine.*

BALLARD: *OK.*

RIVERA: *Can you please tell us exactly what, if anything, the investigators or authorities have told you about--about this case? Have you contacted anyone directly yet?*

BALLARD: *Have I or have they con...*

RIVERA: *Have they contacted you. That's what I mean.*

BALLARD: *I've been contacted by the Boulder police twice, and I've been contacted by Ellis Armistead and Associates numerous times.*

RIVERA: *Now they are the Ramsey family investigators.*

BALLARD: *That's correct.*

RIVERA: *What were the exact dates, if you can recall, Kim, that the Boulder police contacted you?*

BALLARD: *They call--contacted me the first time about a month ago.*

In other words it was roughly April 1997 when the police contacted Ballard. She's also contacted by Ramsey through his "investigators". And now she's on a talk show. Why?

From acandyrose.com:

RIVERA: *And...the second [time you were contacted]?*

BALLARD: *Today.*

RIVERA: *Today.*

BALLARD: *Yes.*

RIVERA: *And to the extent you feel comfortable, what was said or asked of you today by the Boulder authorities?*

BALLARD: *Oh, today was an unbelievable day.*

RIVERA: *Tell us. Tell us everything, Kim.*

BALLARD: *The--they didn't just show up like they did the first time. They came with the Tucson Police Department. The Tucson--my husband went to the door. I was—I've been sick.*

RIVERA: *Oh, I didn't know you were married.*

BALLARD: *Yeah, I'm married.*

RIVERA: *How long were you--are you married?*

BALLARD: *Eight--seven and a half years.*

RIVERA: *Oh, so you were married during your affair with John?*

BALLARD: *Well, we were separated.*

RIVERA: *I see. OK.*

BALLARD: *We weren't together.*

RIVERA: *OK.*

BALLARD: *But they--they came anyway, even though my husband had told them over the phone, 'She's really too sick,' and I had just about lost my voice this morning. They came anyway. And they told my husband that they didn't believe I was alive, that I was well, that something had happened to me. And that unless they saw me alive and well, they were going to call in reserves and they were going to get a search warrant and search our house to make sure I was really alive.*

RIVERA: *How many of them...*

BALLARD: *Before I knew it...*

RIVERA: *How many of them were there, Kim?*

BALLARD: *Our yard was full of Boulder police, Tucson police, reporters, satellite vans. This was all being videotaped by two stations that I know of for sure.*

RIVERA: *Uh-huh.*

BALLARD: *And I was on the phone with the radio station, so it was all on audio. It was maddening.*

RIVERA: *OK. S--and this was j--what time today? Can you recall?*

BALLARD: *It was between 10 AM and 11 AM our--Pacific time.*

RIVERA: *OK. Now did you let them in?*

BALLARD: *No. I did not want to talk with them without an attorney. I decided this is getting too serious.* **I should have an attorney present.** *But they weren't going to leave. They saw that I was alive. They didn't believe I was alive for some reason.*

RIVERA: *So what arrangements have you made to speak substantively with the authorities?*

BALLARD: *Well, I just--they--you know, they said they wouldn't leave until they saw me...*

RIVERA: *Yeah.*

BALLARD: *...so I went to the window and told them that I would not talk with them without an attorney. So they all left--all the police. The press didn't. But all the police did leave, and I haven't spoken with the police since.*

Interestingly, like John Ramsey, Kimberly will talk to the media and Rivera, but when it comes to talking to the cops she needs an attorney. Ironically in a sense that's what's she's getting here because Rivera – the host – *is* an attorney.

From acandyrose.com:

RIVERA: *OK. Now let me ask you a couple of questions, Kim, if I may. Tell me precisely the extent of your relationship with Mr. Ramsey.*

BALLARD: *I met him in August of 1994 and I saw him until approximately April of '95.*

JonBenét's birthday was August 6, and Burke hit JonBenét a day or two after her 4th birthday in August 1994. JonBenét visited a plastic surgeon for the golf blow to her face in October 1994, but it was determined she didn't need surgery. In April 1995 JonBenét Ramsey won Colorado All-Stars Pageant and Patsy was interviewed by Boulder Women's Magazine. Here's an excerpt from that magazine article from acandyrose.com:

*Patsy Ramsey has chosen her lifestyle and has dedicated herself to the role of stay-at-home mother, a title that seems to be a bit of a misnomer, since **[Patsy] Ramsey is rarely at home**. She fills her days with volunteer service to the community and in her children's schools. In addition, she regularly travels with her husband John, CEO and president of Access Graphics...*

The article also provides additional insight into how John's and Patsy's career paths might have crossed [John claims he met Patsy in the same apartment he lived in].

From acandyrose.com:

*Ramsey began her career with McCann-Ericson Advertising Agency, where she focused on doing promotional marketing for Coca-Cola USA. Later she joined **Hayes Microcomputer Products, Inc.**, as Director of Marketing Services, and worked there for five years developing user-friendly product instruction manuals. One of the **software manuals** Patsy Ramsey was responsible for won first place in an **international technical writing** competition.*

If John was having an affair with Kimberly, what was going on with Patsy circa 1993/1994?

From acandyrose.com:

In 1993 [Patsy] was diagnosed with ovarian cancer, an illness she has since learned runs in her family....During [Patsy] Ramsey's battle with cancer, her mother came to live with the family in Boulder for a year. "Coincidentally," Ramsey recalls, "my mother had just retired two days before my diagnosis from a full time job that she had enjoyed for several years after her children were grown - just in time to be a full time mom again! She not only took care of me, but **she helped John take care of our children as well**. We couldn't have gotten along without her." Because [Patsy] Ramsey's father works with John at Access Graphics in Boulder, he was also close during that time, and the family had many friends who offered their support as well. Even though we had only lived in Boulder a short time, our friends and neighbors came to our rescue with prepared meals, and they drove the kids to school and piano lessons -they gave us an overwhelming amount of moral support. We were surely blessed."

Even as everyone around her was so wonderful to her children, says Ramsey, "I knew that ultimately, they were my real reason to fight the cancer and live! No one can take care of my kids and do the things I want to do with them the way I can. And I plan to be around for a long time to see them through."

Before we get back to Kim Ballard and Geraldo there are two final points to highlight from that April article published in *Woman's Magazine*:

1. Patsy's continued involvement in Miss America

2. John Ramsey's connections with top level military defense executives

From acandyrose.com:

As a former Miss West Virginia and Miss America talent winner, Ramsey continues to serve as a judge and patron for the Miss America Scholarship Program. "Miss America awards millions of dollars in scholarships for women annually," she says... [Patsy] serves on the benefit Style Show & Luncheon committee, and she will chair the entire event in the spring of 1997.

Although Ramsey puts a great deal of energy into her local

community, she is hardly confined to activities around Boulder. Being the wife of a busy corporate CEO requires Ramsey to accompany John to many functions around the world. Most recently, the couple attended a formal affair in Washington, D.C., **honoring the retiring CEO of Lockheed- Martin**.**

From acandyrose.com:

RIVERA: *Did [John], at any point, seem to you to be in any way out of the ordinary?*

BALLARD: *I didn't really--well, I saw a little bit at the time that--that the--he was a little unusual, but not that much. I think...*

RIVERA: *In--in what way unusual?*

BALLARD: *Well, he's a grown, professional wealthy man and he wanted me--he--he had --answered a personals ad that I had placed in USA Today. And he wanted to know just what I looked like, what-- how tall I was, how much I weighed, what color my hair was, what color my eyes were; all this before he ever met me.* ***And he was very specific about how I was to dress, how my hair was to be worn, how my nails were to be done, everything.***

RIVERA: *All right. Gen--generally, briefly as you can, tell us what did he want you to be?*

BALLARD: *Oh, well, I'm slightly over five feet tall. I weighed about 90--maybe 90--between 90, 95 pounds at the time. That's what I've weighed all my life until the past couple of years. I've gained weight because of the side effect of medication I'm on. That's...*

Ballard seems quite awkward and embarrassed about her weight. As we'll eventually see, it becomes something of a touchstone when John is asked to comment on Kim Ballard. We'll deal with John's disparaging comments on Kim in *The Day After Christmas 2*.
Before we get there let's try to get as much of the full story from Kim Ballard herself as we possibly can.

From acandyrose.com:

RIVERA: *Wait. You're--so you're five feet tall, 90--90-odd pounds at the time?*

BALLARD: *Yes.*

RIVERA: *So...*

BALLARD: *That's what I've been since I was 14 up until two years ago.*

RIVERA: *So almost childlike size.*

Rivera seems doubtful.

BALLARD: *Yes. That's the way I've always been, wear a size one or three.*

RIVERA: *Mm-hmm.*

BALLARD: *So that--he liked that. And he told me, you know, how he--what he wanted me to--to get, to buy, clothes, and he paid for all the clothes and we met at a restaurant. I drove my own car there and we met. And he stayed in town that first night and then the next time I met him in Denver and then I met him again in Tucson and another time was set up for Tucson, but I did not meet with him and I have not seen him since.*

RIVERA: *OK. Kim, stand by. Stay right where you are.*

At this point the enterprising Geraldo has a brief discussion with a radio reporter on bloodstains in JonBenét's panties and the ransom note. Although this isn't the ambit of our chapter right here and now, let's follow their discussion anyway. Ultimately Geraldo brings it back to Kim Ballard.

From acandyrose.com:

Carol McKinley, our wonderful reporter from KOA Radio is also on the line. Quick comment on this, Carol. Then I want to get on to some other news you have. Then I'll get back to Kim. Go ahead.

McKINLEY (Reporter, KOA Radio): *Well, we talked with Kim earlier this week and, you know, I think what she says is up to the* *people of America to believe or not. But, remember, this has nothing to do with the death of the child; that this has more to do with **the character of John Ramsey, Geraldo.***

RIVERA: *Maybe--may not be separate stories, Carol. May not be. Tell me about the DNA. What do you know, Carol? And then I'll get back to Kim. What do you know about the fact that--is it a fact the authorities have the Cellmark results?*

McKINLEY: *Well, it seems like it--it—it's a fact. I mean, right now I can't get it confirmed, but it would make sense because the DNA landed at Cellmark on March 31st. It's now May 14th. They said four to six weeks. We're at about six weeks right now, so it wouldn't surprise me if the DNA is in. But, remember, **Tom Koby, the Boulder police chief, has told everyone that this is not going to be the magic bullet.***

RIVERA: *Right.*

McKINLEY: *They had three things: They had a hair on a blanket, they had some fingernail cuttings with perhaps some DNA under the cuttings from JonBenét and they had a pair of her underwear that might have had bloodstains on it. But the bloodstains, my sources tell me, had been washed over and over again in the laundry and they might not have been able to get any DNA from those stains. So it might have been old.*

RIVERA: *The child's underwear had bloodstains.*

McKINLEY: *From what my sources say, yes. I have two very good sources who've told me that. But they might not have gotten anything from the DNA because it might have been an old bloodstain.*

RIVERA: *I just remind everybody the Enquirer has been reporting, and is standing by the story, that the DNA indicates Dad. Again, our experts have said almost nightly that it might be, as Tom Koby suggests and Carol now repeats and reports, almost, if not irrelevant, not the--the magic bullet that investigators and the rest of us are waiting for. But I am also promised a bombshell on this topic tomorrow.*

Carol, I know you've got to run.

McKINLEY: *But I want to--to point out...*

RIVERA: *Go ahead, please.*

McKINLEY: *...Geraldo, that--remember the handwriting samples. The comparative analysis is not done, but the chemical analysis still needs to be done and those samples will be destroyed once that happens. So we're still waiting on that, and that could be the best piece of evidence in this case. At this point, I'm hearing from my sources that* **the Ramsey lawyers are going to get that original ransom note** *from the Colorado Bureau of Investigation through the Boulder police. They're going to receive it in a plastic--like a sleeve so that they can look at it through a--a special camera and get a good idea of what the analysis will bring. That's not the chemical, but that's the comparative analysis. So they're actually going to receive that original note in their offices and send it to--to some--some specialists so they can take a look at it, Geraldo, and that's what we really need to be concentrating on.*

RIVERA: *Wha--so, Carol, you're suggesting that the lawyers for the Ramseys will be conducting their own tests and then the destructive tests will be done by the--by the state?*

McKINLEY: *Hopefully, the destructive testing will be done because if those handprints come out, and we talked about the heel of the hand...*

RIVERA: *Right.*

McKINLEY: *...because that's how you write...*

RIVERA: *Right.*

McKINLEY: *If those come out with prints, then that will be very, very important because...*

RIVERA: *I'm demonstrating as you speak. If that heelprint--here it is, right here. Ren, my--here. This--this print. This, right here. That comes out; very, very significant.*

McKINLEY: *It's much more—it's much different than a fingerprint, and what I'm told from the experts at the Colorado Bureau of Investigation is that that heelprint of a hand is just as distinctive as a person's fingerprint.*

RIVERA: *Oh, I am sure. I'm sure.*

McKINLEY: *The one thing that I've heard from my sources is that they hope the person who wrote that note did not wear gloves when they wrote it.*

RIVERA: *Mm-hmm. Oh, obviously. Yeah. OK. Any--anything else, Carol?*

McKINLEY: *That's it.*

Now, back to Kim.

From acandyrose.com:

RIVERA: *Kim Ballard's on the phone, the woman who alleges a relationship with John Ramsey in '94 and '95, during the time Patsy Ramsey was recovering from her ovarian cancer surgery. Kim, did you make a date with the authorities? Is there a date certain for your interviews?*

BALLARD: *No. The way things were today, it was--it was just a--a media and--it was a circus out there, and I only talked to them through the window briefly.*

RIVERA: *So you have not yet made an appointment with Boulder authorities.*

BALLARD: *No, I haven't.*

RIVERA: *But you will talk to them?*

BALLARD: *I will. I--I don't mind talking to the police. I've—I've never minded doing anything...*

It is starting to seem a little fishy isn't it? What the hell does "I've never minded doing anything" even mean?

From acandyrose.com:

RIVERA: *Why are you coming forward?*

BALLARD: *I'm glad you brought that up because when I saw your show Monday night,* **I was pretty upset by the way it came across***. I'm not just coming forward. I never would have talked, never would have come forward.*

RIVERA: *Have you taken any money from anybody, Kim?*

BALLARD: *No. And I'm glad you said that, because that's something I wanted to say right away also, not one nickel from anyone. The Globe article was done completely without my knowledge or consent.*

RIVERA: *OK. Let's—let's...*

BALLARD: *And...*

RIVERA: *...those issues, while important, are very s--and--and significant and I hope you'll join us on camera and tell us all about them.*

BALLARD: *Well, I wanted you to know this. I did "Hard Copy." That was the first person that I talked with, and before they aired-- day before they aired it, they asked me if I would take a polygraph test.*

RIVERA: *Yes.*

BALLARD: *And I said, 'Sure.' And I took it with no problem. So I wanted you to...*

RIVERA: *So you have taken and passed the lie detector test?*

BALLARD: *Oh, yeah, before I was ever on "Hard Copy."*

RIVERA: *OK. Is--is your husband in agreement with you coming forward now?*

BALLARD: *He never wanted this to come out, and he's--he feels like I do. He's furious with the Globe...*

RIVERA: *OK.*

BALLARD: *...for printing my name.*

It's making a little more sense now. A tabloid printed allegations, perhaps with some substance, and now the accused is coming forward to...do...what? If Kim's setting the record straight she's not doing a great job.

From acandyrose.com:

RIVERA: *Let me ask you, Kim, if--what your reaction was when you first heard of JonBenét Ramsey's death.*

BALLARD: *Once I realized who it was, I felt sick. I felt ice cold all over. I started getting a headache that got per--progressively worse as the day went on, and I didn't say anything to anyone, including my husband for about two weeks. I couldn't sleep. It's all I could think about. But I didn't know what to do.*

RIVERA: *OK. Kim--Kim, I--I--you--your story is fascinating. Can you come--come back tomorrow, will you?*

Geraldo passes Kim on, there's not much substance and maybe if he gets her back a second time he can get her to contribute something tangible. But is there something tangible? This is the substance of Rivera's next interview with criminal defense attorney Daniel Recht.

From acandyrose.com:

RIVERA: *Daniel Recht, comment?*

RECHT: *Well, Geraldo, you and I have talked about this before. Although the--the affair might be true and might be titillating, no court anywhere, certainly not in Colorado, would ever allow that evidence in. So no jury is ever going to hear about that affair, unless there's some linkup that I don't know about. It would be different if, let's say, there was some evidence that he was having sex with a little g--girl because what the law says it has to be a signature, as if--as if it's the identical situation with another person.*

RIVERA: *Ninety-two pounds, five foot tall?*

One picks up just four months after the murder, John Ramsey is the prime suspect and there's a suspicion of pedophilia, and if not pedophilia, then some sort of philandering behaviour.

From acandyrose.com:

RECHT: *Wouldn't do it. I'm confident of it, Geraldo. It just wouldn't do it. And I--you know, I'm not going to be the judge, but I've seen enough of this. It ain't coming in.*

RIVERA: *Are the Boulder authorities chasing after rainbows here?*

RECHT: *I'm not necessarily saying that. Now maybe they think they can make a linkup. Maybe they can talk to her about other things that she's not even aware of that might be relevant and that they can glean from her. So maybe there's something there. But the story itself, the affair itself, unless there's more that we don't know about yet, it's not coming into evidence.*

RIVERA: *Oh, she's coming back tomorrow. If there's more, I'll find it.*

RECHT: *I'm sure you will.*

1997-05-15: Boulder Press Release #44 - May 15, 1997 - Attempt to interview with Kim Ballard

FOR IMMEDIATE RELEASE

May 15, 1997

Contact: Leslie Aaholm, Media Relations, 441-3090

RAMSEY UPDATE #44

Boulder Police received DNA test results from Cellmark Diagnostics on Tuesday, May 13. This material was sent to Cellmark on March 4, 1997; tests began the week of March 31. There will be no additional information provided on the content

of the test results by the Boulder Police.

Police are still requesting a fifth handwriting sample from Patricia Ramsey. This request is being coordinated through the Boulder District Attorney's Office.

Boulder Police are in the in the process of analyzing and evaluating over 13,000 pages of transcripts and various test results. During this phase of the investigation there will be a core group of five Boulder Police detectives, two to four attorney's from the Boulder DA's Office, and two investigators from the DA's Office dedicated to this case.

Since January 1, 1997, 470 cases have been assigned to the detective division for follow-up; 364 have been completed. There are 111 cases that merit follow-up, which have not been assigned due to the Ramsey investigation, the investigation of last Friday's murder of Ruediger Jakob-Chien, and other critical cases. Adds Eller, "We need to work other important cases and thus have reassigned some officers. Should there be a need for more assistance on the Ramsey investigation, we will call in officers as needed."

The Boulder press release also refers to Kim Ballard, though not in glowing terms:

Boulder Police Detectives Melissa Hickman and Jane Harmer were in Tucson, Arizona this week to conduct a pre-arranged interview with Kim Ballard. This interview had been arranged through the Tucson Police Department, however, after waiting four hours to conduct the interview, Ms. Ballard declined to be interviewed. This was the second attempt by Boulder Police to interview Ms. Ballard; there will be no additional attempts to interview her. According to Detective Commander John Eller, "At this point, we would have to consider anything Ms. Ballard may say as suspect. We don't plan to set up other interviews with her."

*Geraldo Rivera is an American attorney with a law degree from the Brooklyn Law School, as well as a reporter, author, and talk show host.

** Two additional highlights from October 1995: 1. John Ramsey won Boulder's "Entrepeneur of Distinction" Award 2. In the same month John Ramsey appeared in the Boulder County Business Report

Revisiting Plausible Deniability

"It has to be an inside job." — John Ramsey speaking over the corpse of his dead daughter in the lounge to detective Linda Arndt

Given our narrative focus, it would be a dereliction of duty to skirt around issues of so-called "plausible deniability". I've involved this idea in a prior narrative, and I've emphasized exactly why plausible deniability is so slippery: the more plausible it is, the tougher it is to recognise and that makes it deniable by default.

If that doesn't make sense, or seems murky, let me be specific. In Sharon Stone's sizzling mystery crime thriller *Basic Instinct* [released in 1992] Stone playing millionaire author and seductress wryly notes to Michael Douglas as Detective Nick Curran:

> *I'd have to be pretty stupid to write a book about killing and then kill him the way I described in my book. I'd be announcing myself as the killer. I'm not stupid.*

The detective notes that writing a book about a crime "gives you an alibi." Actually it doesn't, but what it does suggest is this idea of plausible deniability. *Basic Instinct* provides us with an indecent idea of what an alibi actually is, however. Plausible deniability isn't an alibi, although an alibi is certainly deniability – plausible in this sense is a matter of fact. But it can also be a matter of fiction.

To poke at this "plausible deniability" creature we're going to do a number of flybys. We're going to approach the same thing from a few different angles in this chapter. If it feels haphazard and it feels like it's jumping around, there is some method to our madness.

Before we take our first stab at the creature in front of us that we're struggling to see, let's be clear on what we're looking for. In broad strokes the JonBenét Ramsey case involves:

- The murder of a small child
- Found in the family home

- Under suspicious circumstances

We get a first glimpse of the "plausible deniability" narrative when John Ramsey invokes how parents are natural suspects in a situation "like this", where a child is murdered in the home. The statistics bare this out, and John acknowledges this. Of course there's the same wry undertone to this admission. It goes something like this:

I'd have to be pretty stupid to murder my child in my own home if that's what happens in most cases. And why would I report these statistics; I'd be announcing myself as the killer. I'm not stupid.

The flip side is JonBenét's murder was a mess. It wasn't the work of some methodical super-predator, it wasn't the work of a skilled assassin or a meticulously executed pedophile assault. So no one is accusing the criminal [or criminals] involved of being smart. If the crime was executed poorly, what we can say with some conviction is it has been covered up expertly.

It is for the reader to decide what that precisely involves, and who it precisely involves. What we ought to be explicit about however is the interesting disconnect between:

    A.   A poorly executed crime

    B.   A bizarre "over-the-top" cover-up including a new world record length Illiad of Ransom Notes

    C.   A very well executed defensive aftermath, ultimately succeeding in beating not merely a conviction, but even a prosecution

Put even more simply, this mismatch can be rendered as an equation:

$$\text{poorly executed murder} \neq \text{well executed, strategic and successful defense}$$

The disconnect is so dire in the above equation we really need to ponder whether the murderer and those suspects who successfully petitioned for their own exoneration are the same people. We believe the answer is not a question of *either or* but *and*. What makes this case more difficult than most is if three people are involved, there are at least three dimensions to this crime, and it becomes highly speculative where each dimension begins and ends. Besides this, since we are talking about a family and the crime scene is the family home, we believe there is likely to be some overlap.

Specifically, for example, we believe if Patsy wrote the Ransom Note, John Ramsey provided some sort of input. Patsy's hand may be all over the note but we think John's mind may be integral to it too. And the mind around this crime, a topic that has been underestimated this far, is around a strategic attempt at plausible deniability.

The Ransom Note is a big indicator of this, and the direct finger pointing in the note to "Mr Ramsey", to "John" on three occasions, to the very specific Ransom amount, to John's "southern sense" is an explicit attempt to communicate one thing. This one thing is the precise statement John makes, the first effective quote we get in seven hours of skulduggery. When Arndt checks the rigid cadaver with blue lips and the whiff of death for a pulse, when she confirms to John crouched opposite her on the living room floor that JonBenét is dead, John says what we think he has been gagging to say all morning:

"It has to be an inside job."

If we are confused and mystified by not just the contents of the Ransom Note but the material of the note itself, if we can't understand why Patsy would write it using her own kitchen pad with a pen in the kitchen [and not dispose of either of these], if we're puzzled why John simply handed samples of his and Patsy's writing over to police when requested at 09:30 that morning, when Patsy's own paintbrush is used as a garrotte, none of it makes sense. Unless *the staging is intended to reinforce the idea of an inside job.*

When Patsy is asked about the handwriting, she immediately fingers the housekeeper, Linda Hoffman Pugh. Linda also has a key to the house. John seems to finger a disgruntled employee, Jeff Merrick. The curious thing is both Patsy and John are effectively accusing employees – a housekeeper is Patsy's first choice, and for John it's a disgruntled ex-employee at Access Graphics.

What students of this crime need to see up close is this initial acknowledgement from both JonBenét's parents that *it has to be an inside job*. Just the mere fact that JonBenét is found dead in the Ramsey home is massively damning. That fact alone is a huge hurdle for them. The Ransom Note is both massive misdirection to someone outside of the family but with intimate knowledge of the house and also an enormous giveaway. Patsy was doubtless aware of this, which is why some effort is made to disguise not merely the handwriting style, but the psychology of the author. Hence the initial spelling mistakes and the movie-speak. Patsy's entire note is also "plausible deniability":

- It's not my handwriting

- It's not neat enough

- I wouldn't make those spelling mistakes

- Why would I write a Ransom Note in my own kitchen, with my own pen on my own writing pad?

I'd have to be pretty stupid to murder my child in my own home and then write a Ransom Note using a notepad from my own home. I'd be announcing myself as the killer. I'm not stupid.

The Ransom Note is prima facie evidence, but it's also a clue as to the brazen lengths that were attempted in this case, and the goal of those brazen attempts somehow paid off. If that is the case, were those attempts really so brazen? If someone believes they stand a good chance of getting away with something, and they do, is it really so brazen? And if the Ramseys were involved and knew they could pull the strings in Boulder to get away with it, then what did they really have to worry about besides PR? Besides damage control?

When it comes to stupid though, there's an element that clearly *is* stupid. Any lawyer worth his salt will tell guilty clients to shut up. The problem with trying to win a PR campaign when one has potentially broken the law is one invariably puts a version into the public domain. This version can be analysed [as we do] and every subsequent version can then be used to cross-reference and thus decipher the *schema* of deception and misdirection.

It's a basic truth that killers lie, and liars have trouble keeping a handle on their lies. The truth happens to be easier to remember, and tends to be convincing. As such when the truth is out, no further efforts are really required. Lies on the other hand require endless validation because when seen in context they're simply not convincing. Lies in isolation tend to work, and most people only have those sort of attention spans. It's when one contextualises all the data that patterns begin to emerge, and where ripples don't swim together in a pond we find floating logs of bullshit.

Let's deal with a few right now.

1.   Missing Phone Records

One of the biggest hurdles modern criminals have to deal with are phone records. Phone records provide a time-stamped log of communication, but more importantly, phone logs reveal patterns of communication. We will deal briefly rather than exhaustively with the Ramseys phone records in this section. It is sufficient to note the following aberrations, more than a few, courtesy of detective Steve Thomas:

>   A. When the FBI questioned the DA's staff about their evidence file, Deputy DA Pete Hofstrom had a brainwave: "Why don't we ask the Ramseys" [for access to their phone records]. This appeared to show willingness to co-operate when actually what had been going on was a long period of stonewalling and road blocking – delaying tactics. By suddenly having a flashbulb moment Hofstrom was demonstrating "plausible deniability."

>   B. Almost a year after JonBenét's murder, on November 6th 1997 Boulder Police Chief Mark Beckner finally received a *Consent to Release of Telephone Records*. It was signed by Pete Hofstrom and John Ramsey.

C. The data the police were allowed to subpoena was restricted to the period December 1 to December 27, 1996. Police found little of probative value.

The AirTouch cell phone records were useless. Ramsey started the service in January 1994. AirTouch said that 91 minutes of use were logged during the August-September billing period of 1996, and 108 minutes were used in September-October. October-November was just as busy. **December, however, the only period we were allowed to see, was empty. No calls at all.** *I asked if someone could have removed billing records from the computer. "No way," the Airtouch source told me.* — Steve Thomas*

#Shakedown assessment: Yes way – John Ramsey owned a computer company. Did he not have the resources to have computer data, including phone records, wiped? All he needed was to buy a little time, in theory, and then the data could be hacked and erased. Arguably that's exactly what was achieved, time was bought, and by the time the data was procured it had disappeared. Poof!

2. Missing Paper Trail

A. When Steve Thomas resigned from the Boulder Police Department on August 6th 1998 "the district attorney's office was still preventing our access to the Ramsey's complete toll records and credit card receipts." In other words approaching two years after JonBenét's murder the DA's office were blocking the police from viewing ordinary things like credit card bills and phone records.

B. Warrants for Patsy's fur lined boots [suspected as being a source of beaver hair], phone and cellular logs were passed from pillar to post by the then Deputy DA Trip DeMuth [Demuth's superior was another Deputy DA and Ramsey apologist, Pete Hofstrom. The Ramseys often petitioned for Hofstrom to be present during depositions/interrogations to in order to ensure they were "fair". Fair towards the Ramseys or fair towards the cops?]

C. Thomas points out that when the decision was made to apply directly to a judge for these ordinary warrants, DeMuth warned Thomas to "make sure you tell [the judge] it [the warrant] doesn't have the support of the district attorney's office].

#Shakedown assessment: What could credit card bills really show besides...hotel stays and restaurant purchases?

3. **Warning Shot**

A. If The Boulder Police weren't able to salvage any calls, the one call they were able to dig up sent chills down spines. It seemed to have been left there specifically for this purpose.

> *Checking the [home] records, I found a repeat caller to John Ramsey's private office line.* ***Three calls the day after the murder and two more a few days later came from the home phone of the lieutenant governor of the State of Colorado, <u>Gail Schoettler</u>.*** *Treating her like any other witness simply didn't work. <u>The lieutenant governor</u> strutted her political power and stonewalled me until she was damned good and ready to answer questions. Her husband, <u>Don Stevens</u>, a friend of John Ramsey for thirty-five years, had made the calls merely to convey sympathy, Schoettler told me. The experience demonstrated how deeply John Ramsey was now plugged into the Democratic Party power structure.*

#Shakedown assessment: Schoettler provides plausible deniability on two fronts. First it wasn't she who called John, it was her husband. Secondly, all five calls were to "convey sympathy". Five calls to a grieving family just to convey condolences? <u>What more than that</u> governor?

4. **Bosom Buddies**

A. It's a curious thing if John and Patsy Ramsey felt they were being preyed on by members of their own community, an employee or someone else with access to their "inner circle", that the first thing they should do is invite the entire neighborhood over. Two sets of families, the family pastor...even friends of family tagged along to participate in...plausible deniability.

B. It's also interesting that when John finds JonBenét's body, Fleet White is there. Unsurprisingly it is only a matter of days before those implicated in the "inside job" – employees – are outsourced to include the Ramsey's closest friends, Fleet and Priscilla and then Santa Claus [Bill McReynolds]

C. If the Whites fell out of favour immediately, the same process took a while longer with the Fernies. The Fernies provided temporary accommodation for the Ramseys.

A few months after the murder the pile of red flags grew too high and the Fernies could no longer maintain their friendship with the Ramseys either…

From Websleuths.com:

She [Barbara Fernie] indicated [to investigators] that late in the summer, or early fall of 1996, she had observed damages to the latch area of an exterior screen door located on the rear, south side of the Ramsey home. Mrs. Fernie was concerned that perhaps a burglary attempt had been made to the home, and shared this information with Patsy.

*They inspected the door, and determined that the interior door exhibited no damages whatsoever. Patsy expressed no concern about the damaged screen door and suggested that **perhaps John was responsible for the marks**. He reportedly was **always forgetting his keys** and had broken into the house on other occasions.*

How many fucking doors & windows did John supposedly break trying to get into his house? It makes one wonder, what was really going on with all this external damage, especially since we know

John always entered through the garage.

From <u>Websleuths.com</u>:

Mrs. Fernie indicated that she had seen a photograph of this same screen door displayed in an advertisement running in one of the Denver newspapers shortly after the murder [of JonBenét.] The advertisement, placed by Ramsey attorneys and taking up at least half of the page of the newspaper, purported that this may have been a possible point of entry used by the kidnapper of JonBenét.

*This did not sit well with Mrs. Fernie, because **Patsy was fully aware** that these damages had been inflicted upon the screen door **weeks or months prior to the murder** [of JonBenét.] The use of this particular photograph seemed to be **an attempt to mislead** the public about the evidence associated with the crime and the Fernies indicated that they severed their contact with the family following their observation of the advertisement.*

#Shakedown assessment: We believe the entire point of inviting the Fernies and Whites into their ~~home~~ crime scene was for reasons of plausible deniability. Not only could a barrier be created between Patsy and the cops, between Burke and the cops, between John and the cops, but between all three of them and the investigators. This barrier were the friends and family who "interfered" by alternately praying, independently investigating the scene and just being around. While John's interference of the crime scene was the most egregious, Fleet White did handle the duct tape. On the other handle, Linda Arndt also moved the body on her own accord, something that was also unnecessary. However given the results of the investigation we can say in hindsight that some of the most vital evidence was found stuck to the duct tape, and that evidence linked Patsy to the crime.

    5.   Burke's Basement Window?

        A. Imagine the scenario the Ramseys may have been presented with. Their child dead in their home. Inside their home. We will deal with where this occurred and what precisely may have galvanised. But if they were going to cover up the crime through the cold winter's night they were faced with presenting two possible scenarios:

- Someone who had access came in
- The crime took place outside

B. Patsy was quick to indicate many of their friends had keys to their home, which would account for "no forced entry"

C. If the Ramseys wished to show an unknown outsider had killed JonBenét her body would have been dumped outside the home. This may have seemed objectionable to the parents, if not inconvenient and downright indecent.

D. Curiously the broken basement window was never part of the original rationale *of the Ramseys.* Only once certain police and certain detectives picked up on this, and Lou Smit demonstrated someone could actually get in through the window, did John make this part of his narrative.

#Shakedown assessment: We believe there is a specific reason the basement window is left out of the initial narrative. It helps the Ramseys case that someone broke in so why would John say he had broken the window if he hadn't? This is a deeper kind of plausible deniability in our view. The answer to the question is that from the Ramseys perspective and the perspective of the crime being *"an inside job"* the broken basement window doesn't quite fit. If Linda Hoffman-Pugh had a key, why didn't she use it? If the disgruntled employee had come in and commandeered Patsy's notepad and pen in the kitchen, if he'd penned a long note over a long period of time, why would he need to make a stealthy entrance and exit? The open Butler pantry door also opened the door to the suggestion of a friend, neighbor or resident opportunist striking while the iron was hot. Another question that arises is the relevance of John Andrew's Samsonite suitcase. Was this placed there to help the Ramsey family in the house make their case for plausible deniability? John Andrew would have an alibi even if the suitcase pointed weakly at him being involved. Does the Ramsey's plausible deniability narrative extend to John Andrew? If so where does it end, or is it simply a case of if it's not us, then the case is unsolved and we can point to everyone and no one and the deniability can basically extend into an infinity of unsolvable unknowns? Ultimately, that is exactly what happened. The basement window didn't fit the "inside job" narrative, but what's clear is it was actually the best evidence to clear the Ramseys. So why didn't they use it?

In sum what we can say, and this is with two decades of hindsight, **the Ramseys graduated from an "inside job" narrative to an "intruder" narrative within a matter of months.** The intruder theory wasn't theirs, and probably wasn't their first choice, but they probably found it was gaining traction and so they went with it because it helped bolster their plausible deniability. What they perhaps didn't expect is it raised real questions around this aspect – the window. Curiously, two decades later I'm not sure if investigators or the media have seriously interrogated *the who*. We have, and the implications are vast, and there's still more work to do around who broke the window, when did it break, and how was it broken.

What obviously confounds the intruder debate are questions surrounding footprints in snow. We believe these are watertight. If that's true then we're back to square one, and speculation boomerangs back to not just John and Patsy's involvement, but Burke's too. It's especially around the issue of if Burke didn't break the basement window, and it wasn't broken months earlier, then…where does that take us…

Let's face it, the intruder theory basically imports an idea of an unknown individual, someone so mysterious and so unrelated to the Ramseys the only thing that can possibly identify this nameless stranger is a touch DNA match. Let's forget about the fact that recent developments have shown the whole touch DNA ruse to be a false flag, or that some investigators went to factories in Asia to do DNA tests. We haven't relied on the present assessment to know that the DNA narrative has been most central to the "plausible deniability" narrative all along. It's also the least plausible! But let's follow the Ramsey's line of thinking to where it ultimately leads.

It starts with an inside job based around easy access by someone who has a key, who knows the house, who perhaps enters through an open door, who writes a note, using Patsy's paintbrush and on and on. This someone knows the Ramseys movements and the layout of the home. It's an inside job. The basement window in this scenario is irrelevant, and John himself doesn't even mention it to police on December 26th, during the hours the cops are in his house sniffing around for clues. When John tells French he also reconnoitred the house looking for entry or access points, he doesn't mention the window he supposedly broke even though it's a supposedly obvious access point, besides the suspicion around the location of this access point: it's very close to the dead body.

Interestingly in none of Patsy's versions of John does she mention John going outside, looking for JonBenét, or checking the basement**. Patsy can't say this as much as she would perhaps like to because this would seriously degrade John's deniability. What – John was in the basement, saw the broken window but didn't see JonBenét? In contradistinction, Fleet White checked the basement, found the broken window, reported it but failed to see JonBenét's body in the wine cellar when he opened the door. This was exactly the sort of break the Ramseys needed, and it's because Fleet went downstairs and alone calling for JonBenét that suspicion fell so heavily on him for as long as it did.

But when Fleet was exonerated, and all the other spurious accusations against Linda the housekeeper, Santa Claus and other ex-friends and ex-employees fizzled out the "inside job" story fell apart. So what did the Ramseys do, they fell back on the broken window narrative. And that meant an intruder was the culprit, a person so secret, so invisible and so improbable, he has defied investigators to the present day.

*JonBenét: Inside the Ramsey Murder Investigation

**In *The Craven Silence 3* we provide an example of a slip-up where Patsy accidentally mentions John coming up the stairs from the basement early in the morning on December 26th.

"Zonked"

"She was zonked…She just, she was really zonked…She was zonked out asleep, so I put her to bed." — Patsy Ramsey referring to JonBenét

On three occasions while facing police interrogation Patsy Ramsey refers to the last moments of her daughter's life in a truly odd way. On June 23rd, 1998 Patsy under police questioning Patsy uses the word "zonked" to describe her daughter's condition.

She was zonked out asleep, so I put her to bed.

This phraseology is pregnant with plausible deniability too. How can John, Patsy or Burke be responsible for JonBenét's demise if she went to bed, was sound asleep and then they were too? JonBenét not only being asleep but "sound asleep" is essential to the Ramseys Didn't Do It narrative.

John and Patsy are smart people. If they are criminals they are among the smartest we've studied. But even the smartest people make concessions to the authenticities of linguistic expression. The brain learns over a long time to automatically find the best and most accurate way to describe something. So even when we try to malign or manipulate a listener, the brain sometimes allows a more accurate truth than we would want to slip through.

Even a clever liar is going to have trouble keeping track of giveaway words, changing tenses, questionable plurals and sinister singulars or merely the failure to maintain a consistent lexicon. Sometimes the use of contrived words, words that we wouldn't normally use in a particular situation – words that are too formal or too casual – can condemn the criminal playing word games.

Let's highlight one example from a separate case – Oscar Pistorius – and then get back to finalising and fine-tuning our intuition surrounding Patsy's use of the word "zonked".

From independent.co.uk:

> *He told the court he found Ms Steenkamp "seated **on her right buttock** with her right arm on top of the toilet bowl" and her head resting on her shoulder. She was shot in the arm, hip and head…"I crouched over her and I put my left arm underneath her right arm and I checked to see if she was breathing or she had a pulse…I heard her breathing so I tried to get her up and out of the toilet. I wasn't able to so **I scuttled round** on my legs, which is **probably how I kicked** the magazine rack."*

Here Oscar is referring to the very grim moment when he discovers his girlfriend riddled with three mortal bullet wounds. The word buttock feels completely out of place, as does the evidence. Interestingly Lisa and I have viewed the original autopsy photos [not in the public domain] and we've seen the bruise on the right buttock; it's significant. We can imagine Oscar and his defense team studying the evidence and Oscar simply picking up on the terminology under discussion. Buttock is the sort of clinical term a pathologist would use, or a lawyer, but no one else. Can you imagine a young boyfriend or husband referring to his girlfriend's or wife's "buttocks"? Oscar's use of the overly-descriptive "scuttled" instead of "moved" and "probably how I kicked" are totally at odds with the gravity of the situation. In life and death scenarios, real memories are singed into place, and the language used to describe it tends to be stark and to the point.

Think of this as the semantic equivalent of trying to disguise one's handwriting. You might fool some people some of the time but no one is smart enough [or foolish enough] to fool everyone all of the time.

Coming back to Patsy's lexicon: "zonked" is a strange word to describe JonBenét's final moments isn't it? It's almost a slang word, it's almost flippant which makes it seem a tad disrespectful. Imagine your dog dies and you describe to a friend how the dog was "sweating like a pig" and then expired. The idiom doesn't fit what should be a grave appreciation of suffering in a beloved animal. So when Patsy describes JonBenét as "zonked" instead of "exhausted" something is wrong.

> "I loved that child" vs "she was zonked"

What does the word actually mean?

According to dictionary.com:

- *to become unconscious from alcohol or narcotic drugs; pass out.*

- *to fall soundly asleep or relax completely*

But of course there is a third meaning, isn't there?

From dictionary.com:

- **to strike or defeat soundly; knock out; clobber**

Now there's another familiar word – *clobbered*.

John Ramsey, talking about how Burke "accidentally" hit JonBenét with a golf stick told prosecutors:

"She got clobbered. It was a total accident."

So could Patsy's mind have slipped in the same word for "fast asleep" as for "getting clobbered"? Patsy uses the word three times under police interrogation. We see it as almost an interior monologue for JonBenét's final moments on Earth in Patsy's mind. Besides all this, what we're talking about are Patsy's final moments with her daughter. These are a mother's final moments of life with her daughter, and the word she uses is oddly inappropriate, oddly detached, oddly familiar, oddly unsympathetic.

Consider the possible unintentional symbolism from Patsy's full phrase:

She was zonked out asleep, so I put her to bed.

That simple phrase could be code for JonBenét being unconscious and Patsy putting her away, moving her and preparing her for a permanent sleep, a grave. Zonked out asleep is also a flowered way of simply observing that the six year old was "very tired". The order is also worth noting:

1. zonked

2. asleep

3. put to bed

Did Patsy put JonBenét in the wine cellar, out of the way? Given how much of Patsy was found on JonBenét we think this possibility can't be avoided.

But we must also acknowledge a far more frightening possibility. The word "zonk" may be <u>the sort of sound a softball bat makes when it hits an object like a ball or a skull</u>. Since we believe the black softball bat found outside was Patsy's and also the murder weapon, we think there is more to Patsy's use of the word "zonk" than meets the ear. We think it points to specific knowledge and insight into what happened that night. All of it is locked up in Patsy's mind but the word equates to more than a Freudian slip, it suggests also the last sound JonBenét heard before the maw of death closed around her.

FEUDS & FUNERALS

"...when I opened the door – there were no windows in that room, and I turned the light on, and I – that was her." — John Ramsey's bumbling account to CNN on discovering his daughter lying dead in the family basement

"...the friendship between John Ramsey and Fleet White began to disintegrate only days after the murder. White had gone to Atlanta, where JonBenét was buried, to attend the funeral and serve as a pallbearer. When White learned the Ramseys would be staying in Atlanta for a few days to visit with relatives, rather than returning to Boulder to help police, he reportedly was furious." — crimemagazine.com

Cogne#5

We've left off the previous section with some commentary on semantics. More broadly though how would we expect a husband and wife to conduct themselves if one of them is involved in filicide?

The same day, again at the police station, **Mrs. Franzoni had a discussion with her husband, arguing** *that the door was locked as usual, and nervously commenting: "The door was locked, I have locked it, and I know very well what I do or don't do." At this point, her husband suggested: "Do not say so, baby, because this doesn't help you." Franzoni later said she did not lock the door before leaving and that it was not in her habit to do so.* — Wikipedia

There's some muddiness here around the simple subject of security. First Franzoni insists she's security conscious. When she realises that security consciousness doesn't help her case, because it forms a psychological barrier against the possibility of an opportunistic intruder, she then declares herself security unconscious. Besides this, what's different to the Ramsey case is that the couple are:

1. Talking to each other

2. Talking to the police

3. Evidently not able to come up with a singular version of events

A couple of weeks later, Mrs. Franzoni and her husband went to Monteacuto Vallese, a small village near Bologna, hometown to Mrs. Franzoni. There, during a telephone conversation with a friend, the woman, referring to Samuele's death, said: **"I don't know what happened to me"** *and then immediately corrected herself "Ehm... I don't know what happened to him."* — Wikipedia

See how easily and obviously criminals give themselves away by simply being blabbermouths? Patsy Ramsey did something very similar while being fingerprinted. The horror of the black ink on her fingers made her cry out: "I didn't kill my baby." On another occasion she cried: "Why didn't I hear my baby?"

The Feud Against Fleet

JOHN: *We know for a fact that the police went to our friends selectively and said, the Ramseys think you had something to do with the death of their daughter. Would you like to talk with us? That's the...*

KING: *They said that to other people?*

PATSY: *Yes, they did.*

JOHN: *Absolutely. And that's the only thing that I can think perhaps they said to Fleet and that upset him.* — John and Patsy Ramsey in an interview with Larry King in March, 2000

"What would you say if I told you the Ramseys owned Hi-Tec shoes?" — Fleet White to Boulder Police [Schiller]

"We respect your business..." —Third line of Ramsey Ransom Note, mentioned before "we have your daughter".

They skied together, they played softball together. They spent the Christmas of 1995 together. Three days before the Christmas of 1996 the Whites* and their kids attended a lavish extravaganza at the Ramsey mansion – even Santa was there to keep a coterie of rambunctious kids entertained. And then it all blew up.

Even in the beginning of that blow up, Fleet was there for John. He was there in the basement, he was also the first and only friend to mount a search of the home, something he did within minutes of arriving. And approximately an hour later, when it was decided Burke would go to Fleet [it's unclear who came up with that idea], Fleet made Burke's bed while Burke was getting ready.

Hold on, let's back up. We'll deal with Patsy's call to the Whites imminently, and what Patsy says about that but then we need to go back to the dinner party on Christmas night. Strictly speaking that's not our core focus in this narrative, but it's nevertheless important to juxtapose as many before/after contradictions as we can.

This chapter is a big one, the biggest of this particular narrative, but even so we won't address more than a mere fraction of John's feud with Fleet. But we have to start nailing some of it down. We'll deal with the rest in our narratives that address those timelines, so the end of this chapter is by no means the last word on the Whites, or the Fernies for that matter.

To reiterate, although we want to focus on the days after Christmas, we'll be jumping around a tad, but there's a method to our madness, so hold tight.

Let's address Patsy's call to Pricilla White first. When did she call, who did she call first? If the police raced to the scene after the 911 call at 05:52, the Fernies arrived just before the Whites but just after the cops at around 06:04.

Interestingly the Whites even brought their guests with them, Bill and Heather Cox.

From acandyrose.com:

HANEY: *You called the Whites and the Fernies. Do you recall who first or--*

PATSY: *I think I called the Whites first.*

Of course complete phone records would provide definitive confirmation to these questions. The calls to the Whites and Fernies, irrespective of who was called first, were made at approximately 05:55, and likely between 05:52 [when the police were summoned] and 05:59 [when Rick French arrived at the Ramsey front door].

HANEY: *Were they closer to you?*

PATSY: *Well, we had just gone there the night before, you know, and -- and I just dialed them up. They and the Fernies were like our best friends, you know.*

HANEY: *Let's take the call to the Whites first. I think that was the sequence?*

PATSY: *I think so.*

HANEY: *And you called them. Who answered, what is said?*

PATSY: *I think Priscilla answered. And I mean, I don't know what I said exactly. But somehow communicated to her that **JonBenét was gone** and had been kidnapped and could they come over. I don't know. I was just hysterical. Then I hung up the phone and called the Fernies. And I believe John Fernie answered.*

Note it's not: we can't find JonBenét. It's as if Patsy is sending out an official news release that JonBenét is gone and she's definitely been kidnapped. Of course when the friends arrived neither of these "facts" were certain, certainly not to them. It's interesting that they were [or appeared to be] certain to Patsy, doesn't it?

From acandyrose.com:

HANEY: *Do you recall exactly what you told him?*

PATSY: *I said -- I said -- I am not sure if I told him -- I just can't remember what I told. "Oh, please, **you got to come, please can you bring someone over**" or something. I don't remember.*

Didn't John Fernie asks why, and didn't you give them a good [but bogus] reason why, Patsy?

From acandyrose.com:

HANEY: *And understanding that they are close friends, but did you think that, give any thought to having all this traffic coming over?*

PATSY: *No.*

HANEY: *Folks coming to the house?*

PATSY: *No.*

…you got to come, please can you bring someone over…

From acandyrose.com:

HANEY: *You had gotten through that portion of the note that talked about don't call the police, the FBI?*

PATSY: *Right.*

HANEY: *We are watching you or something like that?*

PATSY: *I know.*

HANEY: *How long does it take for them to get over there?*

PATSY: *Well, it would have been just pretty quick.*

HANEY: *How much after the arrival of the first officer?*

PATSY: *Not much. Just, I don't know, 15 minutes, you know.*

More like five Patsy. And we think Patsy was hoping their pals would get to the house before the cops. That way at least the outside would be muddied with footprints. Kudos to the Boulder cops, they got to the Ramsey home first, within four to five minutes after Patsy pulled the plug on the 911 call. That's fast and we think it was a few minutes faster than the Ramseys expected.

On CNN John Ramsey described the arrival of the cops as "reasonably quick". But let's get to it now: why did the Whites declare war on the Ramseys but not the Stines? Where did the Fernies fit in all this? What happened to the Walkers?

We start this interrogation with the Whites because the Whites have the most significant stake in the unsolved murder of JonBenét, not merely as witnesses but as protagonists, antagonists, suspects, victims, multiple exonerees; you name it.

In order to navigate through the mythos surrounding the Whites we must be clear, as we've mentioned earlier, on their involvement with the Ramseys not just after JonBenét's murder but before as well. Strictly speaking, as we've also emphasized, the White's Christmas dinner party paraphernalia is peripheral to this narrative, but it also provides interesting source material to test not merely John and Patsy's versions of events against each other, but also the *Stine's*.

We don't have as much information from the Whites on their own dinner party with the Ramseys as we'd like to have, but according to Schiller**, this is what they shared with investigators:

[Fleet] White told the detectives [on December 27] that he and his wife, Priscilla, had invited relatives and friends from California to join them for the holidays.

On Christmas Day, the Whites were up early opening presents with their kids and Priscilla's parents. That afternoon at about 4:30, the Ramseys, with JonBenét and Burke arrived at the White's house.

The following people attended the White's Christmas night party:

1. Fleet White
2. Priscilla White
3. Fleet Junior
4. Daphne White
5. Heather Cox, Priscilla's niece
6. Bill Cox, Heather's husband
7. Allison Shoeny, Priscilla's sister
8. Cliff Gaston, Allison Shoeny's boyfriend
9. John Ramsey
10. Patsy Ramsey
11. Burke Ramsey
12. JonBenét Ramsey

[At] around 9:30 p.m., White said, the Ramseys left, saying that they were going to drop off gifts for other friends, the Stines and the Walkers. By 11:00 White was in bed, he said. Priscilla and her sister talked in the kitchen until 2:00 in the morning. By then Cliff Gaston was asleep on the couch in the family room, and the Coxes were also asleep, in the White's daughter's room.

Let's go through our interrogation of that dinner party slowly and meticulously by running through Patsy's version of events from the start of that fateful evening to the end. Patsy provided the following account to Boulder police four months after her daughter's death.

From forumsforjustice.org:

TRUJILLO [establishing the sequence of events on the evening of December 25th, 1996]: *Okay. So you had Burke's and JonBenét's suitcases in John Andrew's room, your suitcase was upstairs and John's would have been upstairs too then?*

PATSY: *The best that I can remember, yeah.*

TRUJILLO: *Okay. Right. You left, left for the Whites about five, 6:00, um, family of the Whites over there. Any other friends that weren't related to the Whites or, or your family. Any other people over there at the White's house that night?*

PATSY: *Uh, I don't recall.*

Patsy's first two answers sound like lawyer-speak. It's almost as though this area is a red flag area and Patsy would rather give nothing away. Besides that, she's probably been informed in no uncertain terms by counsel to be tight-lipped about who, where, what and when regarding their visits to pals that fateful night.

Let's refer to another source for another version of the same events.

From acandyrose.com/The Bonita Papers:

*John, Patsy, JonBenét and Burke were also scheduled to leave for Disney World in Florida immediately after they returned to Boulder from Charlevoix. In celebration of Patsy's 40th birthday on December 29, the family was taking the Disney World Cruise. Patsy had to pack for the two separate trips. **A few winter clothes were placed in plastic sacks** for the Charlevoix holiday, and suitcases were packed with summer clothes for the Disney World Cruise. John spent part of the day checking the personal jet, parked at the Jefferson County airport that would fly his family to Michigan the next morning.*

It's unfortunate detectives didn't prod both parents around such simple issues as where they went and how they packed. There's virtually no detail surrounding John's three to four hour absence on Christmas day, and we're given no explanation why Patsy would pack some clothes in plastic bags and the rest in suitcases. Why not put everything in suitcases? Didn't it also make more sense to put bulky winter clothes in a suitcase and the lighter shorts in a smaller bag?

From acandyrose.com/The Bonita Papers:

That evening would bring another holiday gathering dinner with Fleet and Priscilla White and their family and guests. While getting ready to attend the dinner party, Patsy tried to persuade JonBenét to wear a red sweater and black velvet pants that would match the outfit that Patsy was wearing. Like most independently thinking six-year-olds, JonBenét had other ideas about her evening attire. She insisted on wearing her black velvet jeans and matching black velvet best with a white crew-neck sweater with a sequin star on the front – an outfit she had helped pick out at a local Gap store. To complete her outfit, she wore a small gold ring on the middle finger of her right hand, a gift from her maternal grandmother, Nedra Paugh, a bracelet on her right wrist – a Christmas gift from her mother, and a gold cross necklace given to her by her aunt Pam.

Basically we can assume from this that there was a squabble between JonBenét and Patsy on the way to dinner with the Whites.

From acandyrose.com/The Bonita Papers:

The Ramsey family arrived at the White residence at approximately 4:30 p.m. With a houseful of relatives and guests, tables were set up in both the living room and dining room in order to provide everyone with a seat. Seafood, including crab, a favorite of the Ramsey children according to Patsy, was one of the main courses served for the holiday meal. After dinner, John and Fleet planted themselves on the living room floor and helped their daughters construct paper jewelry from kits given out by the Whites as gifts to the children attending the dinner party. The evening ended soon after some local carolers, entertaining in the neighborhood, came to the White's house, and Fleet and his son went outside and joined in the singing. The Ramseys - John, Patsy, Burke and JonBenét - bid goodnight to the Whites at approximately 8:30 p.m.

Notice we don't get any information on Burke. We don't know

what he was wearing, and at the Whites, there is zero indication what he was doing or who he was playing with.

From acandyrose.com/The Bonita Papers:

While driving home, Patsy stopped at the houses of friends to drop off gifts; ***a gift basket*** *for Susan Stine and perfume for Roxanna Walker.* ***Burke accompanied her to the door of the Stine's residence****, but John and JonBenét remained in the car as* ***JonBenét had fallen asleep****. Patsy also had brought along a gift basket for John and Barbara Fernie, but because it was getting late and JonBenét was already asleep, Patsy decided to deliver this last gift some other time. The family arrived home at 9:00 p.m.*

From The Bonita Papers we have a fairly clear timeline – they leave home at 16:30, although Patsy stretches this to 17:00 or 18:00. They arrive home at 21:00 and are apparently in bed by 22:00. We also get an impression that the Whites had their family and extended family over, and the Ramseys were the only non-family guests in attendance. This does suggest the Ramseys held the Whites in some esteem, and vice versa, that the Whites felt comfortable having their close and extended family in the company of their close friends the Ramseys.

Of course Patsy's version of events by comparison is mostly vanilla; there's not much to go on so we must look for lines to read between. As it turns out, there are a few.

From forumsforjustice.org:

TRUJILLO: *Okay. So everybody's, everybody's pretty much related to the Whites.*

PATSY: *Right.*

TRUJILLO: *Was this kind of a spur of the moment or was it planned to go to the White's house that night?*

PATSY: *It was planned to go there.*

TRUJILLO: *Yeah.*

PATSY: *We had gone there last year, Christmas dinner.*

TRUJILLO: *Okay. So it was kind of a, a yearly event then. Everybody was (Inaudible)...*

PATSY: *Well now it was, second time if you call that...*

TRUJILLO: *Starting to (inaudible).*

PATSY: *saying to become yearly.*

It's an interesting point to quibble over. It's as though Patsy doesn't want Trujillo to think they are better friends with the Whites than they actually are, or rather, were. Is there *any* doubt that they were once best of friends?

From tripod.com:

After Ramsey had moved his computer company from Atlanta, to Boulder, in 1991, the Whites and the Ramseys found they had much in common. Fleet White was also a successful tycoon, in the oil business. Both couples enjoyed sailing and had six yr. old girls with older brothers. Neither Patsy nor Priscilla worked, but both were committed volunteers. When John Ramsey had decided to throw his wife a surprise 40th birthday party a month earlier, on Nov.30, **he turned to Priscilla to organize the event** *at the swank Brown Palace in Denver.*

Detective sergeant Trujillo, back to you.

From forumsforjustice.org:

TRUJILLO: *Okay. Who all did you let know that you were going over to the Whites? Did you let the Barnhills know or anybody like that?*

PATSY: *Uh, I don't remember. I think I, seems like I did call Betty that day to see if they had anybody over there with them or, you know, if they were okay or...*

TRUJILLO: *Okay.*

TRUJILLO: *Okay. About what part, what part of the day did you call Betty to make sure she's okay?*

PATSY: *Um, sometime that afternoon.*

In other words before they went out.

From forumsforjustice.org:

TRUJILLO: *Okay. Okay. What did, what did you do at the White's house that night?*

PATSY: *We um, had dinner. I called Fleet's mother, Fleet called his mother and I talked to her. She was ill. She was usually there, because Christmas is her big, she likes Christmas.*

This lends some veracity to the 911 explanation from December 23 – that Fleet was trying to call someone in order to get medicine to his ailing mother. It does seem a little bizarre though how Patsy spends her Christmas dinner in 1996 - by calling old ladies to make sure they're okay.

From forumsforjustice.org:

TRUJILLO: *Um hum.*

PATSY: *And um, she was ill and I talked to her for quite some time.*

TRUJILLO: *Okay. Where does she live at?*

PATSY: *She, there from California, but they have a residence in Aspen.*

TRUJILLO: *Okay.*

PATSY: *And she was in Aspen.*

If Grandma White was so ill, shouldn't she be in California over Christmas, you know somewhere warmer, rather than the white slopes of Aspen in winter?

From forumsforjustice.org:

TRUJILLO: *Okay. So give me kind of a step by step, get to the Whites 5:30, 6:00, 6:30 whatever, what time did you have dinner that night? What did you do before dinner after dinner?*

PATSY: *Well, we had um, I think we had cocktails, kind of, she had some cracked crab left over from their Christmas Eve dinner and we sampled some of that and I remember she kind of, for some reason, made a little plate for JonBenét or I remember her making a special plate for JonBenét for some reason so she would have some crab...*

Cocktails...Some readers may recall one of the excuses given for the accidental 911 call on December 23 was a drunk guest. We think it was likely there was some alcohol consumed, not just at the Whites but throughout December, and likely at the Walker's and Stine's too that night. We think there was a shitload of celebrating going on, whether it was Patsy's 40th milestone, or John's landmark $1 billion in revenue or just Christmas.

From forumsforjustice.org:

TRUJILLO: *Okay.*

PATSY: *....cause my kids like seafood and uh, we nibble on that and I uh, we had dinner and I can't remember what we had.*

TRUJILLO: *Okay. Was it like a buffet, sit down, what kind of dinner was it?*

PATSY: *I just, I just, I don't know. I can't remember.*

Notice how Patsy's clamming up here. You're invited to dinner, the last Christmas dinner of a momentous year, an evening that's been planned in advance, and suddenly Alzheimer's kicks in? It's as though Patsy has remembered she's been told to keep mum about times, what was eaten, who said what, any helpful detail. Just give them the broad strokes Patsy, just give them vague vanilla...

From forumsforjustice.org:

TRUJILLO: *Okay. Was it a formal plates around the table type..*

PATSY: *Well, we had, she usually puts up several tables in her living room. She had several tables in her living room, in her dining room. Just were, there were a lot of us there and uh, we sat at the table, you know, she had a place for everybody.*

Good job Patsy. Now that's how you say a lotta nuthin'!

From forumsforjustice.org:

TRUJILLO: *Okay.*

PATSY: *And uh, she had little gifts for the kids. They had these little paper jewelry things that JonBenét and Daphne got and um.* **Fleet and John were down on the floor** *helping them make those.*

Besides Burke's complete absence, it's interesting that Patsy has John and Fleet both doing something on the floor with their daughters. Around eighteen hours later John and Fleet would be fumbling at an inert JonBenét on the floor of the wine cellar, and then fumbling on the floor in the lounge with a quilt under the Christmas tree.

From forumsforjustice.org:

TRUJILLO: *Okay.*

PATSY: *Jewelry things.*

TRUJILLO: *Okay. About how long did you stay at the White's house?*

PATSY: *Oh, several hours, you know, I, something like 9:00 or so, eight.*

TRUJILLO: *Okay.*

PATSY: *Eight or nine. We had to get up early so we didn't...*

TRUJILLO: *Stay out too late?*

PATSY: *...stay really late.*

We sort of think you did Patsy. Not so much that you stayed at the Whites but that you went out again, and were out kinda late. In any event, to go by Patsy's timeline, they arrived at the Whites at around 18:00 and left at 20:00. Two hours to have cocktails, a big Christmas dinner, some last minute late night Christmas gifts and then getting down on the floor with the kids…all that in two hours? Where's the fire, Patsy?

From forumsforjustice.org:

TRUJILLO: *Okay. So, other than the dinner with the little gifts, any other social activities go on that night, caroling or just socializing? What else happened?*

PATSY: *Uh, I think some carolers came. Some neighbors came to the door caroling and Fleet, big Fleet and little Fleet, I think went out with them for a little bit. Um, maybe Daphne went with them.*

The carollers sort of add an additional time spanner to the works. Who's again mysteriously absent though is Burke. We hear about JonBenét, and Daphne and Fleet Junior. Where the fuck is Burke?

From forumsforjustice.org:

PATSY: *…I don't know. I think some of them went out and sang a little bit with them and…*

TRUJILLO: *Okay.*

PATSY:*…came back in.*

Patsy that's very helpful – they went outside…and then came back in?

From forumsforjustice.org:

TRUJILLO: *JonBenét and Burke go out with them to carol?*

PATSY: *I just can't remember.*

TRUJILLO: O*kay. Got home about 8:30, 9:00. What's the first thing you guys do when you got home that night? Actually, let me* *step back. Before you got home you went over to....*

PATSY: *Walkers and dropped off a little gift.*

TRUJILLO: *Okay.*

PATSY: *And Stines and dropped off a little gift and drove home and JonBenét was asleep. She had fallen asleep in the car.*

TRUJILLO: *Did you have to wake her up to get her inside or...*

PATSY: *And Stines and dropped off a little gift and drove home and JonBenét was asleep. She had fallen asleep in the car.*

Notice how Patsy seems to want to jump clean over the Stines visit. She basically doesn't say more than "and Stines".

From forumsforjustice.org:

TRUJILLO: **Did you have to wake her up to get her inside or...**

PATSY: **Well, she was just really zonked and John carried her up to her room.**

There's something so vague about that question and the way Patsy answers it. It seems vaguely symbolic doesn't it? Did you have to wake her up to get her inside...what, the wine room? No, she was really zonked...John carried her inside...Hmmm.

From forumsforjustice.org:

TRUJILLO: *Okay.*

PATSY: *And I uh, you know, ran up behind him and, or in front of him, I can't remember. Maybe, or it might have been in front of him to turn the bed down.*

TRUJILLO: *Um hum.*

PATSY: *And he laid her down and I got her undressed and put her, I left her shirt on her and uh, went in the bathroom and tried to find some pajama pants and all I could find was some, like long underwear pants...*

There still seems to be something potentially symbolic going on here. Patsy is undressing JonBenét until she realises…well, she didn't completely. JonBenét's <u>white thermal sequin star top</u> was <u>what JonBenét was wearing</u> when <u>she was found dead in the basement</u> the next day. Fortunately Trujillo steers Patsy towards precisely this fact<u>, high-five detective</u>!

From <u>forumsforjustice.org</u>:

TRUJILLO: *Um hum.*

PATSY:*...and put those on.*

TRUJILLO: *What color of top did she wear to bed that night? What color top was she wearing actually to the White's house like?*

PATSY: *Well she wore this little outfit that I had gotten her at the Gap. We had a little, little riff over that, cause I wanted her to wear, I was wearing a red sweater and I wanted her to wear this red sweater with her black velvet pant, cause I was wearing black velvet pants and it was Christmas and all that.*

TRUJILLO: *Um hum.*

PATSY: *And she didn't want to wear the red shirt just because I was wearing it. She wanted to wear the shirt that went with the outfit which was a Gap outfit that I had bought her when we went shopping for her and it was a little white, kind of neck like this, kind of a . .*

TRUJILLO: <u>*Kind of a crew neck*</u>?

PATSY: *.crew neck and it had a little, little rhinestone, little kind of sequin kind of star thing on it.*

TRUJILLO: *Okay.*

PATSY: *So I just left that on her.*

Let's deal with what Patsy's actually saying here. She's saying she put her daughter to bed and went through the hullabaloo of getting her changed…except she didn't really fully change her.

She's wearing the same sequin star top she wore to the Whites. One gets a sense that JonBenét is really clinging to the only things she really knows – her pajamas. They give her comfort and familiarity, and JonBenét has started insisting on wearing them.

Something else I want to highlight while we're here: the Ramseys in my view are pros at confuscation. The Ransom Note is one exhibit where besides the whole thing being confiscation, there's also the confuscation of disguising handwriting, disguising one's education, all to reinforce the ruse of "an inside job". JonBenét's outfit presented the Ramseys with a problem – I mean the outfit she was found dead in. I believe they were unwilling to remove the sequin star top because it had been exposed everywhere all day and was a veritable smorgasbord of touch DNA. On the other hand that item of clothing presented a real problem. It showed a mother who apparently did not change her daughter's sleeping wear from one night to the next. In my view the white blanket thrown over the dead JonBenét was meant to disguise the white sequin star shirt she was wearing. It was muddying the scene with color, just as Patsy muddied and contaminated her own Ransom Note with faux spelling errors***.

From forumsforjustice.org:

TRUJILLO: *Okay. And I'm sorry. What kind of pants, what color of pants...*

PATSY: *They were black velvet. Black velvet jeans, kind of like, from the Gap. Some little black velvet vest.*

TRUJILLO: *And what were you wearing Patsy, a, a red turtleneck and black...*

PATSY: *Velvet jeans, yeah.*

TRUJILLO: *Okay.*

PATSY: *Velvet pants. And I have a Christmas sweater I was wearing.*

Beaver hair was found stuck in the duct tape stuck across

JonBenét's little mouth. Patsy's insistence on "velvet" is odd. More likely the beaver hair came from the lining of expensive boots or gloves Patsy was wearing. Notice Patsy doesn't really mention any of these items. The fibers reportedly found on the duct tape, on the garrotte and in the paint caddy, were red and corresponded to Patsy's turtleneck sweater. Trujillo, let's nail Patsy on that sucker.

From forumsforjustice.org:

PATSY: *I have a Christmas sweater I was wearing.*

TRUJILLO: *And what color was that?*

PATSY: *Red with all kinds of . . .*

This is classic Patsy. She gives you the answer and then tries to overwhelm you with a potpourri of distracting vanilla and confetti. Red Patsy, that's all we need to know.

From forumsforjustice.org:

TRUJILLO: *And that was over the turtleneck.*

PATSY: *Yeah.*

TRUJILLO: *Okay. Okay. What did, what did Burke wear over to the White's house that day?*

PATSY: *Oh, I don't remember. I don't remember.*

TRUJILLO: *Okay. What about John? Remember having any idea what he wore that day?*

PATSY: *Um um. Unless I try to match us up I can't remember.*

Well, whatever that means. Patsy does mention something about John wearing Khaki but let's move on to the dinner party. We eventually want to get to the feuds, so let's abandon this line of questioning and work on another strand of evidence.

The only dinner party the Ramseys attended on the cold Christmas night of 1996 was a big family do at the Whites. As we've emphasised previously, the year 1996 and the Christmas of

1996 were both extra special milestones for the Ramsey family****:

How did the Ramseys spend their Christmas day, arguably the most special day in a very successful year for the Boulder family? They attended a Christmas dinner party at the Whites. But before the end of that week, even before the year was over, the Ramseys friendship with the Whites would be in smithereens. What changed? What happened to break up the bosom buddies?

If the Stines became the new bosom buddies of the Ramseys, what was the difference between the Stines and the Whites to begin with? What got the Whites so riled up that they turned on the Ramseys when they needed them most? By the same token, what did the Whites do to earn the unmitigated ire of the Ramseys?

To understand how everything went south it's important to establish the social hierarchy as it stood on Christmas day and the day after Christmas. The Whites were clearly number one on the Ramsey's list – they were part of the inner circle, Fleet and John were pals, Priscilla and Patsy were pals, Fleet junior and Burke were pals and Daphne and JonBenét were pals. We must add a slight disclaimer to this. If Daphne and JonBenét were buds, Fleet Junior, who was two years younger than Burke, were less so.

From acandyrose.com:

HANEY: -- *to play. Who else did JonBenét play with on Christmas in the daytime, just kind of separating time frames here?*

PATSY: *Well, [JonBenét] and Burke played, Burke played with the Coby kids and these little girls. And then of course we went to the Whites and she and Daphne played with Burke.*

It's interesting in that little extract that Patsy mentions Burke's name, but can't mention JonBenét's name. JonBenét is simply an anonymous "she". What's also curious is Burke is playing with girls. Where's Fleet Junior?

Patsy doesn't seem to want to invoke even the thought of Burke playing with another boy. Obviously if he was at Fleet's, he'd be playing with Fleet Junior, right? So why not say so? When John takes Burke out of the Ramsey home on the morning after Christmas, he tells Burke "we're going to see Fleet Junior…"

If anything ought to convey the solidarity between John Ramsey and Fleet White, it's the moment Fleet searched John's home for his daughter, and the moment John gave his son to Fleet for safekeeping. It's important to stress John didn't accompany Fleet and his son to Fleet's home – he handed Burke to Fleet because this was Burke's best chance.

If Burke seems oddly compliant, oddly mute, and oddly asleep at 07:00 on a cold winter's morning with his home invaded by neighbors and cops, that's because he is oddly compliant. This is the same kid who told Judith Phillips not to touch him and to stay away from him. This is the same kid Mary Ann Kaempfer, the mother of Anthony Pecchio who was a classmate of Burke's, observed at JonBenét's funeral and said Burke did not wish to be hugged and would rather be left alone. We will reinforce these sentiments from another peculiar source**** at the end of this section. What is interesting is John Ramsey isn't specifically putting his son in the care of a cop or an adult, but incredibly under the supervision of another kid – Fleet Junior. That same kid would later be fingered as a suspect in the Ramsey murder, just as his Fleet Junior's father and mother would be.

From forumsforjustice.org:

Never once did Burke ask why policemen were at his house. The only conversation that passed between the two during the ride was [the] occasional mention of Burke's Nintendo he got for Christmas which he had brought with him.

One can only speculate if this is true. Only Fleet White would know for sure exactly what Burke said to him. What's likely, we think, is John Ramsey read his son the riot act earlier in the morning. If John had said "we're not speaking to you" after the 911 call, we think it's possible when the police were on route, Burke was shepherded back to bed and urgently instructed – perhaps by his father – to pretend to be asleep and not make a peep. If he did…<u>he could kiss his birthday horde of presents goodbye</u>. We think Burke was smart enough to keep his trap shut, especially if a big reward was waiting for him *if he obeyed.*

When Fleet White drove John's nine year old son to his own home, were things still good between the two men? Evidently, but within minutes Fleet would discover something that John had withheld from him, something that rocked him to his core.

When Patsy called the Whites that morning, although we don't know the exact words she used, she expressed there was an emergency and to come to their house quickly. When the Whites arrived at the Ramsey's home, they found out that JonBenét was missing. Within minutes, Fleet was off and searching for JonBenét. It wasn't until after he returned to the Ramseys from dropping off Burke that he found out about the Ransom Note. But he didn't hear about it from his best friend John. It took the officers on the scene to bring Fleet up to speed. Kind of an important detail to not tell your friend, don't you think? After all, he summoned Fleet from his home at 06:00 after Christmas and threw him into a nightmare situation. Then he doesn't bother to tell him exactly what's going on. Understandably, Fleet was pissed.

How do we know this? It's something Jim Clemente discussed in one of his Real Crime Profile podcasts about JonBenét after the CBS special aired. Unfortunately, those podcasts are no longer available so we're unable to source or verify the exact conversation.

Before we spend further time examining the devolution of fraternity that held these families together, I want to be very clear where exactly the Whites were positioned in the Ramsey's social scheme of things. We've established that the Whites were the Ramsey's most important and closest friends, but I want to confirm this – or shall we say 'run through' this – with John Ramsey.

From acandyrose.com [June 1998]:

SMIT: *Do you know who took these pictures?*

JOHN: *I would guess Fleet White, because he was taking pictures. But I don't know for sure.*

Nice one John; you're guessing Fleet White took the photo because he was taking photos. That's another classic: say something without saying anything.

Smit is asking John who took photos at John's slightly sinister Christmas party at the Ramsey home on December 23rd. It was sinister because of a mysterious 911 phone call which like the JonBenét murder mystery, has still arguably gone unsolved. John's photos of that party – if he took any – appear to have disappeared. And Fleet's photos in 1998 had become *maybe* Fleet's photos, *maybe* someone else's.

From acandyrose.com [June 1998]:

SMIT: *Just off the top of your head, do you remember who was there?*

JOHN: *Yeah. The Fernies, John and Barbara Fernie. Priscilla and Fleet White. And, of course, their children; both the Fernie's children I think were there. Priscilla's sister and boyfriend who's this fellow. I don't remember what his name is, from California, was there. I can look at the picture and remember some people who were there. Say Don Paugh, Patsy's father. I think that's Glen Stine, Susan and Glen Stine.*

I'm fascinated by the order in which John mentions his friends. He mentions the Stines last. The Stines were very prominent at that party, so was Fleet White. Susan Stine dealt with the police through the front door speaker system when they were summoned by the accidental 911 call. Fleet White apparently made that accidental call, but one wonders why he couldn't have said so, either to the cops directly, or over the phone when they called back. Or if they had answered he could simply have admitted he'd dialled a wrong number. This has echoes of course of if JonBenét's murder had been an accident, one could simply call a hospital and report it as such. Of course, if one knew it didn't even look like an accident, then some other scheme would need to be devised.

Coming back to John's casting of his friends – notice who he mentions first. John mentions the Fernies first, and mentions their children, although not by name. He says the word "Fernies" three times and "Stines" twice. "White" is mentioned once, and Fleet is mentioned after Priscilla, unlike John and Glen, who are both mentioned before their wives. Interesting huh? Of course just two months after John's interview with Lou Smit the grudge match between the Ramseys and the Whites as well as the District Attorney and a swath of Boulder Police Department cops was in high gear.

On August 17th 1998 Fleet and Priscilla penned a 4950 word diatribe addressed to "the people of Colorado." Although it's not the ambit of this narrative to deal thoroughly with the events of 1998, we'll dip into an extract of Fleet and Priscilla White's invective.

From denverpost.com:

After JonBenét Ramsey was killed in Boulder nearly twenty months ago, her parents, John and Patsy Ramsey, immediately hired prominent Democrat criminal defense attorneys with the law firm of Haddon, Morgan and Foreman. This firm and its partners have close professional, political and personal ties to prosecutors, the Denver and Boulder legal and judicial communities, state legislators, and high-ranking members of Colorado government, including Governor Roy Romer.

The investigation of her death has since been characterized by **confusion and delays**.

These words may seem benign. What's wrong with a little confusion? When we dig a little deeper it turns out that the Boulder Police Department are basically being given the run-around. Investigate every lead that doesn't have to do with the Ramseys... That sort of bogus attitude eventually led to the extradition and arrest of John Mark Karr, a suspect who wasn't anywhere near the continental United States, and who turned out to be nowhere near Boulder at the time JonBenét was murdered either. The only thing that linked Karr to the case was child pornography and a few emails he'd sent saying he was obsessed with JonBenét. That sideshow is such a joke we've mostly sidestepped it, but we mention it here merely to highlight how the authorities managed to stymie a case with *confusion and delays*.

Justice delayed is justice denied, and justice in this case has been denied for two decades and counting. And the confusion and delays simply continue. Part and parcel of *The Craven Silence* is exactly this – from the confusing Ransom Note to the delays to interrogating the parents, to the most silent benefactor of all finally deigning to appear on television in September this year to "set the record straight" [while secretly collecting a multi-million dollar paycheque, to add to his other settlements, for his trouble].

From denverpost.com:

*The district attorney and Ramsey defense attorneys started early in the investigation to **condition the public** to believe that these delays and the lack of a prosecution have resulted almost entirely from initial **police bungling** of the case and the **non-cooperation of witnesses**. This has continued to this day. Advising the district attorney since the early days of the investigation have been Denver metropolitan area district attorneys Bob Grant (Adams County), Bill Ritter (Denver County), Jim Peters (18th Judicial District), and Dave Thomas (1st Judicial District).*

*Recently, Boulder police detective Steve Thomas, an investigator on the JonBenét Ramsey murder case, left the department in disgust. In his August 6 letter of resignation, he publicly accused the district attorney of **obstructing the police investigation and allowing politics to "trump" justice.***

Notice the lexicon the Whites use – politics. How did this case involving the death of a six year old child become a political football? Well, the point was so that it never could. So the politics is all about shutting the case down. The political will to prosecute is eclipsed by the political expediencies that revel against it.

From denverpost.com:

*We knew JonBenét and her parents very well and have been closely involved in the **investigation as witnesses**. During the past year, we have also come to know and respect Mr. Thomas and were saddened and discouraged by his departure from the investigation. We share Mr. Thomas' view regarding the district attorney and his* contention that **overwhelming pressure** brought to bear on the district attorney and police leadership from various quarters has thwarted the investigation and delayed justice in the case. While it is unlikely that the district attorney has been corrupted by Ramsey defense attorneys, it is certain that the district attorney and his prosecutors have been greatly influenced by their metro area district attorney advisers and by defense attorneys' **chummy persuasiveness** and threats of reprisals for anyone daring to jeopardize the civil rights of their victim clients.

We explored the "chummy legal culture" in detail in <u>The Craven Silence</u> series.

From denverpost.com:

*Indeed, the district attorney and the Ramsey attorneys have simultaneously rebuked the police for "focusing"' their investigation on the Ramseys when in fact police were simply following evidence. During the course of the investigation, the district attorney has used inexplicable methods including **the recruitment of magazine writers and tabloids to leak information** concerning the case and to needle witnesses, "suspects"', and police detectives. He has provided evidence to Ramsey defense attorneys at their request but denied reasonable requests by witnesses for their own statements to police.*

It is not the ambit of this narrative to fully interrogate these allegations, but what we must stress is the investigation into Kimberly Ballard as a possible mistress of John Ramsey was mysteriously undermined by a tabloid media circus. White suggests here that the tabloids are recruited by the Ramseys for the purpose of "plausible deniability". If the Ramseys decry the tabloids as predatory and pernicious in public, it seems [at least according to White] in private the Ramseys and their colonels strategically leaked information to the tabloids for the purposes of interfering with key witnesses.

Basically they were two big happy families, although Fleet Junior was a little younger than Burke, and Priscilla and Patsy sometimes rubbed each other the wrong way. Right, Lisa?

The two women seemed to be at odds over Patsy's obsession with pageants. How does Patsy respond to that? She basically calls Daphne ugly.

From forumsforjustice.org:

HANEY: *Prior to the death, what was Fleet's behaviour like, especially regarding JonBenét?*

PATSY: *He, I mean, adored our children. You know. They played together a lot. They were at our house, you know, a lot. My children were at their house playing. They had been up to the lake with us, a number of times, for two, three weeks at a time.*

HANEY: *Was there anything in this prior behaviour that looking back now seems unusual?*

PATSY: **Well, Priscilla was never crazy about me doing this whole pageant [thing] with JonBenét**, *she thought that was just totally unnecessary, because she said you know, it's just not the thing to do. Well, you know, I had grown up doing it, I enjoyed it, I had a lot of friends who had done it. I had very good experiences with it. So that's what I brought to the table.* **My daughter was a performer, she was beautiful, she was outgoing, and flourished in that type of environment. Daphne was not.** *You know. So Priscilla would oftentimes say to me, you know, well, you raise your children the way you do and* **we don't all raise our children the same.** *So you know, kind of looking back at that and think, you know, did that really get to her or something. I don't know.*

Now let's confirm the White's position in the Ramsey's social strata before JonBenét's murder. Actions speak louder than words, and on Christmas night the Ramsey's actions towards their friends spoke volumes. Who did they choose to spend the evening with on this most special day on this most special year? Fleet, Priscilla, Fleet Junior and Daphne White were the undisputed besties of the Ramseys. Possibly the exception to everyone getting along like a house on fire was Burke – because Burke's bestie was Doug Stine.

After dinner at the Whites, and a quick visit to the Walkers, that's where the Ramseys went. This is before-Christmas territory, but once again it's important to establish how different things were immediately after Christmas.

From acandyrose.com:

SMIT: *So where did you pull into then at the Walkers [on Christmas night after dinner at the Whites]?*

JOHN: *I think I pulled into the driveway. And it seems like that when Patsy, as I recall, she went in and she stayed a little while like five minutes.*

SMIT: *And she went in to do something?*

JOHN: *Just to give the Walkers their gifts.*

SMIT: *Do you know what that gift was?*

JOHN: *I didn't at the time. I think it was perfume or something like that. I remember her saying, but I didn't at the time. I thought it was a food (INAUDIBLE) or something like that. And she came back out and we went to the Stines and she had a gift for them.*

SMIT: *Now did you and Burke and JonBenét stay in the car, do you remember?*

JOHN: *I don't remember.*

SMIT: *You stayed in the car at the Walkers?*

JOHN: *Oh, the Walkers, yeah. I think **we all three stayed in the car**.*

SMIT: *And then you go to the Stines?*

JOHN: *Right.*

SMIT: *How far a drive is the Stines?*

JOHN: *Two minutes, three minutes. Pulled up out the front of their house. Patsy certainly went in, I don't think I did. I don't remember if Burke did or not. I don't think JonBenét did. But I don't remember for sure. It wouldn't have been unusual for Burke to go in because that was his buddy, Doug.*

It's interesting how clipped John's answers are, and yet when asked about gifts there's a sudden deluge of verbal diarrhea amounting to fuck all, and when asked about how far the Stine's home was, there's an even bigger deluge. John gives the distance in minutes when we know the distance from the Ramsey residence to the Stine's by bicycles was in the order of two minutes.

We're curious whether John may have given any kind of softball gear to their friends especially since John's company was not only sponsoring the team, Moms Gone Bad, but celebrating a billion dollars in revenue milestone. Wouldn't they spread some of that love by offering new kits, or brand new softball bats perhaps?

From acandyrose.com:

SMIT: *Did you have a gift for Doug?*

JOHN: *I don't know. I know Patsy probably, but I don't recall. And then we debated, we had a gift for the Fernies and we debated whether we should go over there. But that's probably 15 minutes away and we wanted to get home and to bed. And we didn't know what time we would get back. So we left the Stines and drove home.*

The thing is John, that's not entirely accurate.

Susan Stine provided this version of events on the 5th of August 1998 in a documentary titled JonBenét's America [which aired on KUSA-Channel 9]

Susan Stine: *"They came to our house and I talked to Patsy for a while maybe 10 or 15 minutes and **they all seemed perfectly normal**. They were all the same - bubbly about Christmas and about where they were going and we, **my husband and I, waved good-bye to them** as they were leaving and **that was the last time we saw them as an intact family.**"*

What's wrong with this picture? One must bear in mind that this documentary was part of the canon of *Apologia* for the Ramseys otherwise "Patsy's pitbull" wouldn't have appeared in it. What's wrong with Stine's version is broadly that it is just too perfect. This may seem cynical until we drill down and see why.

    1.   According to John he does not go inside the Stine's home, and neither does JonBenét. Burke might have. According to Susan Stine she sees the entire family. Besides seeing everyone, they all seem perfectly normal. **How can JonBenét seem normal and bubbly if she's asleep in a car?**

    2.   Susan Stine says she and her husband waved goodbye to them as they were leaving – who? Burke and Patsy? Burke and Doug and Patsy? **Where was Doug in this if he wasn't waving goodbye?**

    3.   Susan Stine uses a strange and strategic word to describe the Ramseys: **an "intact" family.** It's almost as though she knows there are a few screws loose, and she knows that what's about to happen to JonBenét's skull will not only break her apart, but the entire family. The challenge will be to hold it together. Think holding the cracked shell of Humpty Dumpty together to keep all the yellow ooze from coming out. If it does, Access Graphics is fucked.

From the Ramsey's actions on Christmas night we can assume the Whites occupied the top of the Ramsey's social strata, the Walkers and Stines, were in the middle and the Fernies arguably near the bottom.

Now to conclude. The feuds between the Ramseys and Whites really erupted between December 26th and January 1st. A lot happened in this period – a memorial, a funeral with a separate viewing, a church service five days later, numerous statements by Boulder city spokespersons, appeals to the Ramseys to talk to police and it all culminated with the Ramseys going on CNN on New Year's Day. Let's finalise this chapter with three specific insights from three specific sources.

#1 The Grudge according to Steve Thomas******

"...as the days passed, they grew troubled that John and Patsy seemed to be dodging the police, and decided to talk to them about

it."

Interestingly enough, when the Whites flew down to Atlanta to attend JonBenét's funeral, they stayed with John's brother Jeff. When Jeff learned what the Whites intended to say to his brother and sister in law, Jeff contacted Patsy's parents and informed them. Patsy's father Don loaded two pistols and placed them under a couch cushion. Then "the clan" as Thomas describes them, waited for the Whites to show up at their door.

#2 The Grudge according to the Pilot's Wife*******

Pam Archuleta is cryptic about what her husband Mike [John's personal pilot] observed at the Paugh residence. Pam simply says "something did not go well" and an argument between John and Fleet was "loud and very emotional". Fleet and Priscilla flew home that night, not the way they came and not with Mike. They took a commercial flight back to Boulder instead. Whatever happened during Fleet's confrontation with John, a permanent rift had been created which remains to this day.

#3 The Grudge according to James Kolar********

After the funeral in Atlanta, the Ramseys did not return to Boulder. Instead they appeared on CNN. This appearance was arranged by "a friend" of the Ramseys. It's not clear who arranged it, but it seems it could have been Fleet. When the Ramseys were accused of taking the media into their confidence rather than the cops, John fingered Fleet as the culprit – it was his idea. Whether it was or wasn't is less relevant than the Ramseys choosing to appear on CNN when they did, and waiting to co-operate [conditionally] with the Boulder cops about four months later. The instant "lawyering up", the lack of co-operation with the Boulder cops as well as the Ramseys delaying their return to Boulder infuriated Fleet. One reason for this was possibly because Fleet was in Boulder and being treated like a suspect. John was a key, in a sense to Fleet clearing his name. Of course, on the flip side, if John was guilty and the cops were buzzing around the Whites, that suited the Ramseys just fine for the time being.

Another early betrayal of trust for Fleet was not being informed from the get go about the Ransom Note. Fleet was livid with John for not telling him directly about a possible kidnapping for ransom. We can see this from two perspectives though. John might have assumed Priscilla would have told him, after Patsy had spoken to her over the phone [assuming Patsy had mentioned the note to Priscilla]. On the other hand, had Fleet known a kidnapping was involved, or potentially involved, he might not have wanted to involve himself, his wife or his children in the incident, and he may have advised John to honor the contents of the note.

Perhaps it was crucial to suckering the Whites into their scheme to not let them know too much, and this smacked to the Whites of something seditious. Ultimately the Whites bore the brunt of years of malingering and dirty tricks, and Fleet probably rues the day he rushed to his friend's aid without sufficient forewarning from his wife for what was in store.

From denverpost.com:

The Whites moved to Boulder in 1994 and [initially] lived only two doors down from John and Patsy Ramsey. The two families became friendly but were estranged after the murder...White said he agreed to appear before the grand jury investigating JonBenét's death in 1998 only after Ritter assured him that then-Boulder DA Alex Hunter was no longer overseeing the investigation.

White said Hunter spread insinuations about him in interviews with local and national media....Hunter declined to comment....White said his connections to JonBenét's murder have almost ruined his career in the oil and gas business, leading him to consulting work.

Still, despite the troubles, the family remains in Boulder. Their son is in the United States Naval Academy, and their daughter [attended] Boulder High School.

In early 1999 Fleet White was arrested by Boulder police for not paying a traffic ticket. He was handcuffed and taken to jail.

* Fleet himself got caught up in the web around the mysterious 911 call – the reason given was he had tried calling 411 to order medicine for his mother. We will continue digging to see if Fleet still validates that story.

**Perfect Murder Perfect Town

***Business and possession in the first quarter of the first page with the only two spelling errors, both involving the letter 's'. Business had one 's' too many and possession was missing an 's'.

****List of Milestones for the Ramseys in 1996 leading up to Christmas Day:
1. **JonBenét** appeared in four pageants in 1996
2. **Burke**'s little league Baseball team was #1 in 1996.
3. John's daughter Melinda had graduated from Medical College in 1996 and had started working as an emergency pediatrician at Kennestone Hospital in Atlanta
4. John's son John Andrew began his sophomore year at the University of Colorado in 1996.
5. In April 1996 Patsy was profiled in Woman's Magazine.
6. November 30th: Patsy celebrated her 40th birthday with friends in November so as not to disrupt the momentum of back to back Christmas parties and Access Graphic celebrations. Patsy described her birthday party as "the biggest, most outrageous 40th birthday bash I've ever had!"
7. December 6th: **JonBenét** had her own float at the Boulder Lights of December Parade.
8. December 6th: A Christmas shopping spree in New York with the Stines. Susan Stine and Patsy appeared amid a throng of fans on the TODAY show.
9. December 13th: Church party attended by 150 guests
10. December 16th: John celebrated business revenues surpassing $1 billion at an Access Graphics party
11. December 17th: **JonBenét** was crowned Colorado's Little Miss Christmas eight days before her death.
12. December 20th: Access Graphics Luncheon luncheon party for more than 300 employees at the Boulderado Hotel
13. December 20th: **JonBenét** appears in Rock Around the Clock performance at High Peaks Elementary School. If one includes the appearance on the float and this performance, JonBenét appeared in pageant related activities at least six times in 1996, four of these December.
14. December 21st: Access Graphics mints "First Billion Dollar Year" gold coin.
15. December 21st: Boulder Daily Camera business article on Access Graphics reaching $1 billion in sales.
16. December 24th: article appeared in the Boulder Daily Camera regarding the Ramsey Christmas party
17. On December 25th Patsy's actual 40th birthday was just four days away [on December 29th]

18. Patsy's cancer diagnosed in June 1993 appeared to be in remission throughout 1996.
19. The Charlevoix house was on the home tour in July and was scheduled to appear in Better Homes & Gardens in 1997.
20. Morning of December 26th: on the day after Christmas the Ramseys were scheduled to leave to celebrate a second Christmas, this time a family-only gala in Minneapolis followed by a New Year's Disney cruise...

*****Doug Stine
******Source: *JonBenét: Inside the Ramsey Murder Investigation*
*******Source: *The Pilot's Wife*
********Source: *Foreign Faction*

Two Funerals for Lazarus

"Anything I tell you is an alibi for something else." "Then let's be quiet together." — Leonard Cohen, The Favorite Game

The Ramseys liked living large, didn't they? Like Noah they liked seeing and doing things in pairs. That's why Patsy didn't have one 40th birthday party but wanted two, it's why the Ramseys had two mansions and two planes instead of one, why the Ramseys' didn't celebrate Christmas once but twice, and why they essentially held *two funerals* for their daughter.

Besides these two funerals there was also a "visitation", which is like a reception at a wedding, except it happens at a funeral and it happens before the funeral. And besides the visitation on December 30th there was also a sort of valedictory Church reunion on January 5th. As distasteful as that sounds it was meant to appear as a gathering together of the funeral folk for a second fond farewell. In fact it was a lot more distasteful than that – it was a PR blitz for Team Ramsey by Team Ramsey.

Think about what we're actually talking about though. The death of your daughter, in which you are a suspect, is used as a PR event. To use a funeral for marketing begs the question, marketing for who, and for what?

Here'a hint courtesy of John Ramsey:

"I don't know if it was an attack on me, on my company..."

Was the PR around JonBenét's funeral meant to smooth over John's reputation, and indirectly, repair any aspersions that could be cast to the computer juggernaut John owned? Was this all to keep business booming as usual at Access Graphics?

To answer these questions we first have to be clear on whether there was PR of any kind at these funerals and what it looked like. Cameras in church? Pageantry at a funeral? Camera crews camped on church steps? Was any of this going on?

We've touched on this lightly in *The Craven Silence* Trilogy, now it's time for a closer look. Let's examine the broad strokes first by asking an innocent question. What was going on in the first two, three, four, five weeks after JonBenét's death? Were the Ramseys sort of secluded somewhere in mourning? What was happening?

It turns out a lot was happening, and it was energetic stuff for a bereaved family. The double-dealing we're about to reveal is more than merely excessive or over the top, when one drills down it turns out to be really sick. Consider the following circus tricks based on a two week timeline in January 1997:

    1.   *Ramseys appear on CNN [January 1st 1997]*

    2.   *Ramseys hire private detective [Ellis Armistead, January 3rd, 1997]*

    3.   *First search warrant issued to search Ramsey mansion in Charlevoix [January 5th, 1997]*

    4.   *"Staged" church appearance on the same day [January 5th, 1997]*

    5.   *Website created dedicated to the case [January 6th, 1997]*

    6.   *Boulder judge Diane McDonalds seals all search warrants including the one for the Charlevoix home for a period of 30 days [January 6th, 1997]*

    7.   *A tabloid [the Globe] publishes leaked photographs of JonBenét's autopsy [January 13th, 1997]*

    8.   *The media report FBI profiler John Douglas [and author of Mind Hunter, a book alleged to be on John's bedside table, and part of the crime scene photo archive] has been recruited to Team Ramsey along with several handwriting experts. [January 14th, 1997]*

All of this shit happens within three weeks of JonBenét's murder. A long fourteen days after John Douglas joins Team Ramsey the Boulder cops finally get their search warrant to search the house in

Boulder. This warrant is the fourth issued, but the first to be mired in bureaucracy. The process of delaying the investigation and murking it up was now in full swing.

The events of 1997 and beyond, including the role of sexual assault in the crime and Alex Hunter's impact on this case form the narrative core of *The Day After Christmas 2* and *3* respectively.

In order to do our due diligence in this narrative, we must go back to the last days of 1996 in Boulder and peel away the surface, the veneer of what we're being told, to see, and see for ourselves what was really going on. To fully absorb what happened in those first days after Christmas we're going to have to spend a little time in church. We must look at congregants, listen to the odd dirge and get a sense of the ebb and flow of the media throughout.

Steve Thomas provides a useful first-hand account* because the detective actually attended the funeral on December 31st.

*In prayer Patsy's sisters, Pam and Polly [Paulette], waved their arms over their heads and loudly called for heavenly help...their actions were so unusual in Boulder that a little girl in the pew beside me was swept up by their spirit and joined in, twirling her arms and shouting. [Then] John Ramsey rose to say a few words, his arms across his chest and his voice tight. He said **he had grown spiritually** from the death of JonBenét [and] then shared a secret. He said he once missed the talent portion of a pageant in which **his daughter had won a medal. She had given him the medal**, and today he wore it outside his shirt. It was one of the items taken from the house by Pam Paugh that police failed to inventory...*

It's important to establish here that John is claiming he kept a medal JonBenét gave him. We can't be certain how Steve Thomas knows this item was taken by Patsy's sister Pam, but we can assume it came up in crime scene photographs. In any event, what Thomas is suggesting is interesting. If correct, the "secret" John shares to family and friends at his daughter's funeral about his daughter is a heresy.

We have devoted a chapter in the forthcoming narrative to this medal, it is called "Badge of Honor" and John actually mentioned it several times in television interviews after the funeral [hence our chapter title].

What Thomas also observes at the funeral in Atlanta is a "scuffle" breaking out between church dudes and photographers. Ominously Thomas then comes face to face with John Ramsey's eldest son John Andrew who – at the time – shouted at the detective to *"get rid of them!"*

Is this an early indication of how the Ramseys saw the police? As chess pieces? As pawns? At crud to be shat on and shouted at?

In Thomas' account* there's also a great moment where John tries to do his suave thing with detective Thomas but it <u>doesn't have the desired effect</u>.

John Ramsey approached me. After such an emotional service, I thought he might be ready to tell me to find the bastard who killed his little girl. Instead he offered a mild "thank you" and a weak handshake, not making eye contact. I didn't let go of his hand until he looked up, and I said, "Good luck."

Nice one Steve!

Unsurprisingly <u>Pam Archuleta's</u> take** is a lot more sympathetic.

... Patsy came down the stairs and she was a vision of sadness with her <u>black dress, black veil and gloves</u>. As she slowly walked down the stairs she seemed to be held up by friends and family. I thought if they let her go she just might fall over. I walked up to her, hugged her, and [shared my condolences].

Pam is a funny lady. She encourages her pal by reminding her of a *"wonderful memory of [JonBenét] on the night of the Parade of Lights."* Ironically enough Patsy, even in Pam's telling of it, didn't find this tremendously comforting, because Patsy responded: *"Yes, but she was cold."*

There's a sense of Freudian slippage here too, in the sense of JonBenét's cold cadaver lying on a concrete floor in the basement on a very cold Christmas night. If I was concerned my speckled pigeon might be devoured by ants, I suppose in the hours Patsy waited for that little corpse to be discovered, Patsy may have felt a sense of the cold shell of what was her daughter growing colder.

In any event Pam didn't appreciate her well thought out commiserations falling on fallow ground.

"It felt hurtful to me since we had tried so hard to keep her [JonBenét] warm that night, but someone had told Patsy that JonBenét was cold."

Perhaps more valuable than the detectives' observations about Patsy's siblings, John and John Andrew, are Pam's remarks about Burke. What was Burke doing inside the church while his family were saying a permanent goodbye to his dead sister? According to Pam** Burke was playing with a model airplane. Burke was:

"...not paying attention to what was going on around him. [Burke's] parents were grieving [along with] every adult in the room, but Burke was ignoring everything and just flying his plane lost within his own thoughts... Did he realize what had happened? He was smart and nine years old, but was he in shock, too?..."

We'll be addressing airplanes as a category of Christmas gift on its own in the next narrative. We've dealt with bicycles and baseball bats, airplanes are next. We have dealt with Pam's observation of Patsy standing up in church and "giving JonBenét" to God, something that came up in the Dateline documentary. In that documentary Pam confuzzled many by identifying herself as Pam Barday. In any event, let's revisit the same territory, this time via Pam's written observations**.

[When] the minister [spoke] about JonBenét, Patsy stood up in the middle of the service... held both of her arms up...as if to say, "Take her, she is yours." [Patsy walked towards]... the church altar, and then she almost fell down on her knees while John raced up to her rescue. He half picked her up while the minister helped them both up to the altar.

We pondered how much pageantry occurred inside the church,

well here's your answer. Even John got involved. Pam continues:**

The minister knelt down, and talked to both John and Patsy for a short time, but no one could hear what he was saying, although it was absolutely quiet at that time…I doubt this had happened at any other memorial service.

From there Pam relates how Patsy stood up, her hands held high once more [a black doppelganger for her daughter who was carried days earlier with her frozen, doll-like arms raised stiffly upward in the steely grip of death] and headed back to an aisle and sat down.

Pam seems awestruck by her pal, hypnotised by the movement of the spirit in *someone so close* to her. Wow! At this moment Pam observes that Patsy reminded her of Jackie Kennedy, and how Jackie Kennedy looked at JFK's funeral. And shortly after this spectacle the service ended "abruptly".

If Pam saw Patsy as Jackie, perhaps that was by design, because the Jackie Kennedy-look was exactly what patsy was going for. How do we know? Patsy says so:

From acandyrose.com quoting Death of Innocence***:

"On December 28, a department store in Denver sent some clothing to the Fernies' so I could pick something to wear to the funeral, since all our clothes were still in the house. Roxy and my sisters were there to help me sort through the dresses and hopefully come up with something I could wear to my daughter's funeral. I chose a black knit, two-piece dress."

The savvy reader would have picked up something in there that doesn't wash. Yes, Pam Paugh's authorised sortie into the Ramsey residence disguised as a Boulder cop on December 28th was under the pretense of retrieving funeral clothes. Just as we cannot imagine pageant queen Patsy putting on the same clothes she wore to the Whites the next morning, Patsy wouldn't be seen dead in just any old outfit.

From acandyrose.com:***

> "*...a picture of Jackie Kennedy abruptly flashed across my mind. I remembered seeing her wearing a black veil, walking hand in hand with her two children to JFK's grave site. Now I could see why people wore veils at such times. The filmy material surrounds you like a cocoon, over-shadowing your face and closing out the world. With the covering and protection, I could cry, be private in my grief. I decided I wanted to wear a veil to JonBenét's funeral, so **I asked one of my friends to help**. She found a sheer black scarf and attached it to a black felt hat, then packed it for the trip to Atlanta.*"

The above paragraph seems to suggest the scarf was rescued from Patsy's stuff, possibly by her sister Pam. But nowhere does Patsy say the scarf was hers; instead we have a sense of an enterprising friend coming through at the last moment so that Patsy isn't arrested by the fashion police on the occasion of her daughter's funeral [in which she's a suspect]. The craziest part of Patsy's story is this idea of her wanting to be "private in my grief". If Patsy wanted to be private would she have stood up mid-service at the memorial and made a hullabaloo in the front of the church? Would she have gone on CNN? Would there be a memorial service, a visitation and a second church service with open invitations to the media besides the fucking funeral itself?

When Patsy describes the last time she saw JonBenét, she names everyone. Mom, dad, her sisters, John and herself, John Andrew and Melinda, on and on, who gave what to put in the casket. It's all very touching until you realise poor little Burke is left out of this aspect of the narrative too. Curiously John tucks his daughter in a silk scarf. Whenever we hear about John and his last moment with his daughter he seems to be covering her over in something, doesn't he?

What's even more intriguing is at this point Priscilla White is still Patsy's bestie.

From acandyrose.com:***

> "*Suddenly my friend Priscilla White rushed in. She and Fleet had found Sister Socks, a stuffed kitten that was so dear to JonBenét. I couldn't believe that Priscilla had the gray-a-white cat. I had asked to have the toy brought from the house in Boulder [because] the*

stuffed animal that was given to us earlier was the wrong one. Priscilla knew that, and somehow, even though she was now in Atlanta, she had gotten hold of the right Sister socks, the one with the red ribbon around it's neck. I tucked Sister Socks under JonBenét's right arm."

Patsy is pedantic about every detail, she can remember the order when which family members placed the tiara on JonBenét's dead head, the six year old's funeral is a final glorious moment of carefully crafted pageantry for Patsy, and she revels in it. She revels in every detail except one – she forgets about JonBenét. What does she look like? How does it feel to see her there, to say goodbye to her? Does the thought cross her mind what happened to her, and how it happened, and whether the child suffered in her final moments? Does Patsy have the slightest sliver of regret or even reflection? Is there a memory that surfaces of her and JonBenét? And what about her other child? Does she comfort Burke? Does she see Burke as a future for her parental resources and investment?

Let's jump ahead to the funeral on Sunday January 5th, 1997. Again this is the Ramsey version of events*** at the "staged" church Reunion in Boulder.

From acandyrose.com:***

"Unknown to the parishioners, Pat Korten, the media relations guy, had let the media know that we would attend church that day…our attorneys [had hired him] to answer…media requests for information…Pat had made a deal with the media. "The Ramseys will walk out of the front door of the church and give you plenty of time to video them…" …We stopped at the top of the stairway leading from the church, knowing that we were going to get caught on camera, but also knowing we had agreed to get caught. A woman crouched down in front of us with a monster camera… she managed to walk backwards with her knees bent and that big camera on her shoulder. [As] we made our way down the walk…there were several verbal altercations as photographers tried to break through…"

The Ramsey version of events is that Korten arranged the exclusive scoop in exchange for the media backing off. Instead what actually happened was the whole thing backfired, and the public, rightly so, found the media circus which *appeared* organized, and was organized, [printed leaflets were one giveaway] distasteful. In the Ramseys version these events of course they're not willing circus acts but victims of the predatory media. We'll see exactly how this played out over several years, and how the Ramseys were able to turn a hefty profit through alternately canoodling with or otherwise suing the tabloids.

We haven't completed our interrogation of the waltz between the Ramseys, their representatives and the media because it's simply too much to attend to in one narrative, and one chapter. We'll provide more from the media's perspective to the funeral, memorial service and attendant pageantry in *The Day After Christmas 3*.

One nagging question that we have missed thus far is a simple but subtle one. If the Ramseys faced the media in Atlanta as early as January 1st, 1997, why not in Boulder? Why didn't the Ramseys face the media in their home town sooner or later, why go out of state to state their case on CNN?

Surely if they didn't want the nation's attention on them there was a way to make that attention go away – speak to the cops, deal with the media and dispel the momentum of curiosity [and suspicion] that was building. We believe there was a clear and strategic plan behind dodging the local cops and media and it had everything to do with controlling the narrative. The Ramseys didn't wish to suppress the story, they couldn't if they tried. Instead they endeavoured to direct the media flow. Think of it like controlling a fountain through the control and manipulation of a fountainhead.

Why would *individuals* suspected of murder act in this way? We can't think of a similar precedent to the Ramsey case other than Oscar Pistorius. Oscar also lawyered up immediately, Oscar also hired his own investigators, his own crime scene and ballistics experts, his own PR spokesperson. He also hired a big hitter in Stuart Higgins [aka "The Human Sponge"], the former editor of the UK tabloid *The Sun*. It wasn't very long before Oscar got rid of his PR army. Some of their early stunts like a twitter fact-checker imploded after just 16 tweets.

What do the Ramseys have in common with Oscar Pistorius and O.J. Simpson? What is different in the Ramsey, Pistorius and Simpson cases to say, Jodi Arias or Steven Avery? How is the Ramsey and Pistorius case similar to Amanda Knox?

There are various shades of gray between these cases but what we can say with confidence is a lot of treasure was harnessed in an effort to protect an even bigger horde of treasure. Lawsuits are a popular method of *enforcing* legal PR****. In this sense we ought to see the use of media not necessarily to protect or defend individuals, but as a broader strategy to assuage *vested interests*. That is not to say a lot of effort doesn't go into defending and protecting individuals, just that the *modus operandi* is different if it is only one hapless individual accused of a crime. Even in the Arias case to some extent the Mormon faith and a cabal connected to Travis Alexander came under scrutiny.

In the Ramsey case we must be bold enough to look to the very epicentre from which all the cool, dark misdirection springs. None of this aggressive PR and calculated politicking makes sense if it was only one person's fate at stake. If that were the case fewer strings could be pulled than were pulled and less treasure would be available than the mountain that was ultimately set aside to defeat this thing. So what is/was <u>at the epicentre</u>?

"I don't know if it was an attack on me, on my company..."

When we see a corporation with over $1 billion in revenues, affiliated <u>to an American global aerospace, defense, security and advanced technologies company</u> with worldwide interests, then suddenly <u>the large scale legal sleight of hand</u> makes sense.

In any event, barely two months after Korten's stage-managed church circus fuck up Korten was fired*****. Perhaps he'd served his purpose. Perhaps he'd shared his connections with the Department of Justice and perhaps he'd been worth every penny. Whatever the case, and whatever we may think about the effectiveness of a choreographed media fuck up involving a church in Boulder, it wasn't the first, it wouldn't be the last and in the scheme of things, <u>the Ramseys got the last laugh</u>.

* JonBenét: Inside the Ramsey Murder Investigation

**The Pilot's Wife.

***Death of Innocence

****Donald Trump for example has initiated over 3500 lawsuits. From usatoday.com: *[Trump] and his businesses have been involved in at least 3,500 legal actions in federal and state courts during the past three decades. They range from skirmishes with casino patrons to million-dollar real estate suits to personal defamation lawsuits. The sheer volume of lawsuits is unprecedented for a presidential nominee. No candidate of a major party has had anything approaching the number of Trump's courtroom entanglements. Just since he announced his candidacy a year ago, at least 70 new cases have been filed [and]... at least 50 civil lawsuits remain open...*

*****The Ramsey's high powered media man Pat Korten was fired on March 28th, 1997

Cogne #6

All high profile criminal cases involve some form of PR. If that wasn't the case we'd never hear about them. The PR is intended to either counter or control a narrative. PR is never intended to make an entire narrative – as a whole – disappear. As such it's fair to say that anyone who strenuously objects to allegations against them, no matter who they are, ought to harness not just the law but PR as well.

The law in a sense is an aggregate system of rules; it's what people generally agree with. PR in a sense is an aggregate of opinions; it's what people generally think at a particular point [absent the full story or facts]. PR has the ability to powerfully and effectively leverage the law, especially during the early stages. Hijack a narrative early, and hijack it well and the narrative basically continues on a different course from that moment on.

Franzoni almost immediately began releasing interviews to newspapers and TV programs, *initially showing desperation for the tragedy she faced, and later stating that she wanted "to be known",* so that people would not think she was the kind of mother capable of killing her own child. — Wikipedia

We get a similar protest from Patsy. Is there anything wrong with protesting your innocence? Well yes, when you forget to petition for the pursuit of the "actual" murderer of your child.

Soon after her child's death, Mrs. Franzoni released an interview to an Italian TV channel, Italia 1. Despite her perfect make-up and smart dresses, she appeared upset and cried desperately, but, as soon as cameras went off, Franzoni quickly dried her tears and calmly asked a journalist: "I cried too much, didn't I?", and did not seem as sad as she pretended to be. At the same time, Mrs. Franzoni, her husband and his family began to indicate several people living in Cogne as potential killers of their son. — Wikipedia

In a word this is nothing more than self-preserving pageantry, isn't it?

*At first Mrs. Franzoni **pointed her finger against a young couple of friends**, whose baby daughter had recently died after a premature birth; Franzoni alleged that the woman had told her "You should face the death of your son as well," the evening before the murder.* — Wikipedia

Notice the pattern – the first accused are friends, and the accusation is based on little more than hearsay.

*Later, Franzoni changed her mind **and accused the neighbor that first ran to help her** and Samuele on the morning of January 30, Mrs. Daniela Ferrod. She said that Mrs. Ferrod was "as evil as a witch"" and "jealous of my family and my happiness", suggesting that Mrs. Ferrod used to "spy" on her and that probably she killed Samuele as an act of revenge, motivated by jealousy and envy.* — Wikipedia

Priscilla White had a motive to murder JonBenét, because Pricilla supposedly was jealous of Patsy, especially jealous of how beautiful JonBenét was. That's one theory, somewhat reinforced by John Ramsey saying [during a deposition in 2001] that Priscilla White had used the term "fat cat" in his presence.

Later Mrs Franzoni changed version again and, during summer 2004, with her husband and her lawyer (Carlo Taormina, a former member of the Italian Chamber of Deputies) **filed a lawsuit against another neighbor**, *a 35-year-old bachelor called Ulisse Guichardaz, who was also Mrs. Daniela Ferrod's brother-in-law.* **Mr. and Mrs. Franzoni-Lorenzi heavily slandered Mr. Guichardaz**, *describing him as a sexual maniac and arguing that Mrs. Franzoni was terrified of him.* — Wikipedia

A Boulder Journalist Christ Wolf filed a $50 million libel lawsuit against the Ramseys. Wolf claimed the Ramseys had defamed him in their book *The Death of Innocence* as well as in various television interviews. Some of the suspicion around Wolf was warranted.

From denverpost.com:

Wolf's girlfriend called police to say he was acting suspiciously and was not home during the time of the killing. Boulder police investigated Wolf and said they found no evidence to link him to the crime, according to a press report.

Of course the Ramseys took this tip-off as a gift and ran with as far as they could. We'll deal with the details of that 2001 lawsuit in the first *Sequin Star* narrative. Back to Cogne…

This man had an alibi. Lawyer Taormina contradicted himself several times about the identity and possible motives of the murderer. Firstly, the prominent lawyer argued that the crime was dictated by "a sort of revenge against the victim's mother" … but later he claimed that the murderer was a voyeur who sneaked into Mrs Franzoni's house to rape her. Lawyer Taormina stated several times that he knew the name of the murderer and he was willing to reveal it, something that never happened. — Wikipedia

This feels like the same flip-flopping between a disgruntled employee and a pervert who dressed up as Santa Claus. The only thing more incredible than the accusations themselves was the endless variety of people that were accused.

Doug's Back to School Announcement [on behalf of Burke]

"A kite is a victim you are sure of; you love it because it pulls." — Leonard Cohen

In *The Craven Silence* Trilogy we invoked a Lord of the Flies metaphor for this story. We suggested that sibling rivalry may not have been the only ingredient in JonBenét's murder, but perhaps peer pressure as well.

In *Death of Innocence* the Ramseys provide an insight into their son from an unlikely source – his buddy Doug Stine. When the High Peaks school counselor asked Burke's class how they should welcome JonBenét's brother back to school, Doug piped up.

> *"Burke doesn't want any presents...He doesn't want it to be any different."*

I'm not sure if that's entirely true on both counts, but one can imagine Doug having his own reasons for things to just continue as normal, no questions asked. What's worth noting is Doug's urgency in petitioning a certain code of conduct from his peers, not for himself [apparently], but for Burke.

Doug implored his classmates [barely a handful of kids] to not make a big deal out of "all this stuff". When a little girl raised her hand and suggested giving Burke a hug, Doug glared at her and admonished her: "You can't hug Burke." If you really think about it, why not?

One possibility is a personable or enquiring response from the kids would put Burke [and perhaps Doug] on the spot. What happened that night? What did they see? What did they hear? Where were they?

Doug went so far to insist that kids who were mean to Burke should continue being mean to him, and those who had always been nice to him should continue to be nice. What's interesting is how strenuously Doug seems to be interceding for his pal. It's like he wants to shut everyone down, he wants everything to proceed as normal [Doug does] on behalf of Burke.

In the end it's not clear how Burke was received when he arrived back at school, but it's likely there was minimal discussion. For the kid who told Judith Phillips "don't touch me" we can imagine there was a sort of cordon put around Burke at school, thanks to Doug.

After a while a tree was planted in JonBenét's memory in front of the boys' High Peaks school.

UNDERWORLD
"I'm planning a catastrophe." — Leonard Cohen, The Favorite Game

Cogne #7

__The murder weapon was never found__, despite extensive researches. Medical examiner found several traces of copper around the wounds on the child's head and this suggests that the murder weapon was made of copper. The victim had suffered at least 17 blows, which devastated his forehead and face. — Wikipedia

Did the child's head explode or implode? If it exploded could it have exploded 17 times? If the child was murdered in his own by a family member, that person would have had ample time and opportunity to concoct a cover-up, including disposing of vital evidence in and around the home. Dirty clothes? Pop them in the washer.

Police discovered that __a few hours before the murder Mrs Franzoni suffered from a serious panic attack__, and felt so bad that __she pushed her husband to call the emergency doctor__. It was not the first time that she faced panic attacks, but she had always minimized, denied having any problems. — Wikipedia

By the same token, three days before JonBenét's death there was an aborted emergency call. The cover up for that call also included some sort of medical emergency. Patsy's housekeeper Linda Hoffman-Pugh suggested that her early exit at around 17:00 on the evening of the party on December 23rd may have left Patsy frazzled.

According to the Police, Mrs Franzoni had __a violent outburst__ against her son and beat him to death. __Then she covered her wounded child with the comforter, hid her pajamas__ (completely drenched in blood and brain matter) between the sheets, washed, __dressed normally and walked to school her eldest son__. — Wikipedia

There are both similarities here and difference. Burke was the only one having outbursts, according to Judith Phillips, although Patsy had her "psycho" moments to according to Burke. We think it's possible that John or Patsy covered JonBenét's dead body in a white blanket, and it's possible there was bloodied clothing hidden or disposed of. It's also possible Burke's clothing was either washed or somehow removed from the scene. Like Franzoni, Patsy dressed normally the next morning, and this included applying make-up, or fixing her already applied make-up, in time to receive the police and the neighbors.

Several close friends recalled that Mrs Franzoni seemed worried about her younger son's health because, according to her, "his head was too big and too hot". Shortly after Samuele's birth, **Mrs. Franzoni faced post-partum depression, separated from her husband** *and came back to her parents' home with her two babies. However, after a few months the couple reconciled and by the time of the murder, they seemed to be happily married. One year after Samuele's death, Mrs. Franzoni gave birth to another child, a boy named Gioele.* — Wikipedia

Patsy too was concerned about JonBenét's health, which is why JonBenét went to a paediatrician 27 times before her death.

JonBenét's Medical History
"I have tried in my way to be free." — Leonard Cohen

Children are a lot like plants. You may think putting them somewhere in the garden is sufficient as long as they have sufficient sun, soil and water to grow, but plants need more than mere planting to live, let alone to thrive.

I'm fairly new at gardening. I'm ignorant of the underworld of possibilities involved – from the PH of the soil to things like drainage. One ignores the stipulations when buying plants from a nursery at one's peril. Full sun doesn't mean shade, shade doesn't mean full sun, although no one can say for sure what half sun really means. Is it half shade all day or half a days quota of sunlight? The point is if plants are so sensitive to the nuances of sunlight, imagine how sensitive miniature human beings are when their apple carts are upset?

It's been a source of frustration, fascination and even wonder to see how certain plants can thrive with minimal care while others seem to insist on whithering and dying. Recently in a corner of my garden reserved for cuttings, fruit and vegetable offal and my gardening mistakes, I saw a beautiful perky pink flower peeking through the foilage. It turned out whatever was slipping in one area of the garden somehow found its feet [or roots in this case] when left to rot in a sunless, water-forsaken quadrant. It turned out this pile of forgotten detritus was the perfect environment for this plant, and since then four more large, bright, staggeringly beautiful blossoms have emerged.

I've had a similar experience with a bouginvillaea that seemed to insist on dying. No matter how much I watered it or didn't water it, no matter how much research I did, no matter how much I tried to modify the sun, the wind and the rain, the plant just went downhill. I bought four more and planted these within a few feet of my unmitigated siaster, and all of them did okay. It occurred to me to pull out my failure and use it as fuel for a barbeque, but after a particularly drenching summer storm, a miracle. The Bougainvillaea that seemed all twisted sunblasted bark sprouted the tiniest maroon stars. These steadily expanded and now it's clear whatever ailed this insufferable failure had somehow been overcome, and not through any of my doing.

That happens, plants resurrect themselves, but I notice more often one has to save them when they start going downhill. Leaves may brown on the edges, or develop discolorations in their hearts. Stems may lean over. Drooping amongst plants of children is never a good sign. What tends to arrest this degradation is attention – move them somewhere, and attend to them until they improve. If they don't improve, attend to them again in some way until they do. One has to think in so many dimensions when it comes to plants – how much sun, how much water, and what sort of shit their roots have to deal with. And if you get through all this there are the pests to deal with – the snails and the slugs who come out in search of something healthy to chew on. Life comes at the expense of other life, what survives does so on the strata of a moist bed of black and juicy death.

In the Ramsey household very few of the house humans were happy or healthy plants. Patsy had cancer and she eventually died from it. Burke, besides not being perfectly well adjusted socially, seemed to be emotionally...well, a little strange. As for John, his attention was on a billion dollar enterprise, and although that pays for Christmas, it's not great for a family for the rest of the time. In a sense the Ramsey household was whithering not because of too much sun but too little, not because of too much warmth but too little, and not because they were getting food and water at healthy intervals, but because they weren't. Everyone seemed starved of attention even though everyone was getting attention.

In JonBenét's case the endless attention and adulation that came with pageants was a sort of empty and not very nourishing attention for a six year old girl. If Patsy didn't see it, it's perhaps because when she looked at her daughter she didn't see JonBenét, she saw herself becoming Miss America, and those are world's apart.

I know in the gardening sense one can insist on the same thing. For whatever reason one has the impression a certain plant enjoys the sun and needs "no water". The plant deteriorates and one simply insists on the status quo because it's in one's head, it's one's psychology. But the plant isn't adapting and it isn't enjoying the set of circumstances you've imposed. I've often found when checking up what the preferences are of a particular plant, it's not the plant that's gotten them wrong it's me. Sometimes even our undivided attention is no help if our focus is in the wrong place – not on the living thing, but on what we thing about the living thing.

Let's drill down to examine Patsy's attitude to JonBenét's health. We may have touched on some of this before, but it's an important primer for the medical history to follow.

From acandyrose.com:

DeMUTH: *Did Dr. Beuf used to normally prescribe you medications? Did he ever prescribe medications for you?*

PATSY: *I think he did. I mean, he is the children's pediatrician. He, I believe, prescribed something for me immediately the day that we discovered JonBenét.*

DEMUTH: *Had he done that before that?*

PATSY: *No.*

This is classic Patsy though. Did the doctor normally prescribe – I think he did. Had he done that before – no. [WTF](WTF)!

From acandyrose.com:

HANEY: *Did you check the bed on say Christmas day, morning?*

PATSY: *Yeah. (INAUDIBLE).*

HANEY: *Okay. But you distinctly remember going and checking on that?*

PATSY: *Plus she had her pink pajamas on that she had put on the night before. If she had wet it would have been soaking wet and she wouldn't have had those on in the Christmas picture, so --*

Patsy jumping in with the word 'Plus' seems very defensive. She seems to be petitioning the detective; yes of course I checked, and the Christmas photo is evidence. Well the urine stains on the bed were evidence too. Obviously if Patsy was allowing her daughter to walk around in urine-smelling clothing, that's a reflection of Patsy's care and duty for her ~~plants~~ child, or rather, lack of. And it's possible this area in particular may have prodded the Grand Jury to make their pronouncements around child neglect resulting in death. I mean this is possible evidence of exactly that sort of primary neglect that is below the standard of most parents.

From acandyrose.com:

HANEY: *Okay. If that's what she, and you say that's what she wore to bed the night before?*

PATSY: *Yes.*

HANEY: *Okay, all right. Did you ever discuss this with Dr. Beuf, is that her pediatrician?*

PATSY: *Not that I remember.*

HANEY: *It just wasn't a concern?*

PATSY: *No.*

HANEY: *Okay. Were the other children her age pretty much potty trained though?*

PATSY: *The White children were.*

HANEY: *So this was not out of the ordinary, not unusual for you?*

PATSY: *No.*

HANEY: *And you say you don't remember if you discussed it with the doctor or--*

PATSY: *I really don't remember whether I did or not.*

HANEY: *Okay. So if it's in the medical records?*

PATSY: *We would have discussed it.*

HANEY: *Okay. Do you remember anybody suggesting any remedies, any devices, anything to help train JonBenét on the bedwetting?*

PATSY: *No. I didn't consult a lot of people about it.*

HANEY: *Okay?*

PATSY: *Yeah.*

HANEY: *Did you consult anybody about it?*

Nice one Haney – nailing it down.

From acandyrose.com:

PATSY: *No, I mean, I just didn't think it was, you know, I had gone through big children, they wet the bed, I mean just, it wasn't a big deal. I didn't --*

John's kids were both at university when JonBenét died, and by 1997 Patsy had been married to John for seventeen years. So Patsy might have had some, limited exposure to John's kids as three and four year olds perhaps. If she had though, she'd likely not learnt anything.

This is going to sound silly but Patsy's attitude to potty training Jacques, JonBenét's dog came down to exiling the mutt under the stairs and then giving him away. My perception of Patsy is of an extremely high maintenance person with expensive taste and expensive pretentiousness....someone who was simultaneously loath to do chores and too important for such stuff – no cooking or cleaning or child rearing for Patsy.

From acandyrose.com:

HANEY: *Okay?*

PATSY: *I was not alarmed by it, at all.*

HANEY: *So it wasn't something that you might seek some advice about?*

PATSY: *No.*

HANEY: *And if you did, who would you have talked to about it?*

PATSY: *I don't think I did.*

HANEY: *Okay. If you did, this type of a problem?*

PATSY: *If I had thought it was a problem, I probably would have talked with her doctor about it, and I can't remember talking with him about it. So --*

HANEY: *Okay?*

PATSY: *I don't think it was a problem.*

HANEY: *You didn't consider it one?*

PATSY: *No.*

HANEY: *Okay. Do you recall like I say discussing it with anybody?*

PATSY: *I just, I don't remember discussing it with anybody.*

HANEY: *Okay. Do you recall talking to anybody about that as kind of a source of frustration or a little problem, this bed wetting?*

What about her housekeepers? Didn't Patsy ever ask Linda to get the bed cleaned up? Mind Hunter author and FBI profiler John Douglas would write in a book* published in 2000 [the same year the Ramsey's published their book]:

The bed-wetting was so common that Linda Hoffmann-Pugh reported that before she even got to work in the morning, Patsy would routinely strip JonBenét's and put them in the washer/dryer...

It seems odd that Patsy wouldn't mention this, and sinister that she wouldn't mention her housekeeper. Hadn't a single comment passed between the two regarding JonBenét's bedwetting, over a period of months? Oh Linda, won't you put JonBenét's pajamas in her cupboard, I've washed them. Linda let's get these sheets washed... Linda are there any spare sheets? Linda what do you mean all of JonBenét's pajamas are in the wash?

Patsy's attitude to JonBenét's bedwetting was like my attitude to a plant dying in the sun. Despite evidence to the contrary, the plant/JonBenét should make a full recovery...except that as time goes by the organism's resilience is eroded. It begins to die before it is dead.

From acandyrose.com:

PATSY: *You know, it just didn't seem like a problem to me. I have had problems. I had cancer, that's a problem. You know. It didn't seem to be a problem. So I can't really say that I -- that it was on my mind to discuss with anybody.*

HANEY: *Okay. But it doesn't have to be a problem to discuss something with somebody, right?*

PATSY: *I don't remember ever discussing it with anybody, including her doctor.*

Patsy seems to see this as a badge of honor. It's not. Whether Patsy admits that she discussed her daughter's bedwetting with her doctor [and the problem persisted until JonBenét's dying day], or whether she denies, Patsy looks like either a negligent mom, an ignorant mom or an arrogant mom, or all of the above.

From acandyrose.com:

HANEY: *Okay.*

PATSY: *So -- you know, if she wet the bed, if she had an accident, I take the sheets off, throw them in the laundry, you know. Que sera, sera.*

Now let's take a look at JonBenét's medical history as provided by Dr. Beuf to Detective Harmer of the Boulder Police Department.

From forumsforjustice.org**:

6th August, 1990: *JonBenét Ramsey is born.*

12th June, 1991: *First visit with Beuf. Treated for fever, cough and wheezing.*

10 months pass: *JonBenét has a typical pattern of a toddler's colds and coughs.*

January 1993: *Ear infection. Amoxicillin prescribed.*

At two and a half years of age: *JonBenét has a history of fever and coughing.*

March 1993: *JonBenét is diagnosed with her first serious illness. She has difficulty breathing and a severe fever, 102 F. She's almost three years old and coughing up yellow mucous. Beuf describes JonBenét as appearing "droopey".*

July 1993: *Patsy has been diagnosed with cancer, JonBenét is in her grandmother Nedra's care. Beuef notes JonBenét has regressed both in her toilet training and eating habits.*

August 31st, 1993: *Beuf questions Patsy. Patsy says JonBenét has no phobias and JonBenét's sexual education does not need to be discussed.*

September 6th, 1993: *JonBenét's buttocks and vaginal area chafed red from diarrhea.*

November 1993: *JonBenét is sleeping poorly, grouchy from fatigue, bad breath. Chronic sinusitis. Cough and stuffed nose.*

December 31st, 1993: *Still drinking from bottle; parents having trouble weaning her.*

January 1994: *Bad breath, cough and congestion.*

It's possible JonBenét's halitosis comes from a simple lack of hygiene. If she's not brushing her teeth regularly, this is also indicative of an absent or negligent parent. The inability to wean JonBenét off the bottle isn't surprising given the bedwetting regression. Bedwetting and failure to wean off a bottle frequently go hand in hand.

From forumsforjustice.org**:

> **February 4th, 1994:** *Breath still bad, runny rose, little appetite,* **slept poorly, bladder infection and vaginal discharge.** *Diagnosed with vaginitis. Amoxicillin prescribed [second ear infection] and warned against bubble baths.*

One wonders if the neglect was so severe that JonBenét got virtually every infection there was – ear, throat, nose, urinary, vaginal – what other neglect was possible? The answer is if JonBenét's neglect was chronic this would certainly have ushered in the possibility of an older sibling abusing or harming his younger sibling, especially if he felt neglected because of her arrival on the scene [and not because of Patsy's cancer].

From forumsforjustice.org**:

> **April 1994:** *Ear hurting, cranky. Still coughing, stuffy nose, congestion Diagnosed with allergic rhinitis, Benedryl prescribed.*
>
> **April 1994:** *(1 week later) Still coughing, Suprax prescribed.*
>
> **October 5th, 1994**: *JonBenét came in for check-up, doctor notices* **scar on left cheek**. *She'd been hit accidentally by a gold club when the family was in Charlevoix. A week after the accident, a plastic surgeon was consulted. No injury to cheekbone. Beuf is told (at this visit) that she's getting along with brothers and older sister. Wearing pull-ups at night because she's wetting bed. Patsy completes developmental questionnaire, and says there are no aspects of JonBenét's behavior or sex education she needed to discuss, and also notes JonBenét has no fears or phobias.*

JonBenét's fourth birthday was on August 6th, 1994. Burke hit his sister with a golf club within a day or two of her birthday, and then a plastic surgeon is contacted to make sure JonBenét's face doesn't have any permanent scarring.

> **November 1st, 1994:** *Had diarrhea five times and was lethargic. One bowel movement appeared bloody.*
>
> **November 4th, 1994:** *Badly congested, deep cough, bad breath. Diarrhea gone.*
>
> **January 1st, 1995:** *Chickenpox. Rash even appears in vaginal area. Recommended Avino, Benadryl and Lanocaine.*

The thought occurs that if both children suffered chronic neglect, then birthdays and Christmas' were exceptions where children once again became the focus of parents' attention. However if it was another sibling's birthday or another sibling was seen to be preferred in terms of Christmas gifts, the sense of neglect is not only reinforced but validated in the sense that one child is literally costing the other its "right" to life, liberty and more specifically, essential resources [such as material possessions, a tangible thread on which one feels oneself alive].

From forumsforjustice.org**:

> **January 31st, 1995:** *Still has bad cough and **not sleeping well**. Robitussin not helping.*
>
> **Mid-Feb/95:** *Cough. Temp 99.3*
>
> **March 1995:** *Complained of stomach ache but sleeping well.*
>
> **April 1995:** *John Ramsey calls in, says JonBenét has another cough, but he doesn't think daughter needs to be examined.*
>
> **May 8th, 1995:** *JonBenét falls in Alfalfa's food market, lands on face. Hurts nose, but it's not broken.*

December 1995: *JonBenét trips and hits head above left eye. Stuffy nose, bad breath, coughing.*

March 1996: *Coughing a lot.*

May 1996: *Bent nail back on fourth finger, left hand, in **another fall**. Swollen and painful, but no bruising. Ibuprofen recommended.*

August 27, 1996: Patsy reports *JonBenét's sleeping well...**Not interested in opposite sex, behaved modestly in public, and didn't engage in sex play with her friends. She was, however, asking about sex roles and reproduction.** She was not rude or afraid of either parent. Didn't seem to be bossy with brother, didn't react with tantrums, and was active. Loved fruit and some vegetables. Patsy said she was delightful and doing very well. Burke had his annual check-up same day.*

A vaginal exam is conducted on JonBenét by Dr. Beuf on the same day.

This is an odd check-up three weeks after JonBenét's sixth birthday. The check-up appears to be routine except for sexual content. There's a contradiction in her not interested in opposite sex however asking about "sex roles". It's also interesting that Burke is at the doctor the same time, the first mention of Burke with regard to JonBenét's sexual history is around a theme of "sex role playing."

September 1996: *Cough back, Robitussin recommended.*

October 1996: *Stuffy nose, bad breath. Diagnosed with allergic rhinitis.*

November 12, 1996: *Runny nose and cold sore, sneezing.*

December 3rd, 1996: *Sees eye doctor.*

December 1996: *Misses pageant due to illness.*

"I have known for years that Boulder prosecutors did not file charges against John and Patsy Ramsey because the evidence to prosecute them did not exist." — Lin Wood, Atlanta-based lawyer representing John and Burke Ramsey

*The Cases that Haunt Us
**Perfect Murder Perfect Town

Back to the Future of Injustice

"Let judges secretly despair of justice: their verdicts will be more acute." — Leonard Cohen

Before we get to John and Burke's defense attorney Lin Wood, let's go back to the future briefly to revisit the moment the Ramsey case got buried.

In October 1999, after a 13th month Grand Jury investigation Boulder District Attorney Alex Hunter refused to sign the Grand Jury indictment implicating both JonBenét's parents in her death. The following year, Alex Hunter – the longest serving DA in Colorado – did not run for re-election.

From denverpost.com:

"It's been a great run," Hunter said, hours after he announced he won't seek an eighth term as Boulder district attorney. The 63-year-old Hunter is likely to leave unsolved the case that, for many, will define his tenure.

Great run? Well it depends on which team you're on surely. If you're with Team Ramsey, maybe it was a great run, if you aren't, maybe it wasn't.

From denverpost.com:

Hunter stressed Thursday that his departure doesn't signal an end to the investigation into JonBenét Ramsey's killing. "We should not give up on this case," he said.

Think about what's actually going on here. Folks who have been following the Ramsey investigation with concern eventually find the case is washed up, kaput. The Ramseys were on their knees [they say] watching the decision in television, when they found out they'd effectively been exonerated. That decision was criticised and a few years later they'd get a second official exoneration, along with an unprecedented letter of apology from Hunter's successor.

For Hunter to quit during by far the biggest case of his career says something about his commitment to the Ramseys, to himself, and the cause of justice. To quit while saying how great it's been and also that everyone else shouldn't give up on the case [even though he had done just that] speaks volumes.

From denverpost.com:

*Since JonBenét's body was found in the basement of her parents' home Dec. 26, 1996, Hunter has survived several calls - including from Thomas and from former Ramsey family friend **Fleet White** - that he be removed from the case and replaced by a special prosecutor. And the chorus of criticism over his handling of the case resounded anew after his Oct. 13 announcement that after a 13-month grand jury investigation, there would be no indictment in the case. But Hunter said he has shaken off that criticism, thanks to **the certainty that the decision was the right one.***

It's interesting that Hunter would not only shake off criticism, but block and indictment and claim to be resolute and unruffled by criticism, this despite stalling the case he was in charge of. It could be argued that Hunters final action as District Attorney was sufficient to torpedo the Ramsey case to the present day. Personally I find Hunters pride and confidence in his decision surrounding this case illuminating.

From denverpost.com:

*The prosecutors involved were **convinced** that a judge would dismiss an **indictment for lack of evidence** long before it got to a jury, [Hunter] said.*

*"We are a little different in Colorado, I think. **I know we are in Boulder**. The judges up here would throw this thing out," he said. But Hunter said Thursday that even if he believed the JonBenét Ramsey case would be solved soon, he wouldn't seek another term. "This office deserves new eyes, maybe even on this case." Pointing out that he will be 64 when his current term ends in January [2000], Hunter added, **"I've had my shot at it, and I'm very grateful for that shot."** Hunter and the Larimer County district attorney are*

Colorado's longest-serving DAs.

If Hunter left his job with his head held high, feeling grateful for his shot, one wonders what he was so grateful for. The timing of it is also interesting – Hunter buried the Ramsey investigation and then immediately retired, presumably to a life of carefree and comfortable bliss. 64 is a few years shy of what might be considered the benchmark for retirement. Typically Supreme Court justices retire at age 70.

From denverpost.com:

When Hunter leaves his office for the last time, the color photo of JonBenét Ramsey that sat on his desk for more than three years will go with him, Hunter said.

"I will take that along with my rolltop desk and a few other antiques I've salvaged from a couple of marriages." And he'll take disappointment that the little girl's killer has not been brought to justice.

Was Hunter genuinely disappointed the JonBenét Ramsey case hadn't been settled? If he was, why not stick around for another year? The bottom line is when Hunter left he also left a case that was exhausted and bankrupt. The question is, was this by design or by Hunter doing what he thought was right, misguided as that may have been?

From denverpost.com:

...Hunter acknowledges the Ramsey case is a big portion of his term in office, "it's not the most important piece. **What's important is the brand of justice** *I think has come out of this shop, this criminal justice system, this community, that I do not think the media - including local media - has covered as well as they might have."*

It's noteworthy that while Hunter is content to sing his own praises, the media is the villain for not – apparently – focussing on all the good stuff Hunter and his office achieved. You mean zero convictions in ten years? We'll scrutinise Alex Hunter and his successors in *The Day After Christmas* 3. Now let's get back to the arch cheerleader for Team Ramsey, Lin Wood.

Who is this guy? What is his background? Besides being a Trump supporter, we want to get a sense of now only who defended John, Patsy and Burke but how. What was his defense? How did it change, if at all? What did the Ramsey's defense attorney think of the various Boulder District Attorney's vested with the fate of the JonBenét case.

It should come as no surprise that the Ramsey defense attorneys, even those before Lin Wood, thought the world of the Boulder District Attorneys. And why not, every Boulder District Attorney seemed to have their clients – the Ramseys – best interests at heart. Before we get to the why [which we investigate in *The Day After Christmas 2*] we ought to know how. How did a slew of Boulder District Attorneys defer to the Ramseys?

From nytimes.com [December 26 2000]:

*Ms. Keenan has said she plans to bring the agencies closer with several measures, including a weekly review of major cases. "**I'm not going to make any decisions in this office**, minor or major, because I want to be re-elected,"' Ms. Keenan said. "If I do a good job, I'll get re-elected and if I don't, I don't deserve to be re-elected."*

It's an odd thing to say because surely that's how re-election works. More pertinently Keenan appeared to be saying "things aren't going to change now that I'm here." In other words, expect an uninterrupted status quo. Who was she really communicating to here, her Boulder constituents or some shadowy force billowing in the mountains above Boulder?

In a certain sense Keenan seemed not only an obvious choice, but an excellent choice to solve JonBenét's murder. Even though three years had already passed and the case was turning cold, Keenan brought in a woman's touch along with a very special skillset. The only question was, if change was coming she seemed to be announcing her broom wouldn't be doing much sweeping.

From nytimes.com:

Ms. Keenan, a Democrat, earned her law degree at the University of Iowa and joined Mr. Hunter's office in 1985. A single mother of two grown children, she led the sex assault unit. She defeated a lawyer, David Sanderson, in the November election for district attorney.

"'She has a reputation that I think is deserved for being tough and, I also feel, thoughtful in her handling of sex assault cases," Mr. Hunter said. "It is a very difficult area and one of the tributes I think she deserves has been a willingness to tackle tough cases."

An endorsement from Hunter bodes ill, doesn't it? And we know for all the tough talk all Keenan ultimately achieved was extraditing a bogus suspect from Thailand. John Mark Karr was a prime suspect for effectively a few hours before he was released, having zero links to the crime, he wasn't even in Boulder. And Keenan was the ferocious tiger who pursued Karr to that dead-end and back.

From nytimes.com:

L. Lin Wood, the Ramseys' lawyer, said he wanted Ms. Keenan to move the case forward. "'I hope she is also a courageous prosecutor and can resist any pressure from the Boulder Police Department to file charges against my clients,"' Mr. Wood said.

Mr. Wood said the only way to solve the case was to bring in new investigators, perhaps an independent panel of experts, or hand the case over to the Boulder County Sheriff's Office. The Boulder police chief, Mark Beckner, said he was looking forward to working with Ms. Keenan to improve relations between the police and prosecutors.

*"**Anything that increases communication** between the agencies is a positive," Chief Beckner said.*

Beckner was alluding to *The Craven Silence* which had already begun to bury the efforts of the Boulder Police Department, and those efforts have remained buried and unaccounted for to the present day.

"Attorney of the Damned"

"The election of @realDonaldTrump as President is an event of unparalleled magnitude in the history of this country." — Lin Wood via Twitter, 9 November 2016

"They need to go home or better yet, to work. Election is over. You lost. Deal with it." — Lin Wood via Twitter, 10 November 2016

"Always amused by self-important celebrities believing their influence extends beyond their profession to politics." — Lin Wood via Twitter, 13 November 2016

In 2004 John Ramsey gave an interview commemorating the eight year anniversary of his daughter's death. At his side was his attorney Lin Wood. Let's listen in on what Lin Wood said then:

COURIC: *I know Mary Keenan took over the case a while ago. And you believe as a result of her input, that both John and Patsy Ramsey were exonerated. Some legal experts don't necessarily agree. What causes you to say the Ramseys have been exonerated?*

WOOD [seated beside John Ramsey]: *Well I don't think there's any doubt about it, uh, Katie. Uh...Mary Keenan issues in April of 2003 a public statement in which she agreed with a federal judge ruling in Atlanta, uh, that stated that the weight of the evidence in this case established that an intruder uh murdered JonBenét. For a District Attorney to issue that statement, a District Attorney who is familiar with all of the evidence in the case, uh I think that is a very clear statement...that this investigation has moved beyond John and Patsy Ramsey, and Mary Keenan is focusing on the intruder evidence to try to find the killer of this child.*

COURIC: *Let's talk about the DNA evidence that was found in JonBenét's underwear...I know it took a while to isolate that. Tell me what the latest is on that and do you believe that would lead investigators to her killer.*

WOOD: *I do think the DNA evidence will solve this case, Katie. Uh the DNA was found in 1997, uh, but it was not fully tested until*

1999. Uh the results of that testing, uh were ignored by the Boulder Police Department for years. Uh, in December 2002 when Mary Keenan took this case away from the Boulder Police Department she established as her number one priority, to get that DNA certified into the national FBI database. That was finally done in 2003, late in the year. And I believe [blink] one day, hopefully in the near future, there's going to be a hit, a match [blink] and I believe that will identify the killer [blink] of this child.

COURIC: *You know I've covered this story for a long time, and many things have surfaced lately. The most interesting thing is that investigators hired by the Ramseys found that within a two mile radius of their home, 38 of their neighbours at the time of JonBenét's murder were registered sex offenders. And there had been over 100 burglaries months before the murder. First of all, did you find that shocking, and second of all, why didn't this come to light sooner?*

<u>WOOD</u>: *I have to tell ya Katie, not only is it shocking it's reprehensible that the Boulder Police Department had knowledge of this information, they failed for years to fully investigate uh, the people in that neighborhood who were registered sex offenders. Uh failed to follow up on the tremendous number of burglaries in the area...uh. You had a case where what we're learning, and I think what the public is learning with the passage of time, is that there was just a tremendous number of leads...uh a lot of potential suspects who were never investigated. Now Mary Keenan is following those leads, and that evidence...[gulps]...[that's why] I know this is a difficult time for John and his family, this is also a time of hope... Uh because the real breakthrough in this case was when Mary Keenan took the case over.*

A whole lotta nuthin specific there, but Lin Wood sure seems to like Mary Keenan* running the D.A.'s office doesn't he?

COURIC: *Okay so Mr Ramsey, are these 38 registered sex offenders currently being investigated as well as the burglaries?*

Nice one Katie!

JOHN: *Well I don't know specifically [clears throat] that...uh...but uh...*

Uh but John if you're trying to find JonBenét's killer, and your lawyer is pissed at the cops for not following these leads for years, and now they are, shouldn't you know what's being done, who's being followed? Shouldn't you know? Don't you care?

JOHN: *Uh but what we feel is everything that can be done is being done by the [nods] current people...working on the case...and we have great confidence that they uh...that the case is in good hands. And <u>they'll do what it takes</u> [nods]. And [chokes a little] exhaust all op-options.*

There's some discussion about a novice kidnapping up the road from the Ramseys nine months before JonBenét's murder. Once again John blames the Boulder Police Department for being remiss in not investigating that. I think there was a burglary in my neighborhood, here in South Africa a few weeks ago, I guess the Boulder police fucked up in not checking that out too?

Katie, throw him a curveball please!

COURIC: *Mr Ramsey, despite the fact that these new leads are being investigated, many people believe that you and your wife are responsible for JonBenét's death. What would you say to them this morning?*

Now think about if you were asked this question. You've been accused of a crime you didn't commit, and simultaneously lost someone you loved. Would you be angry about your reputation? Would you be angry that your child's murderer still hasn't been found? Wouldn't you want to reassure the public on two counts – first tell them how you can't be involved, what you were doing that night [whatever it was], and second tell them how you are working day and night to pursue this criminal. How you owe it to your daughter... How much you love and miss your daughter. Because that's part of an authentic parent declaring their innocence – part of that is declaring their love for their lost child.

As we so often find in these cases, the victim is never the victim, it's the person on trial [where in the court of public opinion or otherwise] for someone else's loss of life. And all they can talk about is what they have lost. Take a listen.

JOHN: *Well you know [eye twitch] Katie, two things were taken from us in 1996. Our precious child and our family's honor. Uh...**it's very difficult to recover your good name**...uh regardless of what happens after it's taken. And we're struggling with that. And uh there's a line in Shakespeare that says: "my life and my honor are intertwined. **Take away my honor and my life is done**." And it's difficult for us. But uh...we are...individual people, people have been wonderful to us through this process. And that's where we gain our strength.*

WOOD: [Interrupting] *Katie tell those people who think John and Patsy are involved to look at the evidence and they'll learn that they're wrong.*

Lin's a straight shooter right? Do we get a sense that he's not shy to make his presence heard? Two years prior to their interview with Katie Couric, Lin Wood is on the record for some real straight shootin'.

VIDEOTAPED DEPOSITION OF

GIDEON EPSTEIN

May 17, 2002

9:35 a.m.

191 Peachtree Street, N.E.

Atlanta, Georgia

WOOD: *Hey, I made more money handling the Ramsey case than you've made in your whole damn career practicing law, Darnay.*

HOFFMAN: -- *instead of settling for chump change, which you've done in all these other cases, you're actually getting paid a decent* --

WOOD: *I've made more money in the Ramsey case than you've made in your entire career as a lawyer, you want to bet on that?"*

If you're wondering where the "attorney of the damned" moniker comes from, well, not from us, from Wikipedia:

Wood's representation of Richard Jewell propelled Wood from a personal injury lawyer to be known as one of the top libel, defamation and First Amendment lawyers in the U.S. earning him the title of "Attorney for the Damned"

If Jewell was truly innocent – and it appears he was – Wood went on to represent other clients whose innocence was…let's just say not quite as cut and dry.

If you're wondering what happened to Lin Wood after his threat to sue Dr. Werner Spitz for $150 million and CBS both in September 2016, well – Wood appeared on CBS [again] as a guest of Dr. Phil who is also a client [yes, Dr Phil is another client of Lin Wood's].

This time Wood was defending another client, Gary Condit. Condit is a lot more high profile than Jewell, a former politician and member of the Democratic Party suspected of the abduction and murder of Chandra Levy. Her murder has only recently been classified back to unsolved. While Condit was under investigation, a 20-year-old illegal immigrant from El Salvador Ingmar Guandique was arrested and convicted for Levy's murder, essentially on the strength of hearsay. A jailhouse informant claimed Guandique had confessed to the crime, however evidence emerged later that Morales [who ratted Guandique out] had brokered a deal with prosecutors to have his own jail conditions improved in exchange for testifying.

In late October Gary Condit felt he had some PR to do, and Lin Wood was there at his side. Dr. Phil did the honors, it felt like a rerun of the Burke Ramsey interview. Instead of smiling as Burke did, Condit had a sort of bug-eyed look on his face. What was also unexpected was he not only denied having an affair with Levy [29 years younger than him], he said he'd seen her only once. Photos had been taken of the two which seemed to suggest otherwise.

In any event, Lin Wood was there to do damage control, and Dr

Phil punted a special book which seemed to suggest Condit couldn't be involved. The book *Actual Malice* is co-authored by Gary Condit. It appears to be the first true crime book published by Jay McGraw, Dr Phil's son through his publishing company Ghost Mountain Books.

A cursory glance through the portfolio of Ghost Mountain Books appears to show fare dedicated to psychological health, exercise, wellness and health foods. You know, the kind of stuff you'd expect to come up on dad's show. *Actual Malice* sticks out of the wellness stuff like sore thumb. Meanwhile Lin Wood also periodically retweets Woodward's book on the Ramsey case, which no surprise is just another *Apologia*.

One does sense a nice little business going on – crime, defense lawyer, *Apologia* [book, documentary], and a TV talk show to get the money ball rolling.

Curiously enough, Lin Wood has this to say on Dr. Phil about his client:

*"I call it **the unholy alliance between law enforcement and the media**. And that is a real danger if it occurs during a slow news cycle. And **people will watch this show and hopefully they will read this book** but there will still be, unfortunately, a large number of people that will still believe that Gary Condit was somehow involved in what happened to Chandra Levy. The shout of guilty is never overcome by the whisper of innocence. They destroyed this man. It changed his life. It destroyed his reputation, deprived the public of a hell of a good congressman, gone in the blink of a three-month media frenzy fuelled by incompetent law enforcement and leaks of false information."*

Dr. Phil concludes:

"I hope people, if they think they know what happened here, they will see this broadcast, they will look at this book [Dr. Phil is holding the book at the camera], and hear me say, 'Don't fall victim to confirmation bias. Actually guard against that and say, 'Wait a minute, I need to hit the reset button on what I think I know and

check the facts here of the story that you put together [looking at Condit]' ...Cuz it isn't even almost what you think you know. That's my point"

Of course Condit and his lawyer, and Dr. Phil and his lawyer, Lin Wood and the co-author of the book, all grandstanding about the same thing on a talk show wouldn't be about confirmation bias, would it? Each one is a client and/or reinforce of the other, and the book is a cheerleading effort for their particular point of view. Besides points of view, it's also about recycling money, isn't it?

Perhaps that's not the case, perhaps true crime has made us cynical. Whatever is the case, let's wrap with a generic description of Lin Wood from that most generic of online resources, Wikipedia:

*Lin Wood was raised in Georgia after moving to Macon, Georgia, at age 3. Wood has stated in news accounts that his family struggled financially with **frequent episodes of domestic abuse involving his parents**. He has one sibling, Diane Wood Stern born February 1951 and a half sister, Linda Martin born in 1946. After a school dance, the then 16-year-old Wood returned home to find **his father had beaten his mother to death**. L. Lin Wood Sr. pleaded guilty to involuntary manslaughter, a charge reduced from first-degree murder. He served a little over two years in prison. Wood has stated that it was this experience that solidified his earlier decision to become a lawyer.*

---

*Patsy's sister Pam Paugh was also a fan of Mary Keenan: "Mary Keenan Lacy, thank you, thank you. To Boulder county, reelect her; she is one in a million."

Silent Aftermath #1

"It's hard to hold the hand of anyone who is reaching for the sky just to surrender." — Leonard Cohen

It's a small square cardboard box. It lies in the centre of a room called the wine cellar. There is no wine in it. JonBenét is not here yet either, or rather, what will remain of her has not yet arrived.

There is a furnace like heat surrounding the red box. The box itself is like a compact oven – no, a sun. The basement is a sauna of quivering golden light.

And when the searing lid of the red box is opened, the room instantly reverts to an icy black cold. We have travelled to some phantom zone between Christmas and The Day After Christmas. Time and space seems to bend and warp. Dank basement walls become black holes while a ceiling glitters with the cosmos. And somewhere in the centre of it is a tiny golden thread…like a single hair from JonBenét's head, threading across eternity.

It glints gold in the dark.

When we reach out to it, we reach out to death itself. A sound of flies buzzing around a severed head begins to rise and fall, to quiver and hiss.

"The Lord of the Flies…warns of danger…"

SUDDENLY SLOWY OUT OF THE ETHER

A CURIOUS APPARITION

A CURIOUS COMBINATION

OF FEATHERS AND BONES AND ANTS

FLYING IN THE DARK

YOU WANTED TO KNOW WHAT HAPPENED THAT CHRISTMAS NIGHT

DIDN'T YOU

DIDN'T YOU?

    "The Lord of the Flies…warns of danger…"

MAKE AN EFFORT TO ANSWER NOW

                                              YES.

YOU'LL WANT TO WRITE THIS DOWN

              I-DON'T HAVE ANYTHING TO WRITE WITH

                        AND-AND I CAN'T SEE

TAKE ONE OF MY FEATHERS AND OPEN YOURS EYES

LISTEN NOW

LISTEN CAREFULLY!

        YOU WANT TO KNOW WHERE

        YOU WANT TO KNOW WHO

        WELL WE'LL GET THERE

        IF YOU KNOW WHAT TO DO

        NUMBER ONE ON OUR LIST

        IS A BROKEN WINDOW

        SO WRITE IT DOWN

        CURL THOSE FINGERS INTO A FIST

                                                1.

        TWO BOYS PLAYING IN A BASEMENT

        TWO BOYS AND A GIRL

        TWO BOYS IN A BASEMENT

PLAYING BASEBALL AND HOW

2.

THE WINDOW

THE WINDOW

BROKE BY HER BALL

NOT A BASEBALL

NOT A BASEBALL AT ALL

3.

THE MISCHIEF MIGRATED

FROM BALLS TO GIFTS

AND FROM GIFTS TO ONE

LITTLE LITTLE GIRL

NONE WERE ABOUT

SO FIDDLE THEY DID

FIDDLE AND TAUNT UNTIL SHE SQUIRMED AWAY

4.

IT WASN'T THE KNOT

THE KNOT ON HER WRIST

IT WAS THE ONE ON HER NECK

THAT TIGHTENED HER FIRST

5.

IT WASN'T THE FIRST TIME

THIS TAUNTING, THIS TEASING

BUT IT WOULD BE THE LAST

AS SHE GAVE A LAST GASP

6.

SHE SCREAMED AS SHE GASPED

AND HE BEAT HER STILL

BOYS WILL BE BOYS

<u>IN THE BOILER ROOM</u>

7.

FIDDLE THEY DID

FIDDLELEDEE

SHE SLEPT LIKE THEIR TOYS

WHAT ABOUT ME?

8.

EAGER WERE THEY

EAGER IN THEIR PLAY

CHILD'S PLAY, THEY SAY

BUT WHEN SHE SLEPT

SHE NEVER DID AWAKE

9.

A GAME?

NERVOUS LAUGH

A POKE AND A PROD

WELL JAB HER WITH THIS

OR TIGHTEN WITH THAT

                                10.

LET'S SEE HOW SHE COUGHS

BUT FURTHER

SHE SLEEPS

HE WONDERS SO SOON

IF HER TOYS ARE FOR KEEPS

                                11.

HIDE

UNDER THE BED WILL DO

OR MAYBE GO

GO THAT WAY

GO NOW

NO I WON'T SAY!

                                12.

HE TAKES HER BIKE,

A TWO MINUTE TREK

GO TO BED

SAY NOTHING

NOTHING OF HER NECK

                                13.

HOME AND AWAY
AND HOME AGAIN
WHERE OH WHERE
IS JONBENET?

14.

SHE <u>LAYS ON THE FLOOR</u>*
<u>AT THE DOOR</u>
<u>AT ANOTHER DOOR TOO</u>
IT LOOKS LIKE SHE FORGOT
TO GO TO THE LOO
WHAT TO DO,
OH WHAT TO DO
PRAY TO GOD
OR BOO HOO HOO?

15.

WE MUST DO SOMETHING
<u>FOR THE SILVER STAR</u>
THIS HOUSE IS THEIRS
THE TREASURE IS TOO

16.

IT'S ALL UP TO YOU
NOT ME, JUST YOU
I'LL TALK YOU THROUGH

I'LL TALK, NOT TOUCH

17.

WE NEED TO MAKE
WE NEED TO BAKE
HATCH SOME SORT OF PLOT
TO THEM A SHOCK

18.

LET'S GIVE THEM A SHOW
SOMETHING THEY'LL KNOW
AN INSIDE JOB
WHADAYYA KNOW

19.

WE'LL MAKE US A TARGET
A TARGET WE ARE
HOW TO KEEP BUSINESS
BOOMING AFAR

20.

WE'LL WRITE A NOTE
A NOTE ABOUT ME
WE'LL GIVE THEM A RANSOM
A BONUS THEY'LL SEE

21.

YOU START A WRITING

AND GET HER IN THERE
COVER HER MOUTH
GIVE IT A TEAR

      22.

WE'LL BURN THESE CORDS
BURN THIS PIECE OF GARROTTE
BURN THE TAPE
AND THAT FIRST NOTE YOU WROTE

      23.

THIS BAT IS A PROBLEM
IT'S SPONSORED
YOU KNOW
SO IS THE HOUSE
SAY IT AIN'T SO
I'LL THROW THE BAT
ON THE WRONG SIDE
YOU OPEN THE DOOR
LIGHT ON THAT SIDE

      24.

THE NEIGHBOR SOON HEARD**
THE BANGING THE CLANGING
IT RATTLED HIS BRAINS
THE METAL, THE ZONKING

25.

THERE'S ONE PIECE LEFT

TO PUZZLE THE RIDDLE

IT'S SNOWING, IT'S STILL

GET ALLIES ARRIVING

BEFORE THE PIGS DO

26.

YOU WANTED THE WHERE

YOU WANTED THE HOW

THAT'S THE DAY

AFTER CHRISTMAS

FOR NOW

---

*The carpet cut out that was stained in JonBenét's urine was situated at both <u>the entrance</u> to the <u>wine cellar</u> and the boiler room. Patsy's paint tray was situated within arm's length of this area as well.

**The Stanton's home was situated 150 feet [45 metres] South East of the Ramsey home, in other words diagonally across the road. <u>A vent in the boiler room on the East</u> side – in other words the elevation of the Ramsey home facing the 15 Street and the Stanton home – would <u>have allowed JonBenét's scream to reach the Stanton's bedroom far easier</u> than from the window grate. <u>The same applies to the clanging</u> of <u>Patsy's softball bat</u> on the paved concrete area right beside the front door area on the <u>North East side of the Ramsey house</u>.

Cogne #8

*On 21 May 2008 the Court of Last Resort confirmed the decision of the Appeal Court and Franzoni was arrested. She is now in jail, facing a new trial for **defamation against her neighbors**. Her parents never phone or go and visit her in jail, her husband makes monthly visits with both sons, Davide and Gioele.* — Wikipedia

A case seemingly open and shut took 6 years to finalise. Was the murder weapon the copper piping at the end of the bed?

*Mrs. Franzoni, from 2002 to 2008 - when she was finally jailed - **took part in numerous TV shows: in such shows, Mrs Franzoni always appeared well dressed and made-up, aggressive in supporting her innocence**.* — Wikipedia

Ring a bell?

*On several occasions...Franzoni stated that the judges and the prosecutors unfairly persecuted her and that they knew she was innocent, but would never admit it **nor would they seek out for the "real killer"**.* — Wikipedia

"There's someone out there..."

*Because of these allegations **Franzoni was also charged and found guilty of defamation** against the Chief Prosecutor of Aosta.* — Wikipedia

A case can certainly be made by the Boulder Police Department for repeated slander against them by the Ramseys.

*On December 2006, **Franzoni wrote a... book [called] The Truth...** she once again protested [her innocence], **describing her family life as... perfect and unproblematic**, [and] **presenting herself as a doting mother, a happy wife and a devoted catholic, surrounded by cruel and jealous neighbors**. Curiously...Franzoni wrote she had no idea who... the murderer [could be] and [claimed]* *she never blamed or accused anyone.* — Wikipedia

Acknowledgements

In order to piece together this narrative, we've cast a wide net. We've drawn on information from a number of forums, documentaries and online resources which have been cited. We gratefully acknowledge the suggestions and support we've received from our readers while on this shared journey towards justice.

Please report errors, omissions or corrections directly to @lisawJ13.

CORRECTION: In the chapter Gravity Bites of our previous narrative *The Craven Silence 3*, the image linked to the ** footnote was hyperlinked in error. The image attached at that link shows fingerprint dust left on JonBenét's door from the crime scene technicians, not feces.

About the Authors

Lisa Wilson (aka Juror13) *is a trial blogger who resides in California, USA. She's a marketer by day and true crime maestro by night.*

After years of discussing cases online with fellow armchair detectives and trial watchers, Lisa started her own blog in 2013. Since then, she and Nick van der Leek have formed a True Crime-themed partnership. Under the #Shakedown banner they have begun conducting deep investigations into the narratives of Oscar Pistorius, Jodi Arias, O.J. Simpson and Amanda Knox cases, and have co-authored several books on these criminals, with many more in the works.

Nick van der Leek (@Shakedowntitle) *is the author of over 50 narratives. He has a background in law and photojournalism. His great grandfather is a famous South African landscape artist.*

If you've found The Day After Christmas *a worthwhile read, look out for* The Day After Christmas 2 *which focuses on the sexual dimension of the murder of JonBenét Ramsey.*

To share your insights with the authors leave a comment on our Shakedowntitle blog or join our true crime discussions on Facebook.

Made in the USA
Lexington, KY
15 January 2017